European Union and its Neighbours in a Globalized World

Volume 32

The series publishes monographs and edited volumes in the field of European and international law and policy. A special focus is put on the European neighbourhood policy, current problems in European and international law and policy as well as the role of the European Union as a global actor. The series supports the publishing and distribution of research results of cross-border research consortia. Besides renowned scientists the series is also open for publication projects of young academics. The series emphasizes the interplay of the European Union and its neighbouring countries as well as the important role of the European Union as a key player in the international context of law, economics and politics.

Alessandro Ferrara

Bioethical Reflections on the Border between Life and Death

Springer

Alessandro Ferrara
Magna Graecia University of Catanzaro
Catanzaro, Italy

ISSN 2524-8928 ISSN 2524-8936 (electronic)
European Union and its Neighbours in a Globalized World
ISBN 978-3-032-09984-6 ISBN 978-3-032-09985-3 (eBook)
https://doi.org/10.1007/978-3-032-09985-3

This Springer imprint is published by the registered company Springer Nature Switzerland AG.
The registered company address is: Gewerbestrasse 11, 6330 Cham, Switzerland

To my family
everything good
I am or do
is thanks to them

Acknowledgments I would like to express my profound gratitude to all those who, in different ways, contributed to the realisation of this book.

In particular, I am deeply grateful to Professor Alberto Scerbo for introducing me to this discipline and for encouraging me to explore and challenge my own limits.

To Professor Paola Chiarella, for her unfailing ability to offer the right advice or reassurance at just the right moment.

To Professors Wouter Veraart and Bart van Klink, for their warm welcome, their trust in me, and for listening when I had no voice.

To Professor Britta van Beers, whose inspiring lectures ignited in me a deep and lasting passion for bioethics.

To my Dutch friends, Professors Luigi Corrias and Bertjan Wolthuis, for their help, candid advice, closeness, and the trust they inspired in me.

Finally, to my future wife, Roberta, whose support, patience, and love sustained me through every phase of this work.

Alessandro Ferrara

Competing Interests The author has no competing interests to declare that are relevant to the content of this manuscript.

Contents

About the Author

Alessandro Ferrara is a legal scholar affiliated with the Magna Graecia University of Catanzaro, where he serves as a teaching assistant and subject expert in Philosophy of Law. He holds a PhD in Theory of Law and the European Legal and Economic Order and has been a research fellow working on the digitalization of justice and artificial intelligence. His academic interests focus on the ethical and philosophical challenges surrounding the beginning and end of human life, with particular attention to medically assisted death, surrogacy, and triage as well as the ethical implications of emerging technologies. He has published peer-reviewed articles in international journals such as *Ratio Juris*—where his article "The Ethical Triage Dilemma" was ranked among the top 10% most read papers of 2023 according to Wiley—*German Law Journal*, *BioLaw Journal* and *Ragion Pratica* and has presented his work at leading academic venues, including the Vrije Universiteit Amsterdam and the national conferences of the Italian Society for Philosophy of Law and the Italian Society for Law and Literature. Dr. Ferrara was a visiting scholar at Vrije Universiteit Amsterdam and conducted advanced research in bioethics, philosophy and legal theory. His current research lies at the intersection of bioethics, legal normativity, and technological innovation.

Chapter 1
Introduction

In ancient Greek mythology, the Acheron[1]—along with the rivers Styx, Cocytus, Lethe and Phlegethon—is represented as the river that traces the border between the realm of the living and the realm of the dead.

Plato states in the Phaedo that the Acheron is the second largest river in the world and the only one that flows in the opposite direction, from the ocean towards the land (Plato 2002). Its best-known representation, however, goes back to the third canto of Dante's Inferno where it is depicted as the boundary between hell and Anti-Inferno (Abardo 2001) and is crossed, by means of Charon, only by the souls of those who have received a worthy burial (Petrella 2013).

The Acheron constituted more than merely an element of hell geography; in Greek culture, it also embodied the concept of purification and transition. The river was occasionally linked to rites of passage, in which the water of the Acheron was believed to serve as a symbol of purification from earthly sins prior to entry into the realm of the dead (Pausanias 1918).

The dualism between death and purification that is embodied by the Acheron functions as a powerful metaphor for the exploration of the themes of life and death, as well as the ethical decisions and philosophical reflections that lie on their borderline.

The text's objective is to provide a thorough examination of the border, the passage, from being to non-being and from non-being to being, or rather, from existing to non-existing and from non-existing to existing.

It is on the banks of the Acheron that the reader is invited to consider how the 'souls', in contrast to the aforementioned representations, move back and forth in both directions, from existence to non-existence and vice versa. In this manner,

[1] From ancient Greek Ἀχέρων (Acheron), traditionally related to the Greek verb ἀχέω (acheo), meaning 'to groan' or 'to lament'. Etymology suggests that the name Acheron might evoke the idea of a river of lamentation or sorrow, reflecting its association with the realm of the dead, a place of suffering and sadness.

A. Ferrara, *Bioethical Reflections on the Border between Life and Death*, European Union and its Neighbours in a Globalized World 32,
https://doi.org/10.1007/978-3-032-09985-3_1

they transition from mere solipsism to self-determination, and decide to cross those boundaries, both of life and death.

It is precisely in situations on the borderline between birth and death that the ever-increasing possibility of choice and self-determination—also thanks to scientific and technological evolution[2]—manifests its most problematic aspects.[3] This is not only with respect to the possibility of determining the end of one's own life, but also of determining the birth and/or death of another person.

In order to cross the boundaries of life and death, the human being is called upon to cross further boundaries, the boundaries of science and technology and thus of what is technically and scientifically possible, the boundaries of law and thus of what is legally and legally possible, and the boundaries of ethics and morality and thus of what is just and unjust. While the boundaries of science and technology are insurmountable (at least in a given space of time), those of ethics and morality represent a structure that is mainly internal to the human being. The latter, in conjunction with those of the law, are crossable, influence, and are influenced by the law itself in a continuous shift that attempts to bring the legal structure closer to the moral structure and vice versa. The endeavour to transgress the confines of the legally permissible has, in certain instances, given rise to a phenomenon termed 'human rights tourism'.[4] This phenomenon refers to the practice whereby individuals seek to circumvent the restrictions and prohibitions imposed by the law within their own state by temporarily relocating to other states to engage in activities that they would not be permitted to undertake within their own. They assert the right to undertake these activities in other states. The aim of this book is to provide food for thought through the legal-philosophical analysis of some of the issues that raise ethical and moral questions more than any other and that hold important implications for human dignity, autonomy and the rights of the individuals involved.

The present volume will address the cases previously outlined, with a particular focus on surrogacy, the early termination of life (whether through suicide assistance or euthanasia), and triage, a phenomenon that emerged during the course of the COVID-19 pandemic. The term 'triage' is understood here as the process of allocating healthcare resources in situations where their availability is insufficient in relation to demand, typically in emergency circumstances.

---

[2] "The reality is that it is technology that celebrates its overwhelming power", in a universe in which "the horizon of immortality, madly cultivated over the centuries, today no longer seems to be outside the horizon of the possible, to belong to science fiction" (Zagrebelsky 2018, pp. 336–337). *Translation by the author from the Italian edition.*

[3] The principle of self-determination in relation to further fundamental rights undermines constitutional principles both with reference to health treatments in the terminal phase of existence and in the procreation phase, generating a fervent debate also by virtue of the different modes of regulation adopted by each State (Rodotà 2012, p. 291). In this regard, see, among others, Gusmai, (2017a); Gusmai, (2017b).

[4] On so-called human rights tourism, see: Poli (2015); Rodotà (2006); Korstanje (2023); Cole and Eriksson (2010).

In the latter case, the decision to cross the boundary between life and death cannot be attributed to individual autonomy as a result of the individual's free self-determination. Instead, it is hetero-produced, sometimes by the application of guidelines, and sometimes by protocols or recommendations. During the period of the global pandemic, the established boundaries were found to be wholly impassable in both technological and territorial terms. The technological boundary was characterised by the unavailability of adequate medical instruments to combat the development of the disease for all those who required them. The territorial boundary was found to be impassable due to the restrictions imposed on movement, which resulted in the closure of national and regional borders.

Surrogacy, voluntary termination of life and triage are topics that deeply touch our conceptions of life, death and human dignity. Surrogacy raises complex questions regarding the commodification of the body, the rights of surrogate mothers and the children born through such arrangements. The voluntary interruption of life, or the so-called 'good death', forces one to confront the right to self-determination in the face of the unbearable suffering of a terminal illness and the end of life with the duty to protect the weak and vulnerable, entailing moral implications—even in assisting others to die—that are far from simple. Triage, the practice of assigning medical treatment priorities in situations of limited resources to some patients rather than others, confronts us with difficult choices about who should live and who should die, involving the need to bear the 'burden of proof'.[5]

The second chapter, therefore, will explore the new concepts of parenthood that are now detached from that of maternity, both biological and genetic, and will address the topic of surrogacy by analysing the main issues that have arisen in the international bioethical debate after briefly conducting a quick overview of the different regulatory methods adopted at the international level, highlighting the existence of absolutely opposing visions.

Conversely, the third chapter will address euthanasia and assisted suicide, practices that, despite the existence of widely shared perceptions at an international level, continue to exhibit ambiguities that appear to mask contentious issues, including the potential recognition of a legitimate right to die or to receive assistance in dying.

In the fourth chapter, the topic of triage will be explored in depth, drawing on the experiences during the pandemic to determine how to distribute insufficient healthcare resources. The chapter will also refer to the debate that has arisen on the subject, with particular reference to the lack of uniform regulation at European and

[5] As Mill explains, "the burden of proof is supposed to be with those who are against liberty; who contend for any restriction or prohibition [. . .] The a priori presumption is in favour of liberty, and it is the duty of those who would restrain it, to show why" (Mill 1977, p. 260). Mill introduces the idea of the burden of proof in the context of liberty restrictions, but the concept is extendable to triage. It implies the need for transparency and moral justification of decisions. In triage, those making decisions must provide reasons and evidence to avoid arbitrariness and ensure fairness. From a utilitarian perspective, they must also demonstrate that the outcomes benefit the collective.

international level. The chapter will refer to cases that occurred in some states, including, above all, the United States, to provide useful food for thought.

A common theme running through this volume is the need to reflect on the power and responsibility of choices. This is particularly pertinent when choices affect the two unalterable aspects of human existence: birth and death. In this context, the choices in question are not only those made by the individuals directly concerned, but also those made by the legislator, which directly impact the role of law. Law is particularly important when the outcomes of choices are definitive and affect the weakest and most vulnerable individuals, as is often the case. In such situations, law is called upon to perform its typical protective function. When human intervention through technology and medicine alters the natural course of events, determining the birth or death of an individual, the law must guarantee the freedom and autonomy of those who make the choices, while ensuring that the human dignity of the most vulnerable individuals is protected, including their own.

References

Abardo R (2001) Fra fonti, intertestualità, auto- ed eteromnesi. Lettura del canto III dell'Inferno. Rivista di studi danteschi 2/2001

Cole S, Eriksson J (2010) Tourism and human rights. In: Cole S, Morgan N (eds) Tourism and Inequality: problems and prospects. CABI, Wallingford, pp 107–125

Gusmai A (2017a) Madre e padre (in)certi: brevi riflessioni sulla omogenitorialità a partire da alcune recenti decisioni della giurisprudenza comune in tema di trascrivibilità dell'atto di nascita. Federalismi.it, 23/2017

Gusmai A (2017b) Il concetto di famiglia inter-costituzionale. In: Mezzetti L, Ferioli E (eds) Giustizia e costituzione agli albori del XXI Secolo. Bonomo Editore, Bologna, pp 173

Korstanje ME (2023) Tourism, poverty, and human rights: an unspeakable relationship. In: Korstanje ME, Vgb G (eds) Global perspectives on human rights and the impact of tourism consumption in the twenty-first century. advances in hospitality, tourism, and the services industry. IGI Global, 129–152

Mill JS (1977) On Liberty. In: Robson JM (ed) Collected works of John Stuart Mill, Vol. XVIII: essays on politics and society part I. University of Toronto Press, Toronto, pp 213–310

Pausanias (1918) Description of Greece. Translated by Jones WHS, Ormerod HA. Cambridge, MA: Harvard University Press; William Heinemann, London

Petrella G (2013) Iconografia dantesca ed elementi paratestuali nell'edizione della Commedia Brescia, Bonino Bonini, 1487. Paratesto: rivista internazionale, 10:1825–9537

Plato (2002) Phaedo. Translated by Grube GMA, revised by Cooper JM. In: Cooper JM (ed), Plato, Complete Works. Hackett Publishing, Indianapolis

Poli L (2015) Maternità surrogata e diritti umani: una pratica controversa che necessita di una regolamentazione internazionale? Biolaw J 3/2015

Rodotà S (2006) La vita e le regole: tra diritto e non diritto. Laterza, Roma-Bari

Rodotà S (2012) Il diritto di avere diritti. Laterza, Roma-Bari

Zagrebelsky G (2018) Diritto allo specchio. Einaudi, Torino

Chapter 2
A Bioethical Analysis of the Surrogability of the Act of Procreation

In order to pursue our reflections on the ethical admissibility of gestational surrogacy in a sufficiently clear manner, it is necessary to briefly outline the scientific contours of our field of enquiry.

Surrogacy is one of the Assisted Reproductive Technologies (ART) used to enable conception in all cases where conception is spontaneously not possible or extremely difficult and where other pharmacological and/or surgical interventions are inappropriate.

The techniques employed are designed to promote conception by facilitating the interaction between the spermatozoon and the oocyte.[1] In some cases, these techniques are derived directly from the couple desiring to conceive, while in other cases, they are sourced from a donor.

The principal techniques that medical science has developed to achieve this are as follows: Artificial insemination (AI) is a reproductive technology that involves the direct deposition of laboratory-processed sperm into the woman's uterus, typically during the period of ovulation, with the objective of enhancing the probability of conception. In vitro fertilisation (IVF) is a well-established technique that has gained significant popularity in the field of assisted reproduction. The process entails the collection of oocytes from the female patient and subsequent in vitro insemination with sperm from the patient's partner or a donor. The inseminated oocytes are then transferred into the patient's uterus for embryo development. A related technique is intracytoplasmic sperm injection (ICSI), a variant of IVF in which a sperm is injected directly into the oocyte, rather than being fertilised on its own in a culture dish.

The performance of these procedures frequently necessitates the utilisation of both gamete donation and frozen embryo transfer (FET). The ethical acceptability

[1] Artificial Insemination (AI), In Vitro Fertilisation (IVF), Intracytoplasmic Sperm Injection (ICSI).

A. Ferrara, *Bioethical Reflections on the Border between Life and Death*, European Union and its Neighbours in a Globalized World 32,
https://doi.org/10.1007/978-3-032-09985-3_2

of these techniques has been the subject of extensive academic discourse,[2] although they will not be the focus of this chapter.

In addition to the aforementioned techniques, there is a more controversial and ethically debated case—which this study will focus on—in which a woman makes herself available to take an embryo conceived through one of the above techniques into her uterus on behalf of a commissioning couple or single person. The woman carries the pregnancy to term and renounces,[3] at the moment of delivery, any parental claim to the newborn child in order to hand it over to its so-called intended parents (Sgorbati 2016).

This technique is referred to by various names, including uterus for rent, surrogacy and gestation for others, among others, depending on the conception that is intended to be communicated. The subsequent section will be devoted to this topic.

2.1 A Terminological Premise

In order to understand the essence of the issues to be discussed in this chapter, if it is true that language is the house of being (Heidegger 1947/1977), a terminological premise is appropriate.

The practice whereby a woman carries a pregnancy to term on behalf of another person or couple, who after the birth become the legal parents of the child was originally referred to as 'surrogacy'. The term originates from the English word *surrogacy* (from Latin *surrogatus*, *subrogare*, meaning 'appointed to act in place of') by which the practice has been defined in the United States since the 1970s.[4] It is evident that, over the years,

[2] See, among others: Birkhäuser (2013); Chen (2013); Quaas and Pennings (2018); Richards et al. (2012); May (2009).

[3] The prior renunciation of future parental rights depends on the legislation in force in each state. In fact, there are some legislations that recognise the surrogate mother's right not to surrender her newborn child and to maintain the parental relationship with it.

[4] The first documented practice of surrogacy dates back to 1985 in the United States. The procedure was handled by the Surrogacy Centre of Noel Keane, a lawyer who had opened the first surrogacy centre in the 1970s. However, the most famous case that attracted international attention was that of Baby M in 1986, in which a woman, Mary Beth Whitehead, carried a surrogate pregnancy to term on behalf of a couple, William and Elizabeth Stern, but later changed her mind and sought to retain custody of the child. This case led to a wide-ranging legal and ethical debate on the practice of surrogacy. The court eventually held that the surrogacy contract could not be fully enforced, but that custody should be decided based on the best interests of the child. The Baby M case marked a pivotal moment in the regulation and public perception of surrogacy in the United States and internationally (Feldman 2018; Cahill 1988; Annas 1988). In 1988, a key testimony came with the publication of Birth Mother: The Story of America's First Legal Surrogate Mother by Elisabeth Kane (1988), the pseudonym of a woman who had entered into a surrogacy agreement in 1980. Seven years later, she wrote a book that revealed her growing opposition to the practice.

a phenomenon of semantic remodelling has occurred, which has been concealed, to a certain extent, by the desire to change the perceptual aspect of the practice through its conceptual restructuring. The practice was formerly referred to as'womb for rent' by proponents of a morally critical approach that regarded it as a form of exploitation or commodification of the female body. In recent years, however, the term 'gestation for others' has gained traction, with the objective of enhancing its acceptability by emphasising the altruistic facets that should substantiate its ethical and legal legitimacy.[5]

According to Vitale, the definition of 'gestation for others' expresses the "will of technical thought to take possession of motherhood starting from the lexical dimension itself [. . .] because it fails to give an account of the legal relevance of the whole operation that borrows its economy from the civil law institution of surrogacy, so that only the term 'surrogate motherhood' can be the one that is concretely appropriate to define the operation" (Vitale 2018 *trans. by the author*). According to some (Agacinski 2013, pp. 89–92)[6] therefore, the definition 'surrogacy' would be better able to describe the phenomenon in line with the real need for lexical and conceptual rigour inherent in language that "by nature is deputed to show, and not conceal, the being of reality" (Agacinski 2013, p. 92).

Notwithstanding the author's conviction that the most appropriate term to describe the subject under consideration is 'surrogate gestation', given the evident disconnection between the conventional conception of motherhood and the biological process of childbirth from legal, formal, and emotional/substantial perspectives, this work has been undertaken with the utilisation of the term "surrogate motherhood" and its derivatives (surrogate mother, intended parents, etc.) as a more neutral term, generally recognised and immediately perceptible to the reader. In the course of this work, we have decided to use the term 'surrogacy' without wishing that such a choice should give rise to a value judgement, which we shall attempt to bring out in the course of the reading.

---

[5] In reality, as pointed out by Chini (2016, p. 174), this locution marginalises the mother's role and contributes to the perception of a practice that is not always altruistic.

[6] "Mais le nom de gestatrice et le formule gestation pour autrui, ou GPA, tendent de plus en plus à s'imposer. Ces trois lettres semblent faites pour inspirer confiance, comme le sigle d'une compagnie d'assurances, mais elles contribuent largement à masquer la nature de cette inquiétante nouveauté [. . .]. Les trois petites lettres GPA sont sans doute rassurantes, mais elles constituent une mystification et maquillent une forme inédite de servitude et d'abaissement des femmes" (Agacinski 2013, pp. 89–92). *Translation by the author*: "But the term *gestatrice* and the phrase *gestation pour autrui*, or GPA, are becoming more and more widespread. These three letters seem designed to inspire trust, like the acronym of an insurance company, but they largely serve to conceal the nature of this disturbing novelty [. . .]. The three small letters GPA are certainly reassuring, but they are a mystification and disguise an unprecedented form of servitude and degradation of women."

2.2 On Surrogacy

The ethical admissibility of surrogacy is certainly among the most debated issues in doctrine over the last two decades.

A necessary distinction underlying the theoretical discussion is that between 'traditional' and 'gestational' surrogacy. In the former case, the fertilised oocyte belongs to the woman who will carry the pregnancy, entailing a genetic and consequently emotional connection between surrogate mother and child;[7] in the latter case, on the other hand, the oocytes do not belong to the surrogate mother, who is absolutely unrelated to the unborn child from a genetic point of view.

In the academic debate the specificities that characterise the prodromal relations to the fertilising act—namely the existence of a parental/genetic bond between the surrogate mother and the intended parents the possible biological connection between one or both of the intended parents and the newborn child—and the specific regulatory precautions taken against the parties—including the surrogate mother's right to refuse external influences on her lifestyle during pregnancy rather than the right to keep the child for herself after birth while retaining parental responsibility—have led to different conclusions regarding the ethical admissibility of the practice.

In any case, surrogacy agreements provide that the pregnancy is carried out by a woman who will not become the child's 'social' mother after delivery.

It is acknowledged that disparities may be observed between one clinical practice and another with respect to the genetic composition resulting from pregnancy. Indeed, in certain instances, the male and female gametes originate from the intended couple. Conversely, in other scenarios, one or the other may be sourced from a donor and subsequently implanted in the surrogate mother's womb.[8] It should be noted that the feasibility of such implantation is contingent on the legal framework governing surrogacy practices in the specific country where the procedure is conducted. In some cases, neither gamete belongs to the intended couple. Finally, the surrogate mother may also donate the egg. In addition to carrying the pregnancy to term by becoming the child's genetic mother, as previously mentioned, this modality may raise complex legal and ethical issues, especially regarding custody rights and the emotional relationship with the child (Richards et al. 2012). In other cases, the surrogate mother has no genetic link with the child, since the embryo is created in vitro using the gametes of the intended parents or donors and then implanted in the surrogate mother's uterus. This form of surrogacy is the most prevalent today and is favoured due to its complete separation of the gestational role from the genetic link (Schroeder 2002).

---

[7] This is precisely why in most legal systems where surrogacy is legal an essential requirement is that the fertilised egg does not belong to the surrogate mother.

[8] There are some countries, in fact, that require there to be a genetic connection between at least one of the two intended parents and the unborn child.

Moreover, according to the applicable legislation, the practice may also be requested by singles or same-sex couples, in some cases compulsorily married and or resident in the country where the fertilisation takes place.

Having traced the scientific contours that identify the main characteristics of surrogacy, it is appropriate to make a further distinction from which derive, in the academic debate, relevant consequences regarding the admissibility of the practice. Surrogacy, in fact, can be carried out in an altruistic form and therefore provide for the surrogate mother to receive no remuneration for her service, but only reimbursement of expenses incurred or reimbursement of potential loss of earnings due to the pregnancy, or in a commercial form with the provision of actual remuneration for her gestational service. As will be discussed in more detail below, the academic debate on this point has been—and continues to be—extremely vigorous at the international level (Gheaus 2024; van Niekerk and van Zyl 1995; Brandão and Garrido 2022). While commercial surrogacy is highly controversial from an ethical point of view, as it is criticised for the potential commodification of the female body and the risks of exploitation of women, especially in poverty-stricken contexts and is consequently legal in a limited number of states, altruistic surrogacy is permitted in a larger number of countries due to the fact that no remuneration is received, but of a simple reimbursement of expenses, or in any case compensation for the 'damage' suffered by the surrogate mother would tend to exclude the risk of exploitation of the woman's body and trafficking in human beings as—at least in appearance—the newborn child is not the subject of a commercial transaction as the result of a production process.

However, this case gives rise to a number of questions concerning the social and familial pressures that may motivate a woman to become a surrogate, and there are still uncertainties regarding the true extent of the sums received by surrogate mothers.

2.3 The Relationship Between Surrogacy and Motherhood. Reflections on Motherhood From Ancient to Contemporary Philosophy

The advent of assisted reproductive technologies has undoubtedly contributed to the evolution of the concept of motherhood, historically connected to the act of giving birth—hence the Latin proverb *mater semper certa est*—but now increasingly autonomously connected to the *animus* of the parent rather than to the pregnancy, birth and the sex of the latter.

Dealing with surrogacy necessarily implies prior reflection on the concept of procreation and motherhood. All living species are united by the possibility—at least theoretically—to reproduce, to procreate, to ensure the continuity of the species.

Throughout history, fertility, pregnancy and motherhood have played a central role in society. The approximately 35,000-year-old Venus of Willendorf, considered the oldest representation of fertility worship, is proof of this. The importance of the ability to procreate was so great that some of the earliest fertility deities were also associated with agriculture, testifying to how essential both processes were for the survival of humanity (Behjati-Ardakani et al. 2016).

The study of religious iconography since 4000 BC reveals that representations of deities connected to male and female fertility are prevalent. Simultaneously, the initial documentation of a practice of 'surrogate motherhood' can be traced back 4000 years to the Turkish region of Kayseri. There, historical records have been found that suggest the presence of prenuptial agreements, whereby in the event of childbirth complications, the offspring could be entrusted to a third party. In ancient Egypt, pregnancy was regarded as one of the most significant phases in a woman's life. The concepts of fertility, pregnancy and motherhood were regarded as divine endowments, and the ability to conceive and carry a pregnancy was perceived as a blessing. An examination of conceptions of motherhood in ancient philosophy discloses significant insights into fundamental notions of human nature, the role of women, and the social function of procreation.

Greek philosophers, in particular, explored these ideas in a context that deeply connected biology to cosmology and ethics. Plato, in the *Timaeus* (1997, 41a-b–c), offers a vision of procreation that transcends its mere biological function, placing it within a broader cosmic order. Procreation, according to Plato, is a means by which human beings participate in immortality. He states that the desire to procreate is rooted in a fundamental need to perpetuate the species and, in this way, to participate in an eternal and divine order. This view, where reproduction is considered an almost sacred act, carries with it a significant philosophical implication: motherhood is not just a biological act, but a connection between the mortal and the immortal, between the temporal and the eternal. Plato, however, seems to treat motherhood rather abstractly, focusing more on the concept of procreation as a universal function than on motherhood as an individual experience. This approach reflects the Platonic tendency to value universal ideas over the particularities of concrete experience.

Aristotle, in *De Generatione Animalium*,[9] takes an empirical-biological approach compared to Plato, considering procreation as a natural and necessary

[9] For Aristotle, the woman is characterised by a certain biological inferiority in comparison to the man, and this is caused by a thermal defect: the female animal, in fact, is physiologically unable to complete coition (pepsis), which the male body, on the other hand, fully realises, by transforming blood into sperm, thanks to its own vital heat. This causes the two sexes to exercise very different roles in the reproductive process. The female, in fact, provides the necessary matter for reproduction, the menstruum, while the male provides that which processes, shapes and animates this matter. According to Aristotle, in effect, it is the pneuma contained in the sperm that actively induces in the material constitution of the unborn child the eidos, and thus its specific nature as a living being. In Aristotelian thought, therefore, the concept of 'innate pneuma' plays an essential role in all the major biological problems, from the more general one of reproduction to the more specific ones of the transmission of the soul and hereditary traits, the functioning of the sense

function for the perpetuation of the species. His view of motherhood is strongly influenced by the theory of formal and material cause according to which woman provides the substance (*hylé*), thus making a material contribution, while man provides the form (*eidos*) through the seed. In this perspective, woman is seen as the passive vessel in which life develops, while man is the active agent that gives form and direction to the reproductive process. This conception has had a major influence on Western philosophy, entrenching the idea that woman is intrinsically linked to matter and passivity, while man represents form, activity and intellect. This dualism has contributed to a long tradition of thought that sees motherhood as primarily biological and subordinate to man's active function.

Before Plato and Aristotle, pre-Socratic philosophical schools had also reflected on procreation and, implicitly, motherhood. The Pythagoreans, for instance, regarded procreation as a manifestation of cosmic harmony. Pythagorean number theory saw the world as a harmonic unity, and procreation was an expression of this harmony. Although they did not focus specifically on motherhood, their ideas implied that the reproductive process was part of a universal and sacred order (Kirk et al. 1963). Hippocrates, with his philosophy of medicine had an indirect impact on the philosophy of motherhood. His work reflects an approach to human health that integrates empirical observation with a natural and rational view of the body and its processes that sees motherhood as a phenomenon deeply rooted in nature and in the cycle of life, in which the female body plays an essential role, while at the same time highlighting how it represents a highly vulnerable moment in a woman's life (Hippocrates 1931, Chaps. 1–5).

Even in ancient Rome, the subject of motherhood was addressed within the broader discussion of ethics, virtue and the role of the family. Cicero saw the family as the essential core of the state and motherhood as a fundamental function for the continuity and stability of the family and, by extension, of the state itself. In particular, Cicero writes about *pietas*, a concept that includes duty and respect towards the family and the gods, which is also reflected in a mother's devotion to her children and family (Cicero 2008, I, 17).

---

organs and locomotion. Precisely because of this 'new physiology', Aristotle can state that the embryo's acquisition of the nutritive and sensory faculties occurs through the paternal contribution to generation. Having left the body of the male parent, the semen, being composed of water and pneuma, does not materially participate in conception, i.e. becoming part of the foetus, but evaporates, immediately after having transmitted the movement with which it is endowed. Female matter, which in turn contains potential movements derived from the mother's body, exclusively receives this impulse, which is nothing more than a form, i.e. a soul, in potency. The latter, which resides in the organ that is generated first during the embryogenetic process, namely the heart, the archè of psychic and vital processes, presides, through the blood, over the growth of the embryo, i.e. the constitution of its material and organic parts. According to Aristotle, at first, that is, when it is still only seed, the unborn child has a soul only in potency. Subsequently, after the new living being has become a proper embryo, thanks to the union of the male and female contributions, this soul, transmitted to it by the paternal sperm and, more precisely, by the pneuma it contains, becomes actualised, i.e. it passes from potency to act (Aristotle 1943, I, 20).

Seneca, on the other hand, one of the leading Stoic philosophers, discusses motherhood in terms of virtue and duty. In his letters and philosophical works, he reflects on how mothers must face the loss of a child with serenity and resignation, seeing motherhood as a part of the great cycle of natural life that must be accepted with wisdom (Seneca 2014, pp.16–18).

The various philosophical theories on the function of motherhood point to a certain conception of women, which in an early stage of history was considered primarily as tools and means to achieve social ends and devoid of individual value.

The approaches just mentioned—at the basis of the evolution of modern philosophical thought—can be considered useful contributions in order to arrive at the most comprehensive analysis of the subject and above all to understand how

With the advent of modern philosophy, the conception of motherhood has undergone significant transformations. Whereas in ancient philosophy motherhood was often viewed through a biological or cosmological lens, with the emergence of modern thought, it is reinterpreted in ways that reflect new ethical, political and social concerns. However, despite these changes, motherhood continues to be treated primarily as a natural function, anchored in biology, with implications that resonate in the contemporary debate on surrogacy.

John Locke, one of the founding fathers of modern liberalism, addresses the issue of motherhood in the broader context of family and society. In his *Second Treatise on Government*, Locke sees the family as a social microstructure, a unit that not only reproduces the population but is also fundamental to the transmission of social values and norms (Locke 1980). In this sense, procreation is seen as an act of responsibility, not only towards children, but also towards society as a whole. Locke sees motherhood as an integral part of this social responsibility. However, he treats motherhood more as a biological function, necessary for the perpetuation of the species and society, rather than as a relational or existential experience. This view reflects Locke's empirical and utilitarian approach, in which the family serves as an instrument to ensure social order and stability. Motherhood, therefore, while acknowledged in its importance, remains confined to the role of a means to wider social ends.

Rousseau, on the other hand, offers a more nuanced view of motherhood, emphasising the mother's role as the child's first educator and arguing that motherhood cannot be regarded only as a biological task, but also as an essential educational function. The mother is seen as the child's first moral and intellectual guide, responsible for the child's growth not only physically, but also emotionally and intellectually (Rousseau 1979). On the other hand, Rousseau offers a more nuanced view of motherhood. He emphasises the mother's role as the child's first educator, arguing that motherhood is not only a biological task, but also an essential educational function. The mother is seen as the child's initial moral and intellectual guide, responsible for their growth, both physical and emotional (Rousseau 1979). He idealises motherhood as a return to nature, whereby the mother participates in a natural process that strengthens family and social ties by nursing and caring for her children. However, this view of motherhood is closely linked to biology and nature; therefore, the maternal role is considered inalienable and non-delegable. In this context, surrogacy would represent an anomaly and an interruption to the natural process that Rousseau considers essential for the formation of a healthy, morally sound individual.

The implications of the idea of surrogacy for the philosophy of Immanuel Kant, one of the most influential thinkers of the modern era, are even more obvious. With his emphasis on autonomy and the concept of human dignity, Kant enunciates the principle that every human being must always be treated as an end and never as a means (Kant 1998, 4:428). This concept as a categorical imperative has profound implications for the understanding of motherhood, especially in relation to bioethical issues. According to Kant, the human body—including the female body—should never be used as a means to an end. This principle comes into tension with the practice of surrogacy, which could be interpreted as the exploitation of a woman's body. In this context, the woman becomes a 'means' through which other people's desire to become parents is realised, which violates the Kantian principles of dignity and autonomy. The Kantian perspective invites us to consider motherhood as both a natural function and an experience deeply connected to a woman's dignity and autonomy. Despite the fact that Kantian philosophy is often borrowed as a classical argument to contest the ethical admissibility of surrogacy at the end of this chapter, an alternative interpretation will be attempted to justify its admissibility.

Modern philosophy, in any case, transforms and enriches the understanding of motherhood, shifting the emphasis from mere biological function to more complex ethical, social and relational considerations. Locke, Rousseau and Kant, among others, although coming from different philosophical traditions, all contribute to a deeper discussion of motherhood, which begins to be interpreted not only as a natural process, but as an experience charged with ethical and social significance.

In the twentieth century, thanks in part to scientific and technological advances that have led to the expansion of procreation techniques, there has been a growing interest in motherhood not only as a biological function, but as a complex phenomenon involving issues of identity, ethics and politics. Several contemporary philosophers have examined motherhood through the lenses of feminism, psychoanalysis and phenomenology, bringing to light new perspectives on a topic that, historically, has often been marginalised or treated reductively.

Simone de Beauvoir analysed the condition of women in patriarchal societies, devoting ample space to the question of motherhood. She argued that motherhood has historically been used to oppress women by forcing them into a limiting role that denies them autonomy and the opportunity to develop a sense of self. According to de Beauvoir, patriarchal society reduces women to a reproductive function, alienating them from their own bodies: 'In motherhood, woman is reduced to an instrument of the species, alienated in her body, which becomes a mere means of procreation' (de Beauvoir 2010, p. 461). This critical view of motherhood has had a profound impact on feminist thought, stimulating reflections on the relationship between gender, the body, and power.

Similarly, Luce Irigaray criticised the Western philosophical tradition for reducing the mother figure to a mere biological function and denying women's subjectivity and experience. She proposed a new conception of motherhood that recognises the unique female experience, valuing its physical and emotional aspects. Irigaray states that 'in Western discourse, the mother has always been relegated to a biological function, denying her subjectivity and voice' (Irigaray 1985, p. 133). However, she argues that motherhood should not only be understood as a natural process, but also as an experience with the potential to transform and restore meaning to female identity. This would challenge the patriarchal structures that have traditionally dominated discourse on motherhood.

Julia Kristeva's reflections on motherhood from a psychoanalytic perspective are an important contribution to our understanding of its complexity, highlighting the ambivalence that characterises the experience. She introduces the concept of 'abjection' to describe the internal conflict a mother can experience when she is torn between loving and rejecting her child, who is both part of herself and different from herself. 'Motherhood is an experience of abjection, in which the mother finds herself negotiating her own identity through the otherness represented by the child' (Kristeva 1987, p. 92). This highlights the psychological complexity of motherhood, which is not only a biological function, but also a process involving deep identity and relational aspects.

Maurice Merleau-Ponty is equally opposed to the objectification of the female body. His philosophy of corporeality has had a profound influence on contemporary philosophical understandings of maternity. Merleau-Ponty argues that the body is a subject that experiences and perceives the world, not simply an object. This conception of the body as 'living flesh' has enabled motherhood to be redefined as an embodied experience in which 'the body is never merely an object, but always an embodied subject living in and constituting the world' (Merleau-Ponty 2012, p. 158). Therefore, the mother's body is not merely a passive container, but an active participant in creating and caring for life. Adrienne Rich, on the other hand, proposes a fundamental distinction between motherhood as a personal experience and motherhood as a social institution. She argues that, although the experience of motherhood can be empowering and fulfilling for women, the institution of motherhood has historically been used to control and subordinate them. According to her feminist understanding, 'motherhood is the experience through which society seeks to shape women, but it is also an opportunity for women to redefine their own power' (Rich 1976, p. 24). This distinction opens up new perspectives on how motherhood can be both an emancipatory experience and a form of oppression depending on how it is experienced and institutionalised.

This brief overview of the evolution of philosophical thought with respect to the concept of motherhood is certainly not exhaustive, but it does make it easier to understand the diversity of interests at play in the current academic debate on surrogacy. To gain a comprehensive understanding, it is crucial to consider the various consequences and implications of motherhood, including biological, psychological, and social aspects.

Originally, motherhood was understood as being functional to the preservation of the species and the evolution of society, with women being considered almost as instruments to achieve procreation. In the Italian context, evidence of this can be seen in the fact that sexual violence was included in Title IX of the Rocco Penal Code of 1930, entitled 'Crimes against public morality and morals'. Within this title, sexual offences, including sexual violence, were treated as crimes that threatened not only individuals, but also public morality and, indirectly, the species—understood as all Italian citizens and their moral and physical integrity. This concept reflected the ideology of the time, which viewed sexuality as primarily functional for reproduction and the protection of the nation's purity and morality. According to this perspective, a woman's body was often viewed as merely a means of reproduction, and sexual violence was more often considered an assault on the honour of the family and society than a crime against the victim.

Over time, this approach has been subject to strong criticism, leading to a major legislative revision. Following the reform of the Italian penal code in 1996, sexual violence was reclassified as an offence against the individual, shifting the focus of penal protection from public morals to the individual's fundamental rights.

As philosophical and scientific thought has evolved, we have therefore witnessed the individualisation of the concept of motherhood, through which women have acquired a central role in the procreation process. This is not only because they are pregnant and therefore vulnerable, but also because they have autonomous and specific interests and rights relating to motherhood, pregnancy and parenthood.

The existence and validity of these interests and rights are still being debated today, with some theorising that they are owned by virtue of the natural connection[10] between mother and child, while others hypothesise that these interests and rights may be detached from the biological and genetic relationship and based on a contractual or intentional one instead. Such hypotheses have emerged as parenthood has increasingly taken on the connotations of a right (without ever really being one), rising—for many—to the status of an essential element for achieving a fulfilling life. This is all under the guise of respect for the right to autonomy and private life, the substance of which has gradually expanded over time. For this reason, since the early 1970s, advances in medical science have focused on enabling those unable to procreate naturally to fulfil the desire to give life to another human being for whom they can take on parental responsibility.

Some of these techniques involve the participation of third parties (donors and/or surrogate mothers), who will have no link with the newborn child at the end of the procreative process. These techniques have generated a wide-ranging debate about their ethical acceptability from the outset. The most debated issue concerns surrogacy, as it calls into question the principle that the mother is always certain, and challenges the concept of parenthood by separating the biological act of giving birth from the parental bond and responsibility.

[10] Natural refers to the relationship between she who gives birth and he/she who is given birth.

2.4 Assisted Reproductive Technologies (ART) and New Forms of Parenthood: Towards Ectogenesis and Synthetic Embryos

What has been said so far highlights the profound changes modern society has undergone in recent years on the subject of family and parenthood.

The report of the International Bioethics Committee (ICB) set up at UNESCO on assisted reproductive technologies (ART) and parenting, published in 2019,[11] contains an in-depth analysis of the main issues related to the relationship between assisted reproductive technologies and parenting.

The ICB is a transnational body established to develop opinions, reports, guidelines and recommendations on the most relevant bioethical issues from a global perspective, as shared as possible.

The paper addresses the relationship between assisted reproductive technologies (ART) and parenting, examining the interactions between social and technological developments leading to new concepts and forms of parenting. The report discusses various aspects of ART, including the causes of infertility, gamete and embryo donation and storage, uterine transplantation, artificial wombs and artificial gametes, *post-mortem* reproduction, and surrogacy, delving into the most problematic ethical and legal aspects.

The report discusses the main ethical, bioethical and bio-legal issues related to the implementation of reproductive technologies in view of how they may impact on the evolution of the concept of parenthood.

In the Committee's view, the new assisted reproductive techniques developed to combat cases of infertility or difficulty in conceiving have made it possible to increasingly develop in individuals and couples the desire for parenthood and to overcome the constraints of 'natural' procreation.

The implementation of these techniques, including surrogacy, carries profound implications for a wide array of domains, including economics, culture, science, ideology, ethics, and religion. The report analyses the various reproductive technologies, providing useful indications on the most problematic bioethical issues associated with each of them, focusing on the positions of the most vulnerable subjects, i.e. the unborn child and the third party (be it the donor or the surrogate mother).

The ICB defines parenthood as the social condition of being a parent, which presupposes the relationship between one or two parents and a child towards whom there are rights, duties and responsibilities.

The notion of parenthood is one that has undergone and is undergoing evolutions over time. The concept of the family unit has historically been intertwined with the Aristotelian framework, which posits the duality and sexual differentiation

[11] UNESCO, International Bioethics Committee (2019) Report of the IBC on Assisted Reproductive Technologies and Parenthood, available at: https://unesdoc.unesco.org/ark:/48223/pf0000367957.

of the parents (mother, father, child). However, the family unit has also exhibited a range of characteristics, including monogamous, polygamous, mononuclear, or extended structures, among others.

The development of reproductive technologies has resulted in the separation of the sexual and reproductive aspects, leading to the differentiation of the genetic, gestational and social levels of parenthood. Consequently, the concept of parenthood has been divided, with the traditional understanding of parenthood being limited to the relationship between a man and a woman (both genetic, social and gestational) from which another human being is given birth. The ICB has observed that this division has led to the emergence of novel challenges and issues in the field of bioethics. These challenges and issues require bioethics to articulate its position, with a view to balancing technological progress and its beneficial effects with the risks for the protection of fundamental human rights, especially of the most fragile and vulnerable subjects.

The traditional family unit has long since experienced a period of flux, commencing with the dissolution of the need for a relationship between individuals of the opposite sex, and thus the acknowledgement of an equivalent parental capacity for homosexual couples and singles, to the point of demands for legal recognition of multi-parent relationships, a concept already advanced in the Netherlands, where through private agreements, there are already groups of four or more individuals exercising parental responsibility over a child. Furthermore, in certain common law countries, such as the United States and Canada, a distinction has been in existence for a considerable period between parentage, parenthood and parental responsibility.

Parentage is defined as referring to those who have biological ties to the child, including gamete donors and surrogate mothers. Parenthood, on the other hand, refers to those who are recognised as the child's legal parents, such as intended parents exercising parental responsibility. Lastly, parental responsibility refers to the person or entity temporarily or permanently exercising parental responsibility over the child in all cases where the exercise of parenthood is not possible or permitted.

For instance, the Californian Family Code establishes a judicial procedure for the recognition of multiple parenthood[12] in cases where there is a need to protect all children who consider their parents to be more than two persons, or where there are individuals who already have an active role in the child's life and who exercise the function of 'de facto' parent over them.

In the Canadian province of British Columbia, the multi-parent relationship may instead originate from a simple agreement between the parties. The Family Law Act[13] stipulates that the biological mother of the child (and potentially a surrogate mother) may be joined by the intended parents, as well as other third parties.

---

[12] California Family Code, § 7612, available at: https://law.justia.com/codes/california/code-fam/division-12/part-3/chapter-2/section-7612/.

[13] Family Law Act, SBC 2011, c. 25 (British Columbia), available at: https://www.canlii.org/en/bc/laws/stat/sbc-2011-c-25/latest/sbc-2011-c-25.html.

In contrast, the province of Ontario has established a framework that allows for the establishment of pre-conception agreements. These agreements, in essence, grant legal recognition to up to four individuals as parents, even in cases of natural conception. This framework has the potential to exclude the 'natural' father from assuming parental responsibilities, should he be qualified as a donor.[14]

The scientific development of medically assisted procreation techniques, in conjunction with the evolution of contemporary family models that are increasingly heterogeneous, necessitates an effective evolutionary response from legal systems and, most crucially, from the jurisprudential categories that underpin the theory of law in the bioethical field (Lam 2024).

Indeed, the categorisation of the various forms of parenting that are the subject of contemporary discourse can be traced back to the initial genetic classification, which is attributable to those who are identified as the 'owners' of the gametes that gave rise to the embryo. A second gestational type is recognised in respect of the woman who gives birth to the child and carries the pregnancy to term. A third of a legal kind is attributed instead to those who concretely manifest the desire for parenthood and the will to have parental responsibility attributed to them. This is an area which is still evolving, thanks in part to the implementation of new reproductive technologies, among which recent scientific studies on ectogenesis and synthetic embryos stand out.

Ectogenesis, otherwise referred to as artificial womb, is defined as the process of functional evolution of a foetus outside the natural womb, in an artificial environment. Ectogenesis can be categorised as either partial or complete. Partial ectogenesis[15] occurs when a pregnancy takes place outside the woman's body, for example, when babies born prematurely continue their growth and development in an incubator. In contrast, complete ectogenesis occurs when the pregnancy takes place from the beginning of the embryonic phase until delivery in an artificial environment (Segers 2021). In order to successfully carry a pregnancy to term, it is essential that the gestational sac containing the foetus is filled with amniotic fluid, which provides a protective environment for the developing embryo. The umbilical cord serves the vital function of supplying the foetus with oxygen, hormones and nutrients.

To date, biobags[16] have successfully supported the growth of a premature lamb foetus for a period of 28 days (Partridge et al. 2017). However, the development of an artificial womb for human use has given rise to significant ethical questions concerning the social and identity implications for the child, as well as the consequences of the absence of sensory experiences and emotional development typically associated with natural pregnancy (Stratman 2023).

---

[14] Children's Law Reform Act, RSO 1990, c. C.12, s. 7.4 (Ontario), available at: https://www.canlii.org/en/on/laws/stat/rso-1990-c-c12/latest/rso-1990-c-c12.html.

[15] Partial ectogenesis is also defined as the use of biobags that attempt to reproduce what happens inside the uterine sac, Romanis (2020), p. 392.

[16] This is what amniotic sacs that mimic the activity of amniotic sacs are called.

Concurrently, the advancement of ectogenesis holds the potential to enhance the survival prospects of numerous premature infants, particularly in developing countries, and to serve as a sustainable solution to maternal-fetal conflict by subsequent reduction of abortion rates (Okesanya et al. 2024).

It is evident that ectogenesis may serve as a viable alternative to surrogacy (Tumanishvili and Poli 2017; Poli 2015) or in instances of unwanted pregnancies (Segers et al. 2020), thereby eradicating the disparities between men and women associated with pregnancy. This approach liberates women from the physical, financial and social burdens associated with procreation (Kennedy 2020) and the risks and constraints of pregnancy, labour and delivery (Horn 2020; Knight 2020).

The issue has been shown to have multiple social, psychological and ethical implications. The potential implications of ectogenesis extend beyond the realm of reproductive biology, encompassing ethical, legal and social considerations. These include the re-definition of parental roles, concerns regarding privacy and psychological well-being of children, and the potential emotional detachment of the latter from their biological parents. Conversely, ectogenesis holds the promise of promoting reproductive equality, mitigating clinical risks and offering alternatives to existing practices such as surrogacy and abortion. However, a number of challenges have been identified that may hinder progress in this area. These include technical difficulties, ethical issues, consent problems and various challenges related to regulatory frameworks (Okesanya et al. 2024).

In any event, the appropriate incorporation of ectogenesis within the domain of reproductive medicine is contingent upon ongoing discourse, with the objective of elucidating the implications of emerging knowledge and addressing the emergence of novel ethical concerns.[17]

It is evident that artificial embryos represent one of the most fascinating and controversial frontiers of biological research and bioethical speculation. Although ectogenesis is more recently developed, it is nevertheless inextricably linked to artificial embryos. Synthetic embryos are also known to be the result of a particular technology (Aguilera-Castrejon et al. 2021) that does not require the use of ova or sperm. Instead, this technology uses the reprogramming of stem cells capable of self-organising themselves to form embryo-like structures in their early stages of development (Shahbazi and Zernicka-Goetz 2018). The study of this process, which has hitherto been exclusively tested on mouse cells, gives rise to significant ethical questions, closely linked to the dignity of the synthetic embryo and the risk of the instrumentalisation of human life.

On the one hand, there are compelling reasons to pursue experimentation and research in the attempt to create embryos through stem cells. These reasons include the implementation of basic scientific knowledge in the first days after embryo formation, as well as the potential applications of regenerative medicine in organ

[17] For a more detailed discussion on the visual and ethical aspects of artificial womb technologies and related innovations, see Kendal (2022), Sahoo and Gulla (2019), and Hammond-Browning and Williams (2020).

transplantation and assisted reproduction. On the other hand, however, the process gives rise to several worrying ethical issues.

Among a multitude of other scholars (Villalba et al. 2023), a significant number have pondered the potential outcomes of the creation of functional primitive nerve structures during their ectogestation. Indeed, establishing a parallel with abortion, which is only considered legal before a certain stage of foetal development,[18] and assuming the existence of synthetic embryos, would their destruction also only be considered legal before a certain stage of development?

Furthermore, the legal status of these embryos would be a cause of considerable legal uncertainty, since they would not fall under the traditional definitions of a human embryo established by many national and international laws (Hyun et al. 2020). These innovations have the potential to separate the notion of an 'embryo' from the fertilisation of an egg with sperm and its maternal gestation, leading to significant uncertainty about the moral status of artificial embryos. The extent to which these cells can be considered 'true embryos' is a contentious issue, given the already highly controversial definition of a human embryo.[19] The question of how such entities should be considered during the process of development ex utero is a complex one. In the event of the development of a future child in an artificial womb from the initial stage, who would be held accountable from a moral and legal standpoint? In light of the prevailing legal framework in numerous nations that attributes legal responsibility to the individual who gives birth to the child, irrespective of the child's genetic origins, it cannot be assumed that this responsibility can be attributed to the donors of the genetic material.

[18] With respect to the ultimate moment by which abortion can be performed, the concept of 'life' as a moral category comes to the fore. According to some, life begins at the moment of fertilisation according to an immediate conception of life based on the fact that the zygote is genetically human and potentially a person; according to others, the embryo acquires a moral status progressively through certain key stages such as implantation in the uterus, the development of the nervous system or the ability to perceive pain according to a *gradual conception*; others argue that the beginning of 'life' is linked to the moment when the embryo can sustain an independent life (viability, usually around the 24th week of gestation) according to a *functional conception*. On fetal pain, see Derbyshire and Bockmann (2020).

[19] Some countries, including Spain, maintain that only fertilised eggs may be considered embryos. Others, such as the Netherlands and Belgium, adopt a broader definition, recognising as embryos any cell or group of cells with the potential to develop into a human being, regardless of the method by which development is initiated. In 2011, the Court of Justice of the European Union (CJEU) ruled in Brüstle v Greenpeace (Case C-34/10) that the concept of "human embryo" must be interpreted broadly, holding that every human ovum, once fertilised, must be regarded as a human embryo if that fertilisation is capable of initiating the process of human development. However, the same Court appeared to revise this approach in a subsequent decision, International Stem Cell Corporation v Comptroller General of Patents, Designs, and Trade Marks (Case C-364/13), where it adopted a more restrictive definition. In that judgment, the CJEU held that only those unfertilised human ova—activated by techniques such as somatic cell nuclear transfer—that are capable of initiating the process of development in a manner comparable to that of a fertilised egg may be considered embryos. For an in-depth analysis of the implications of these rulings in the context of biotechnology and patent law, see de Miguel Beriain (2017), pp. 263–273.

The question of whether children born under the legal and moral responsibility of the state could be considered as conceivable is a complex one.

The implementation of these technologies could revolutionise biomedical research, making it possible to study human embryonic development without using embryos derived from in-vitro fertilisation, thus reducing the ethical implications of destroying the embryos themselves (Aach et al. 2017). However, the use of artificial embryos in clinical applications is still a long way off, hampered by complex technical and moral problems. The interplay between scientific innovation and regulation will be crucial to ensure that progress in this field is accompanied by a robust ethical and regulatory *framework* that can change most of our current paradigms on reproductive ethics.

2.5 Reproductive Tourism and Surrogacy

As previously stated, the aspiration to become parents through surrogacy has motivated couples and individuals to travel to countries where the practice is legally recognised or where the legislation aligns with their personal preferences or financial circumstances to enter into international surrogacy agreements (Fenton-Glynn 2016). These surrogacy agreements are distinguished by the fact that the intended parents possess a nationality other than that of the state where fertilisation occurs and have the intention of taking the child with them after birth.

The phenomenon of reproductive tourism, which has been the subject of much debate in recent years, is characterised by the travel of individuals to foreign countries with the primary objective of undergoing assisted conception treatment. This trend is intricately interwoven with the divergent legislation observed across various states, both within Europe and beyond. Additionally, it is noteworthy that supranational jurisprudence has come to acknowledge the possibility of obtaining recognition of the filiation relationship and the attribution of parental responsibility, even in countries where such practices are prohibited on the basis of the *logique du fait accompli* and the best interests of the child.[20]

The logic of du fait accompli necessitates the determination of the legal and economic ramifications for intended parents who have engaged in surrogacy practices abroad, despite the prohibition of such activities within their own national jurisdiction. It is imperative to recognise that the birth of a child through surrogacy is irrevocable, and the implications of this act cannot be undone. It is precisely for this reason that, in addition to the fact that the child is not a party to the surrogacy agreement but is the result of it and thus the subject who, more than any other, has the right to be protected, case law and consequently a significant proportion of the regulations governing the effects of international surrogacy agreements obligate states to act in what is considered to be the best interests of the child.

[20] This topic will be dealt with in detail in Sect. 2.11.

In the following paragraph, an attempt will be made to stimulate further reflection by offering a comparative overview of some of the laws on surrogacy. This will involve highlighting some of the commonly accepted or most divergent aspects, and distinguishing between countries where there is no specific legislation on the subject, those where surrogacy is prohibited in any form (such as Italy, where it is considered a universal crime), and those where only altruistic surrogacy is legal. The paragraph will conclude with a look at countries where it is legal to enter into commercial surrogacy contracts.

As of the present moment, the European states[21] that have implemented a prohibition on all forms of surrogacy include Austria, Estonia, France, Germany, Italy, Lithuania, Norway, Spain, Sweden and Switzerland (Piersanti et al. 2021). At the international level, the aforementioned prohibition has been enacted in Uruguay, Turkey, Cambodia, Singapore, Nepal and Egypt. In contrast, commercial surrogacy agreements are legally recognised in Georgia, Russia, Ukraine, Canada and several US states.

In the other countries where surrogacy has been specifically regulated, it is only legal in its altruistic form (Guerra-Palmero 2017; Raposo 2017), such as the United Kingdom, Portugal, Greece and, after changes in recent years, also Ireland, India and Thailand (two of the most notorious countries where commercial surrogacy had taken on the features of a real industry). Finally, certain countries, including Belgium, the Netherlands, Albania and several African states, have no specific regulations yet tolerate the existence of surrogacy agreements.

2.6 The Absolute Prohibition of Surrogacy

In the majority of European countries, surrogacy is explicitly prohibited by law and is subject to criminal prosecution, which can result in imprisonment or a fine.

In Germany, the prohibition is stated in section 1 of the Embryo Protection Act[22] (Embryonenschutzgesetz), which provides for a maximum custodial sentence of three years. Similarly, the German Civil Code, in section 1591, states that "the legal mother of the child is she who gives birth to it".[23]

---

[21] For a comparative study of the regime in the European states see Brunet et al. (2013) available at https://www.europarl.europa.eu/RegData/etudes/STUD/2013/474403/IPOL-JURI_ET(2013)474403_EN.pdf.

[22] *Gesetz zum Schutz von Embryonen* (*Embryonenschutzgesetz*—ESchG), BGBl. I S. 2746, 13 December 1990. [Act for the Protection of Embryos (Embryo Protection Act] Available at: https://www.gesetze-im-internet.de/eschg/BJNR027460990.html.

[23] Art. 1591, *Bürgerliches Gesetzbuch* (BGB), "Mutter eines Kindes ist die Frau, die es geboren hat" [Civil Code (BGB), "The mother of a child is the woman who gave birth to it] (*trans. by the author*), available at: https://www.buzer.de/1591_BGB.htm.

In Spain, surrogacy is expressly prohibited by Article 10 of Law 14/2006[24] on Assisted Human Reproduction Techniques, which states that gestation contracts for third parties are null and void. The regulation stipulates that maternity is attributed to the woman who gives birth to the child, irrespective of any pre-existing agreements between the parties involved.

In France, Article 16–7[25] of the Civil Code as amended by the 1994 Law on Creation[26] stipulates that any convention for procreation or gestation for third parties is null and void. As stipulated in both Article 119 of the Federal Constitution[27] and Article 4 of the Federal Act on Reproductive Medicine[28] (LPMA), Switzerland has also prohibited surrogacy.

In Italy, the prohibition of surrogacy is codified in Article 12(6) of Law 40/2004,[29] which stipulates criminal and administrative penalties for individuals who promote or execute the practice within Italy. This legislation also renders any agreements concluded internationally illegal. In recent developments, the government has expanded the scope of the offence of surrogacy to a universal offence, thereby extending the reach of legal consequences to individuals who engage in surrogacy activities in foreign countries where such practices are legally recognised.

In Norway, the Biotechnology Act[30] (*Bioteknologiloven*), in Article 16, prohibits surrogacy and marketing and brokering in activities involving surrogacy in order to avoid the economic or physical exploitation of pregnant women.

---

[24] Art. 10, *Ley 14/2006, de 26 de mayo, sobre técnicas de reproducción humana asistida*, "Será nulo de pleno derecho el contrato por el que se convenga la gestación, con o sin precio, a cargo de una mujer que renuncia a la filiación materna a favor del contratante o de un tercero" [Any agreement whereby a woman undertakes to carry a pregnancy, with or without remuneration, and relinquishes maternal affiliation in favour of the contracting party or a third party shall be null and void] (*trans. by the author*). Available at: https://www.boe.es/buscar/act.php?id=BOE-A-2006-9292.

[25] Art. 16–7, *Code civil*, "Toute convention portant sur la procréation ou la gestation pour le compte d'autrui est nulle" [Any agreement relating to procreation or gestation on behalf of another person is null and void] (*trans. by the author*). Available at: https://www.legifrance.gouv.fr/codes/article_lc/LEGIARTI000006419302.

[26] Art. 3, *Loi n°94-653 du 29 juillet 1994*, *Journal Officiel de la République Française* (JORF), 30 juillet 1994 [Law No. 94–653 of 29 July 1994, Article 3, prohibiting surrogacy contracts in France]. Available at: https://www.legifrance.gouv.fr/loda/id/LEGIARTI000006284447/1994-07-30.

[27] Art. 119, *Constitution fédérale de la Confédération suisse, Médecine de la procréation et génie génétique chez l'être humain* [Federal Constitution of the Swiss Confederation, Art. 119, Reproductive Medicine and Genetic Engineering in Humans]. Available at: https://www.fedlex.admin.ch/eli/cc/1999/404/it.

[28] Art. 4, *Loi fédérale sur la procréation médicalement assistée* (LPMA), art. 4 [Swiss Law on Reproductive Medicine]. Available at: https://www.fedlex.admin.ch/eli/cc/2000/554/it.

[29] *Legge 19 febbraio 2004, n. 40, Norme in materia di procreazione medicalmente assistita* (Law No. 40 of 19 February 2004 on Medically Assisted Procreation), *Gazzetta Ufficiale della Repubblica Italiana*, No. 45 of 24 February 2004. Available at: https://www.gazzettaufficiale.it/eli/id/2004/02/24/004G0062/sg.

[30] *Bioteknologiloven* [Biotechnology Act], *lov 5 desember 2003 nr 100, art. 16.* Available at: https://lovdata.no/dokument/NL/lov/2003-12-05-100.

Austria, with Article 3 of the Law on Medically Assisted Reproduction[31] (*Fortpflanzungsmedizingesetz*), prohibits all surrogacy contracts. Outside Europe, for instance, in China, the 2001 Administrative Regulation on Assisted Reproductive Technology issued by the Chinese Ministry of Health expressly prohibits medical institutions and health personnel from offering surrogacy services. Specifically, Article 3 of the regulation states that "any form of surrogacy is prohibited"[32] prevents hospitals from providing surrogacy services.

In South Korea, the Bioethics and Safety Act[33] is the primary legislative instrument that governs assisted reproductive technologies (ART). The act establishes a regulatory framework that is characterised by a strict approach, with the sanctioning of the illegality of commercial practice in the context of medical ethics. The Medical Service Act prohibits medical professionals from participating in procedures that violate ethical principles, including surrogacy.

Finally, in Saudi Arabia, surrogacy is prohibited based on Sharia principles, as it is considered to be contrary to Islamic precepts on family and kinship. The Ulema Council has issued guidelines that prohibit surrogacy, considering the practice to be in violation of the purity of the lineage and family ties established by the Koran.

The prohibition of surrogacy practices, brokering activities, non-recognition of parental responsibility in the hands of intended parents, and the resulting criminal sanctions for offenders continually clash with the internationally formally recognised principle of the best interests of the child. This principle, based on the *logique du fait accompli*, treats the child born of surrogacy as a fait accompli from which there is no turning back. Furthermore, it recognises the child's absolute blamelessness, providing that the child's life interests may not be affected. This has given rise to difficulties in coordinating the need to protect children born through international surrogacy with the national laws of countries that prohibit surrogacy. Such difficulties include the imposition of sanctions and the recognition of the filiation relationship and parental responsibility, which is usually from a judicial source.

2.7 The Regulation of Altruistic Surrogacy

In order to identify the essential legislative aspects that have been identified for the protection of the parties involved in surrogacy agreements, it may be particularly useful to review, albeit briefly, the essential elements of European and international surrogacy legislation.

---

[31] *Fortpflanzungsmedizingesetz* [Reproductive Medicine Act], 4 June 1992, as amended, §3. Available at: https://lovdata.no/dokument/NL/lov/2003-12-05-100.

[32] Administrative Regulation on Human Assisted Reproductive Technology, issued by the Ministry of Health of the People's Republic of China, Order No. 47 (2001), art. 3. English translation available at: https://www.gov.cn/english/laws/2005-10/10/content_75023.htm.

[33] Enforcement Decree of the Fertiliser Control Act, Korea, available at: https://elaw.klri.re.kr/eng_service/lawView.do?hseq=28880&lang=ENG.

The United Kingdom was one of the first countries on the European continent to regulate surrogacy. As early as 1985 with the Surrogacy Arrangements Act[34] established the regulatory framework for surrogacy arrangements, a framework subsequently supplemented by the Human Fertilisation and Embryology Act in 1990.[35]

The legal framework reflects a balance between scientific progress, ethical considerations and the protection of the welfare of the child and the surrogate. Specifically, the 1985 Act defines surrogacy agreements as not legally binding, stipulating that the surrogate mother retains all parental rights over the child until these are transferred to the intended parents through a court order.[36] It is important to note that even in the event of a formal agreement being in place between the surrogate mother and the intended parents, the surrogate retains the right to change her mind following the birth of the child. This necessitates her consent for the transfer of parental rights.[37]

Moreover, the legislation provides for an absolute ban on commercial surrogacy agreements, allowing only 'altruistic' agreements. This implies that the surrogate mother may only receive reimbursement for expenses actually incurred or for other costs considered reasonable in connection with the pregnancy, while any form of compensation is prohibited.[38] Furthermore, commercial intermediation is prohibited, with specific prohibitions on the activities of agencies that aim to make a profit from the 'placement' of surrogate mothers or the promotion of agreements between the parties.[39]

Parental transfer, which is a key process in the context of surrogacy, is regulated by the Human Fertilisation and Embryology Act of 2008, which provides that intended parents can apply for a so-called *Parental Order*. This procedure allows parental rights to be transferred from the surrogate mother to the intended parents and can be requested within 6 months after the birth of the child.[40] In order for the parental relationship to be transferred, the law stipulates that at least one of the intended parents must be genetically related to the child.

[34] Surrogacy Arrangements Act 1985, United Kingdom. Available at: https://www.legislation.gov.uk/ukpga/1985/49.

[35] Human Fertilisation and Embryology Act 1990, United Kingdom. Available at: https://www.legislation.gov.uk/ukpga/1990/37.

[36] Surrogacy Arrangements Act 1985, Section 1, United Kingdom. Available at: https://www.legislation.gov.uk/ukpga/1985/49/section/1.

[37] Surrogacy Arrangements Act 1985, Section 1B, United Kingdom. Available at: https://www.legislation.gov.uk/ukpga/1985/49/section/1B.

[38] Surrogacy Arrangements Act 1985, Section 2(1), United Kingdom. Available at: https://www.legislation.gov.uk/ukpga/1985/49/section/2.

[39] Surrogacy Arrangements Act 1985, Section 3, United Kingdom. Available at: https://www.legislation.gov.uk/ukpga/1985/49/section/3.

[40] Human Fertilisation and Embryology Act 2008, Section 54, United Kingdom. Available at: https://www.legislation.gov.uk/ukpga/2008/22/section/54.

Furthermore, the surrogate mother must have given her free and fully informed consent to the transfer no earlier than six weeks after the birth. The intended parents must also be married, in a civil union, or cohabiting, or they may be single.[41]

These provisions reflect the UK's approach to surrogacy, which seeks to prioritise the welfare of the child and the protection of the surrogate mother by ensuring that the transfer of parenthood is carried out without any profit motive. This system aims to prevent the commercial exploitation of surrogate mothers and to protect the rights of the child by restricting surrogacy to a process based on informed and altruistic consent.

Ireland with a recent law enacted in 2024 after a 2-year legislative process has regulated in a single piece of legislation of 234 articles medically assisted reproduction procedures including surrogacy by distinguishing between domestic surrogacy[42] and the recognition of international surrogacy agreements.[43] In addition, the new regulation also allows—under certain conditions—the recognition of the parental relationship based on surrogacy agreements concluded before the law came into force.

Domestic surrogacy agreements are entered into between a surrogate mother who has been resident in Ireland for at least 2 years and an intended parent couple, at least one of whom must have been lawfully resident in Ireland for at least 2 years (in the case of singles, the latter must also have been lawfully resident for at least 2 years) and the implantation of the embryo takes place within the State.

The law provides for the establishment of the Assisted Human Reproduction Regulatory Authority (AHRRA), which is responsible for carrying out all the necessary activities (licensing, regulatory, monitoring, etc.) needed to protect, promote and guarantee the health of the parties involved in medically assisted reproductive techniques (donors, surrogate mothers and children).[44]

Surrogacy is only permitted when the agreement is approved by AHRRA because the surrogate mother: (a) has already given birth to a child; (b) is at least 25 years old; (c) has a positive report from the AHR (*Assisted Human Reproduction*) clinic; (d) has been assessed by a medical specialist as capable of carrying a pregnancy; (e) the surrogate mother must not have been a surrogate mother on more than one occasion or must have already carried two clinical pregnancies.[45]

---

[41] Human Fertilisation and Embryology Act 2008, Section 54(2), United Kingdom. Available at: https://www.legislation.gov.uk/ukpga/2008/22/section/54.

[42] Health (Assisted Human Reproduction) Act 2024, Part 7—Domestic Surrogacy, Ireland. Available at: https://www.irishstatutebook.ie/eli/2024/act/18/enacted/en/print#sec51.

[43] Health (Assisted Human Reproduction) Act 2024, Part 8—Domestic Surrogacy, Ireland. Available at: https://www.irishstatutebook.ie/eli/2024/act/18/enacted/en/print#sec51.

[44] Health (Assisted Human Reproduction) Act 2024, Part 9—Assisted Human Reproduction Regulatory Authority, Ireland. Available at: https://www.irishstatutebook.ie/eli/2024/act/18/enacted/en/print#sec122.

[45] A clinical pregnancy is defined as a pregnancy of at least six weeks ascertained ultrasound.

The request for surrogacy is admissible for couples and singles of at least 21 years of age, through the use of at least 1 gamete from them provided that at least one of them has a reasonable life expectancy to raise the child until the child reaches the age of 18.

In order to perform surrogacy, the woman of the couple or the applicant woman must not be able to conceive a child even after the application of one of the medically assisted reproductive techniques; she must not be able to carry a pregnancy to term. Furthermore, she must be unlikely to survive a pregnancy; or it must be highly probable that her health will be compromised as a result of a pregnancy. The intended parents (or intended parent) must undertake within the surrogacy agreement to provide protection and care for the child and to submit a request to the court to issue a *parental order* in order to transfer the parental relationship from the surrogate mother to the intended parents.

Any commercial surrogacy arrangement is prohibited, meaning an arrangement whereby a person offers, accepts or receives payment or reward for entering into or performing the arrangement or for brokering or facilitating the entering into or performance of surrogacy arrangements except for the surrogate mother's reasonable advice and expenses.

Reasonable expenses are considered to be those expenses associated with attempting to initiate the pregnancy and childbirth and entering into or implementing the contract. These include any pre-natal or post-natal medical expenses, any travel or accommodation expenses associated with the pregnancy or delivery, expenses to reimburse the surrogate mother for any net loss of income resulting from the surrogate mother being unable to work for medical reasons related to the pregnancy or delivery for a period not exceeding 12 months in total.

The following expenses are considered reasonable when entering into and executing a surrogacy agreement: the costs of medically assisted procreation counselling related to the agreement; independent, related travel and accommodation costs; and the costs incurred in the procedure for granting the parental order.

Reasonable expenses within the meaning of the Health Act include all expenses resulting from obligations arising from the execution of the Act and lastly the Act also specifies those for: (a) maternity clothes; (b) paid housework or childcare carried out by persons other than the surrogate mother and her spouse, civil partner or cohabitee (if any); (c) pregnancy aids that contribute to the surrogate mother's comfort and well-being; (d) any other expenses typically incurred in the course of a pregnancy.

The legislation also provides for the establishment of a National Surrogacy Registry in which all relevant information on the agreements, their execution and births including the identities of the gamete donors used and the surrogate mother must be recorded.

The regulation stipulates the possibility, through the implementation of a designated procedure, to acknowledge the validity of surrogacy agreements concluded internationally in accordance with alternative provisions, thereby facilitating a more efficient process to attain a parental order.

The court grants the parental order if the child resides with one or both intended parents and there is a regular surrogacy contract.

In the event that the surrogacy contract predates the enactment of the Health Act, the application must be filed within three years of the law coming into force or within six months of the birth of the child. In any event, it is imperative that the aforementioned agreement is in accordance with the stipulated requirements for domestic surrogacy agreements.

In the southern Mediterranean region, Greece and Portugal have enacted two of the most significant pieces of legislation aimed at regulating surrogacy.

The first piece of legislation in this area was Law No. 3089 of 2002[46], which amended Chapter Eight of the Greek Civil Code (articles 1455 to 1460). This legislation allowed surrogacy of motherhood exclusively for couples or single women unable to initiate or carry a pregnancy in a natural way, or to avoid the transmission of a serious illness to the child. The matter was definitively regulated by Law No. 3305/2005, subsequently amended by Law No. 4272/2014,[47] which extended its scope to both residents of Greece and those with only temporary residence

Law 3305[48] stipulates that medically assisted fertilisation techniques, including surrogacy techniques, may be performed on and requested by women up to 50 years of age (up to 54 years of age with a special authorisation from the judicial authority) subject to the following conditions: informed consent must be obtained, and the woman must undergo specific tests for HIV, Hepatitis B, C and syphilis. Furthermore, it is imperative that the surrogacy activity and the biological material used are prohibited from any form of commercialisation. The implementation of the practice is only possible following the granting of judicial authorisation prior to the transfer of the ova. This is subject to the condition that there is a written agreement, unrelated to financial compensation, between the persons wishing to have a child and the surrogate mother. In the case of the surrogate mother being married, the agreement must also be with her spouse.

At the same time, the Act identifies that the payment of sums necessary for cryopreservation of gametes, for obtaining gametes and in any case the reimbursement of the payment of expenses necessary to achieve pregnancy, gestation, childbirth, puerperium and any positive damage suffered by the pregnant woman due to absence from work, as well as the payment of wages for work she has been deprived of due to absence, for the purpose of achieving pregnancy, during pregnancy, childbirth, puerperium or following a caesarean section, is not to be considered commercialisation.[49]

---

[46] Νόμος 3089/2022 [Law 3089/2022], Greece. Available at: https://www.kodiko.gr/nomothesia/document/175735/nomos-3089-2002.

[47] Νόμος 4272/2014 [Law 4272/2014], Greece. Available at: https://www.kodiko.gr/nomothesia/document/97577/nomos-4272-2014.

[48] *Νόμος 3305/2005* [Law 3305/2005], Greece. Available at: https://www.kodiko.gr/nomothesia/document/164338/nomos-3305-2005.

[49] Law 3305/2005, Article 13(4), Greece: *"Η συμφωνία για κυοφορία από τρίτη γυναίκα γίνεται χωρίς οποιοδήποτε αντάλλαγμα. Δεν συνιστά αντάλλαγμα: α. η καταβολή των δαπανών που απαιτούνται για την επίτευξη της εγκυμοσύνης, την κυοφορία, τον τοκετό και τη λοχεία, β. κάθε θετική ζημία της κυοφόρου εξαιτίας αποχής από την εργασία της, καθώς και οι αμοιβές για*

The surrogate mother must be aged between 25 and 45 years, must already have given birth to at least one child, and must not have undergone more than two caesarean sections.[50] The aforementioned sums in each case are settled by the court and paid directly by the clinic, which in turn will be paid by the intended parents.

The parental relationship between the child born by surrogacy and the intended parents is recognised immediately, pursuant to Article 1464 of the Civil Code, provided that the requirements of Article 1458 of the Civil Code have been met. This is because surrogacy is presumed to have been preceded by the relevant judicial authorisation.

Information pertaining to the identity of the surrogate mother or third-party donors is stored in coded form in a national registry at the time of the child's birth. This information may only be disclosed to the child once they have reached the age of majority, if they so request.

Portugal, on the other hand, adopted regulations to make surrogacy legal with *Regulamentar Decree* No. 6/2017[51] which implemented Law 25/2016[52] on surrogacy, which supplemented the 2006 law on medically assisted procreation.[53]

The regulations enacted by the Portuguese Parliament and their implementing regulations stipulate that medically assisted procreation through surrogacy is subject to prior authorisation. This authorisation is granted by the National Committee for Medically Assisted Procreation (CNPMA) upon request by the intended parents and the surrogate mother, following the submission of a report by a psychologist/

εξαρτημένη εργασία, τις οποίες στερήθηκε λόγω απουσίας, με σκοπό την επίτευξη της εγκυμοσύνης, την κυοφορία, τον τοκετό και τη λοχεία. Το ύψος των καλυπτόμενων δαπανών και αποζημιώσεων καθορίζεται με απόφαση της Αρχής". ["*The agreement for gestation by a third woman is made without any consideration. Not considered consideration are: (a) the reimbursement of expenses required for achieving pregnancy, gestation, childbirth, and postnatal care; (b) any positive loss of the surrogate resulting from abstention from work, as well as wages lost due to absence for the purpose of pregnancy, gestation, childbirth, and postnatal care. The amount of reimbursable expenses and compensation is determined by decision of the Authority*"] (*trans. by the author*). Available at: https://www.kodiko.gr/nomothesia/document/164338/nomos-3305-2005.

[50] *Κώδικας Δεοντολογίας για την Ιατρικά Υποβοηθούμενη Αναπαραγωγή*, Απόφαση 73/24-1-2017, *ΦΕΚ* 293/B/7-2-2017, [Code of Ethics for Medically Assisted Reproduction] Art. 9 "*Ο ιατρικός επιστήμονας οφείλει να λαμβάνει τη συγκατάθεση του ζευγαριού …*" ["The medical practitioner must obtain the couple's consent …"] (*trans. by the author*). Available at: https://www.e-nomothesia.gr/kat-ygeia/tekhnete-gonimopoiese/apophase-73-24-1-2017-fek-293b-7-2-2017.html.

[51] *Decreto Regulamentar nº 6/2017 de 31 de julho* (Regulatory Decree No. 6/2017 of 31 July, 2017), Portugal. Available at: https://diariodarepublica.pt/dr/detalhe/decreto-regulamentar/6-2017-107785481.

[52] *Lei nº 25/2016 de 22 de agosto—Regula o acesso à gestação de substituição, procedendo à terceira alteração à Lei n.º 32/2006 de 26 de julho (procriação medicamente assistida)* [Law No. 25/2016 of 22 August regulating access to surrogacy and amending Law No. 32/2006 on medically assisted reproduction], Portugal. Available at: https://diariodarepublica.pt/dr/detalhe/lei/25-2016-75177806.

[53] *Lei n.º 32/2006 de 26 de julho—Procriação medicamente assistida* [Law No. 32/2006 of 26 July on medically assisted reproduction], Portugal. Available at: https://diariodarepublica.pt/dr/detalhe/lei/32-2006-539239.

psychiatrist. The director of the Medically Assisted Procreation Centre where the fertilisation is to be conducted and the relevant Medical Association must also provide their consent.

The surrogacy contract must be drafted in accordance with a model prepared by the legislator and must be verified by the CNPMA. Specifically, the practice of surrogacy is only legal in the event that the recipient woman or intended mother is without a uterus or due to a disease or dysfunction of the uterus or another specific condition is unable to initiate or carry a pregnancy.

In any event, it is not possible for there to be a biological connection between the surrogate mother and the child. Consequently, it can be deduced that the gametes must be from third parties other than the mother.

It is prohibited for beneficiaries to offer any form of payment or donation, including goods, to the surrogate mother for the gestation of the child. This prohibition does not apply to the amount corresponding to the expenses arising from the health monitoring provided, including transport, on the condition that these expenses are duly justified;[54] furthermore, it is prohibited to carry out the practice in the event of any economic subordination or employment relationship between the parties involved.

Access to surrogacy techniques within the Portuguese National Health Service also results in equal access to the practice for all citizens.

The requirements for access to surrogacy are the same as for the other medically assisted procreation techniques within Law 32/2006, i.e. it is only applicable to couples of different sexes who are married or have been cohabiting for more than two years, are of full age, and are capable of consent. Both the intended parents and the surrogate mother undergo thorough medical tests and psychological interviews, also with the CNPMA, in order to verify that all the conditions for proceeding with fertilisation are met.

India has been a significant destination for reproductive tourism for a considerable number of years. The issue of surrogacy has undergone a complex regulatory evolution, shifting from an initially permissive model due to the absence of a regulatory apparatus to a more restrictive regulation aimed at protecting what appeared to be massive exploitation. Since the 1990s, India has distinguished itself as a popular destination for international surrogacy by virtue of its low costs and the significant number of women willing to act as surrogate mothers. The disparity in the value of the Indian currency, particularly in comparison to that of Western states, resulted in a scenario wherein the compensation received by some women for surrogacy arrangements exceeded five times the annual salary of the average Indian.

Commercial surrogacy was considered legal by virtue of a legal loophole, until the Indian Supreme Court, in the *Baby Manji Yamada vs. Union of India* judgment,

[54] Art. 8, para. 5, Law No. 25/2016 Regulating access to surrogacy and amending Law No. 32/2006 on medically assisted reproduction], Portugal. Available at: https://diariodarepublica.pt/dr/detalhe/lei/25-2016-75177806.

formally recognised the legitimacy of surrogacy agreements that had been entered into up to that point, while pointing out the existence of a real surrogacy industry[55] and without providing a clear legislative framework.

Until then, the practice was exclusively regulated by the National Guidelines for Accreditation, Supervision and Regulation of Assisted Reproductive Technology (ART) Clinics formulated by the Indian Council of Medical Research (ICMR).[56] These guidelines established certain minimum requirements, such as the need for written contracts between the principals and the pregnant woman, and the need for authorised clinics to be listed in a register maintained by the Ministry of Health, but lacked binding legal force. The absence of regulation led to the proliferation of an uncontrolled industry, often characterised by abuse and exploitation of pregnant women, many of whom came from vulnerable socio-economic backgrounds.[57]

The pivotal moment that marked a significant shift in the legal landscape was the introduction of the Surrogacy (Regulation) Act,[58] initially proposed in 2016 and subsequently enacted into law in 2021. This Act prohibited commercial surrogacy, allowing only altruistic surrogacy, and imposed several stringent criteria to access the practice. Principals must be Indian citizens, married and childless. Furthermore, the surrogate mother cannot receive any compensation except for medical and insurance costs.

A further new element was the establishment of national and state authorities to regulate the practice and register clinics, to ensure transparency and compliance. However, the new law has attracted criticism from the scientific community and women's rights groups, who point out that the excessive restrictions may be an incentive to bring surrogacy to the black market, increasing the risk of exploitation and commodification of women's bodies. In summary, the regulation of surrogacy in India represents an attempt to balance ethical, social and medical needs, but the practical impact of the new regulations and their effectiveness in preventing abuse remains a matter of debate.

---

[55] In *Baby Manji Yamada v. Union of India*, Supreme Court of India, Writ Petition (Crl.) No. 112 of 2008, para. 9, the Court observes: "This medical procedure is legal in several countries including in India where, due to excellent medical infrastructure, high international demand and ready availability of poor surrogates, it is reaching industry proportions. Commercial surrogacy is sometimes referred to by the emotionally charged and potentially offensive terms 'wombs for rent', 'outsourced pregnancies' or 'baby farms'." Available at: https://indiankanoon.org/doc/854968/.

[56] Since 2005, surrogacy practices were regulated by the National Guidelines for Accreditation, Supervision and Regulation of Assisted Reproductive Technology (ART) Clinics in India, Indian Council of Medical Research, 2005. Available at: https://www.medbox.org/pdf/5e148832db60a2044c2d1f02.

[57] See Sama Resource Group for Women and Health (2012), Surrogacy: A Sneak Peek into the Contractual World. Available at: https://india.unfpa.org/sites/default/files/pub-pdf/SurrogacyInfobrief-1.pdf.

[58] Surrogacy (Regulation) Act, 2021. Available at: https://www.indiacode.nic.in/handle/123456789/17046.

Thailand has also been a major destination for international surrogacy for many years due to its initially permissive regulations and significantly lower costs compared to other countries.[59] As long as Thailand lacked specific regulations governing surrogacy arrangements, they were considered illegal under Section 150 of the Thai Civil Code, which deemed the practice contrary to public order or morality. However, the growing number of disputes and cases of exploitation and commodification of women's bodies,[60] prompted the Thai legislature to intervene to regulate the practice more strictly. The crucial change came with the enactment of the Protection of Children Born from Assisted Reproductive Technologies Act (also known as the *Surrogacy Act*), which came into force in 2015 (Stasi 2017).

This law introduced strict regulations, limiting surrogacy to Thai citizens only. More precisely, only heterosexual couples who have been legally married for at least three years, of which at least one of the spouses must be a Thai citizen, are eligible for surrogacy. The legislation imposes a ban on commercial surrogacy or egg donation, as well as sex selection, and does not allow intermediaries or brokers to enter into surrogacy agreements. It is an essential prerequisite for surrogate mothers that they are female relatives of the couples requesting surrogacy. Furthermore, the surrogate mother is required to be a close relative (up to the second degree) of one of the intended parents, unless exceptions to this rule are approved by a competent ethics committee. The law explicitly prohibits all forms of surrogacy for commercial purposes, allowing only altruistic surrogacy, with the aim of avoiding the economic exploitation of women.

The legislation also provides for severe criminal sanctions for violators, with penalties including high fines and imprisonment of up to ten years.

A distinctive feature of Thai discipline is the emphasis placed on the protection of children's rights. In accordance with the provisions stipulated within the Surrogacy Act, intending parents are obligated to initiate a legal proceeding before a court of law in order to obtain legal recognition of their parenthood. This procedural measure is deemed essential in ensuring the optimal interests of the child are safeguarded. The objective of this system is to prevent situations of abandonment or legal disputes.

In Thailand, too, restrictive legislation has generated concern about the possible flourishing of a black market and illegal forms of surrogacy, so much so that the

[59] On the regulatory evolution in Thaliandia on surrogacy see Whittaker (2016), p. 73.

[60] Two of the most well-known cases are: (a) the '*Baby 101*' case, a private clinic that offered full surrogacy services including gamete donation for $5000.00 and with a choice of donors and surrogate mother, whose owners were indicted for exploitation and *eugenic surrogacy,* see for more details Hibino and Shimazono (2013); Rozée and Unisa (2016) and (b) the '*Gammy* case', the case of a child with Down syndrome who had been abandoned in Thailand by his Australian-born intended parents to be cared for by his gestational surrogate mother, while his twin sister, born without the syndrome had been brought to Australia. The surrogate mother had appeared in the media explaining that she had agreed to be a surrogate mother to pay family debts and had refused to have an abortion when it was discovered that one of the twins she was carrying had Down syndrome. For further discussion see, Murdoch (2014); Whiteman (2014).

government in March 2024 planned a bill that would make surrogacy legal also for foreign intended-parent couples.[61]

An examination of the historical landscape reveals that societies across the globe have encountered, embrace or reject diverse approaches to assisted reproduction. This demonstrates that ethical norms are not universally applicable and that local particularities must be taken into account.

2.8 The Absence of Regulation and Cases of Implicit Legality

The Netherlands does not have any specific legislation that governs surrogacy. Instead, this matter is left exclusively to private contracts, with certain articles of the Criminal Code providing some restrictions. Initially, Dutch legislation adopted a very restrictive stance towards commercial surrogacy, expressly prohibiting any form of financial compensation other than the reimbursement of expenses strictly related to pregnancy and childbirth (Dutch Ministry of Justice, 2004). This prohibition is codified in Article 151ter of the Wetboek van Strafrecht (Dutch Criminal Code), which punishes commercial surrogacy practices and especially those who promote or profit from them.

However, as early as the 2000s, legislative authorities initiated the development of a pivotal distinction between altruistic surrogacy (*altruïstische draagmoederschap*) and commercial surrogacy (*commerciële draagmoederschap*), sanctioning the former in designated cases, contingent on the absence of a profit motive (*Kamerstukken* II 2001/02, 28 457, no. 3).

Legal developments have been influenced by case law that has placed the belang van het kind (best interests of the child), a cardinal principle of Dutch family law, at the centre of the debate. In judicial rulings pertaining to surrogacy, there has been a gradual shift in emphasis towards the protection of the child's right to access information regarding their origins. In this context, the Netherlands has introduced the Assisted Reproductive Donor Data Act (Wet Donorgegevens Kunstmatige Bevruchting, 2004), which establishes a birth register for children born through assisted reproductive techniques, including surrogacy. The aim of this register is to ensure transparency and to protect the children's right to know the identity of the donor or surrogate mother.

In addition, in 2011, the Child Protection Council (*Raad voor de Kinderbescherming*) published guidelines for the application of the law in transnational surrogacy cases. These guidelines have proven to be essential in addressing the issues related to the globalisation of the practice, as many Dutch citizens choose to use surrogate mothers abroad, in countries where legislation is less restrictive or allows commercial surrogacy. In this regard, the Netherlands has imposed strict

[61] VOA News (2024) Thailand Prepares to Lift Commercial Surrogacy Ban. Available at: https://www.voanews.com/a/thailand-prepares-to-lift-commercial-surrogacy-ban/7521512.html.

limits on the adoption of children born through surrogacy in foreign countries. Among other things, these limits require that the national ethical and legal principles of the country of origin are complied with, in order to avoid situations of exploitation or violation of human rights.

The current Dutch legal framework aims to balance various interests. On the one hand, it recognises the right of intended parents to form a family by providing them with a relatively clear legal framework to access altruistic surrogacy. On the other, it places emphasis on the protection of the surrogate mother, who must be fully consented to and protected against any form of coercion, and, above all, on the welfare of the child, whose right to know his or her origins is considered fundamental. With this in mind, the Dutch legislator has tried to develop ethically balanced legislation that, while allowing altruistic surrogacy, strictly forbids any form of commercial exploitation, emphasising the need for strict and controlled regulation of the practice.

It is also important to note that the entire surrogacy process in the Netherlands is strictly regulated by licensed medical facilities. Dutch fertility clinics offering surrogacy services are obliged to ensure that all medical procedures are conducted in accordance with the ethical and scientific guidelines established by the Netherlands Association of Obstetrics and Gynaecology (NVOG). This obligation is particularly stringent in terms of compliance with the rules set out in the Special Medical Practices Act (Wet op besondere medische verrichtingen, 1997). Adherence to these guidelines is essential to ensure the safety of the surrogate mother and the child, as well as the proper application of assisted reproductive techniques. In Belgium, the absence of specific legislation has resulted in a legislative vacuum, giving rise to significant ethical and legal issues for all parties involved. Notwithstanding the fact that the Law on Medical Assisted Reproduction and the Assignment of Surplus Embryos and Gametes[62] of 6 July 2007 (No. 2,007,023,090) regulates certain aspects concerning the donation and preservation of oocytes and genetic material, it does not contain precise provisions on surrogacy. Consequently, the performance of surrogacy practices has become a contentious area, giving rise to divergent interpretations and different decisions between one court and another.

Despite the absence of a specific regulation, surrogacy is frequently practised in Belgium, partly due to the presence of specialised clinics that also offer such services to foreign citizens, same-sex couples and single individuals. However, the performance of such practices is based on agreements made through the clinics' internal protocols, rather than legislative guidelines, with significant implications in terms of safety for intended parents and, above all, protection for surrogate mothers and children. In particular, in the absence of clear legislation, the surrogate mother is considered, under Belgian law, the legal mother of the child until any change in the child's marital status. As a result, agreements between surrogate mothers and

[62] *Wet van 6 juli 2007 tot wijziging van de gerechtelijke organisatie* [Law of 6 July 2007 to amend the judicial organization], Belgium. Available at: https://etaamb.openjustice.be/nl/wet-van-06-juli-2007_n2007023090.html.

intended parents are not enforceable, implying that the surrogate mother may refuse to surrender the child to the intended parents, also by virtue of the fact that Belgian courts tend to uphold the surrogate mother's right to retain custody of the newborn, leaving the intended parents in a vulnerable position. Transfer of parental responsibility, on the other hand, is possible through adoption procedures.

The European Court of Human Rights intervened in a number of cases concerning Belgium, emphasising that national authorities must ensure that the fundamental rights of children born through surrogacy are adequately protected. In particular, the Court made it clear that the best interests of the child, which includes issues of citizenship and legal recognition of intended parents, cannot be subordinated to procedural obstacles or regulatory loopholes. This emerged in judgments such as *D. and others v. Belgium*,[63] where the Court reminded Belgium of the need to provide clear procedures for the recognition of the marital status of children born through surrogacy.

Finally, the absence of clear national regulations not only makes arrangements between intended parents and surrogate mothers more complex, but also opens the way for potential abuses, such as illegal commercialisation of the practice. Although commercial surrogacy is generally prohibited in Belgium, the absence of controls makes it difficult to prevent surrogate mothers or intended parents from seeking more favourable conditions in other countries or acting outside official medical procedures.

2.9 Commercial Surrogacy: the Cases of Russia, Ukraine and Israel

In Russia, surrogacy is one of the most regulated practices in the world, representing an accessible option for many couples and individuals, both Russian and foreign. The primary legislation is contained in Federal Law No. 323-FZ of 21 November 2011,[64]

[63] D. and Others v. Belgium (dec.), no. 29176/13, Decision of 8 July 2014 [Section II], available at: https://hudoc.echr.coe.int/eng#{%22itemid%22:[%22002-10163%22]}. In *D. and Others v. Belgium* (No. 29176/2013), the Belgian authorities denied a Belgian couple the issuance of a travel document for a child born through surrogacy in Ukraine. The applicants had to return to Belgium without the child as their lawful stay in Ukraine had expired. The European Court of Human Rights found Article 8 ECHR applicable and acknowledged that the refusal to issue the document constituted an interference with family life. However, the interference was deemed legitimate, falling within the state's wide margin of appreciation. The Convention, in fact, does not require states to automatically allow entry of children born through surrogacy without the necessary legal checks. In the meantime, the child's travel document was issued, and the Court declared the matter resolved.

[64] Federal Law of 19 December 2022 No. 538-FZ (as amended on 28 April 2023) "On Amendments to Certain Legislative Acts of the Russian Federation". Available at: https://www.consultant.ru/document/cons_doc_LAW_434588/ad890e68b83c920baeae9bb9fdc9b94feb1af0ad/.

as amended by Federal Law No. 538-FZ of 19 December 2022 "On the Basis of the Protection of the Health of Citizens in the Russian Federation" (Russian: Federalnyj Gesetz ot 21 nojabrja 2011 g. The third part of the Federal Law No. 323-FZ) contains provisions that regulate various aspects of motherhood surrogacy, both commercial and altruistic. The Russian Family Code also contains further provisions, enshrined in particular Articles 51 and 52.[65] The law stipulates that only married couples and single women are eligible for surrogacy, provided they prove through medical certification that they are unable to carry a pregnancy. Married couples must present a valid marriage certificate, while single women are required to present a medical certificate justifying access to surrogacy. On the other hand, surrogate mothers must meet strict requirements: they must be between 20 and 35 years old, have Russian citizenship, already be the mother of at least one healthy child and provide medical certification of physical and psychological fitness to carry the pregnancy to term. In addition, the law prohibits any genetic link between the surrogate mother and the child, requiring that the genetic material come exclusively from the intended parents or, alternatively, from donors.

Russian law requires the conclusion of a written contract between the intended parents and the surrogate mother, in which the terms of the collaboration are defined, including medical conditions, fees and termination clauses. However, the contract is not conclusive for the registration of parenthood, as the law requires the surrogate mother to provide her written consent to transfer parental rights to the intended parents after the birth of the child.[66] This can generate legal disputes, as the surrogate mother retains the right to retain the child until consent is formally given. Despite this complexity, the Russian system is considered to be one of the most stable and attractive surrogacy systems globally.

One element that distinguishes Russian legislation is the openness of the practice to foreign citizens. In fact, Russia does not require intended parents to have permanent residence in the country, making the country an important destination for reproductive tourism. However, foreign parents may encounter legal difficulties in their home countries, especially since it is considered legal in Russia to enter into commercial surrogacy agreements. In fact, Russian legislation allows the payment of significant fees to surrogate mothers, which include reimbursements for medical expenses, living expenses and an additional fee for the service. As there is no upper limit on fees, this has led to several criticisms of the Russian legislation, as the practice encourages the commercialisation of surrogacy.

One controversial aspect is the treatment of same-sex couples. Although the law does not contain explicit restrictions on the sexual orientation of the intended parents, Russia's conservative political climate and the ban on same-sex marriages make it almost impossible for same-sex couples to access this practice and obtain parental responsibility for their children. As regards the citizenship of the child born through surrogacy, the legislation states that the newborn child

[65] Family Code of the Russian Federation. Available at: https://stskrf.ru/.

[66] Family Code of the Russian Federation, Art. 51. Available at: https://stskrf.ru/51.

automatically acquires Russian citizenship if at least one of the intended parents is a Russian citizen. However, for foreign parents, the registration of the child's marital status and the procedure for the recognition of parenthood can be particularly complicated.

In summary, Russia offers a detailed regulatory framework that makes surrogacy accessible and regulated, attracting both local and foreign citizens. However, significant challenges remain related to ethical implications, possible legal disputes and the rights of the parties involved, highlighting the need for an ongoing debate on this practice and its regulation.

In Ukraine, surrogacy is a legal and regulated practice. Indeed, the country has become a leading destination for reproductive tourism on a global scale. The relevant legislation is set out in the Family Code of Ukraine (Сімейного кодексу України) and health laws, approved by the Decree of the Ministry of Justice of Ukraine No. 52/5 of 18 October 2000, and the Decree of the Ministry of Health of Ukraine 'On the Approval of the Procedure for the Use of Assisted Reproductive Technologies in Ukraine' No. 787 of 9 September 2013. Surrogacy is permitted under the law only for heterosexual married couples who can demonstrate, by means of medical certification, that they are unable to conceive or carry a pregnancy. This requirement excludes single individuals and same-sex couples, thus rendering the Ukrainian system inaccessible to a significant part of the international community.

One of the distinctive aspects of Ukrainian legislation is the automatic legal recognition of intended parents as parents of the child from birth. According to Article 123 of the Family Code,[67] "if an embryo conceived by spouses (man and woman) is implanted into another woman as a result of the use of assisted reproductive technologies, the spouses shall be considered the parents of the child" and as a result, the names of the intended parents are immediately recorded on the birth certificate, without the surrogate mother having any parental rights over the child. This provision greatly simplifies the procedures for the recognition of the parental relationship by reducing the risk of postnatal disputes and at the same time poses a serious risk to the surrogate mother's rights when she is forced to separate from the child. At the same time, these facilities are one of the main reasons why many international couples choose Ukraine.

The surrogate mother must meet strict requirements in the Ukrainian legislative system: she must be between 21 and 35 years old, be the mother of at least one healthy child, have given her informed and written consent, and have no medical or psychological contraindications to the pregnancy.

---

[67] Art. 123, Determination of the origin of a child born as a result of the use of assisted reproductive technologies, Family Code of Ukraine (Сімейний кодекс України): "If a human embryo conceived by a married couple (a man and a woman) through assisted reproductive technologies is transferred into the body of another woman, the parents of the child are the married couple". (*trans. by the author*). Available at: https://protocol.ua/ua/simeyniy_kodeks_ukraini_stattya_123/.

The surrogate mother cannot have any genetic link to the child, whereas at least one of the intended parents must have a genetic link to the child. In addition, the process requires a detailed contract between the intended parents and the surrogate mother, which regulates the terms of the collaboration, remuneration, medical conditions and termination clauses. In the context of Ukrainian surrogacy, the compensation provided to the surrogate mother is a subject of particular interest. The compensation is typically comprised of two components: firstly, reimbursement of medical expenses and, secondly, additional payment for the service. This aspect of the practice, although it is commercial in nature, is subject to regulation.

Ukrainian legislation also allows foreign citizens access to surrogacy, without requiring permanent residence in the country. This has made Ukraine a major destination for reproductive tourism, especially after other countries, such as India and Thailand, which we will discuss later, introduced stricter restrictions. However, this has raised ethical concerns, especially during periods of political instability, such as the ongoing armed conflict, which has exposed surrogate mothers and children born through this practice to significant risks.

Another critical issue concerns the citizenship of children born through surrogacy. For foreign parents, the child generally acquires the citizenship of the intended parents, but the registration process may vary depending on the laws of the parents' country of origin. In some cases, newborns are at risk of being deprived of citizenship due to regulatory conflicts between Ukrainian law and the law of the country of origin of the parents, who often have to resort to judicial protection to obtain recognition, often to protect the *best interest of the child.*

In conclusion, surrogacy in Ukraine offers a favourable and clearly defined legal framework that has attracted many international couples, but the practice raises significant ethical and logistical questions. The combination of a legal system guaranteeing rights to intended parents and an accessible business environment has made Ukraine a benchmark in this field, albeit with challenges associated with the protection of surrogate mothers and newborns in such complex contexts.

In the state of Israel, the regulatory framework pertaining to surrogacy is characterised by its detailed and unique nature, a reflection of the country's cultural, religious and legal particularities. The main legislation on the subject is the 1996 Gestation for Others Agreement Law,[68] which regulates the terms and conditions for access to surrogacy. Israel was among the first countries worldwide to introduce a specific law on this practice, combining a permissive and highly regulated approach that balances the needs of the parties involved with ethical and social considerations.

The law permits surrogacy solely for heterosexual married couples, on the condition that they demonstrate the absence of viable options for conception or the presence of medical contraindications to pregnancy, which must be substantiated by a medical report. However, more recent amendments (2022) have

[68] Gestation for Others Agreement Act of 1996 (Israel). Available at: https://www.nevo.co.il/law_html/law00/71740.htm.

expanded access to surrogacy to include single men and same-sex couples. This expansion was precipitated by a series of legal disputes and a ruling by the Israeli Supreme Court that declared the exclusion of same-sex couples and individuals from surrogacy rights to be unconstitutional.

A distinctive element of the Israeli system is the strict state supervision of the process. It is imperative to note that the approval of every surrogacy contract is contingent upon the endorsement of a State Committee for Gestation for Others, a body comprising medical practitioners, legal professionals, ethics experts and religious representatives. The committee's remit includes the examination of medical compatibility, the terms of the contract, and the motives of the parties involved. This ensures that the procedure is carried out in accordance with the law.

The surrogate mother must undergo psychological counselling in order to verify her suitability for the practice, be between the ages of 22 and 38, be the mother of at least one child and no more than four, and not have had any complications during previous pregnancies or illnesses that could endanger her health or that of the child; she must not have had more than two pregnancies as a surrogate mother and must not have given birth to more than one other child. In addition, both the surrogate mother and the intended parents must be citizens or permanent residents of Israel. The fertilised egg must not belong to the surrogate mother. Before making its decision, the committee will schedule a hearing during which it will hear all parties involved. Intended parents must also meet certain requirements: they must be between 18 and 54 years old; if married, they must not have more than two children.

An important aspect of Israeli legislation is the integration of religious norms into the legal process. In a country where personal status laws are strongly influenced by the Halakhah (Jewish law), surrogacy must comply with religious precepts. For example, in the case of Jewish couples, it is required that the surrogate mother also be Jewish to avoid complications regarding the child's religious status. This element, although not universally applicable, reflects the importance of religious tradition in Israeli law.

The contract must also provide for clear informed consent on the part of the surrogate mother, and although it excludes financial compensation, it provides for the possibility of agreeing on a monthly reimbursement of expenses taking into account the costs of legal advice and insurance premiums, compensation for time, suffering, loss of income or temporary loss of earning capacity related to the pregnancy, and in any case any other reasonable compensation that is approved by the Committee.

The intending parents, to whom the child will be immediately entrusted, must notify the social workers of the birth within 24 hours, and the social worker—in whose presence the child will be entrusted to the intending parents—will be the child's sole guardian until a parenting order or *status* order is issued.

Within seven days, the prospective parents are required to submit a request for the issuance of a parenting order to the court, accompanied by a report from the social worker regarding the best interests of the child.

Furthermore, should there be a change in circumstances that would justify such a request, the surrogate mother may apply to the court for permission to withdraw from the surrogacy contract and become the child's sole guardian. This would be contingent on a report by the social worker confirming that the child's best interests would not be harmed by such a change.

Despite the fact that the system has been regulated for several years, the issue of surrogacy in Israel has raised extensive ethical and social debates. On the one hand, the approach ensures the protection of the parties involved, with a strong focus on consent and transparency. On the other hand, limited access and lengthy approval procedures have prompted and continue to prompt several Israeli couples to turn to foreign countries for quicker or cheaper options, especially before the widening of eligibility criteria.

In conclusion, surrogacy in Israel is a legally permitted and closely monitored practice, with a regulatory framework that combines ethical, medical and religious considerations. State supervision offers a high level of protection for both intended parents and surrogate mothers, thus establishing the Israeli system as a distinctive and intricate model within the international context. Notwithstanding, the flexibility exhibited with regard to the potential for agreeing on reimbursement of expenses and compensation for the surrogate mother does not appear to be entirely consistent with the prohibition on commercial surrogacy.

2.10 Surrogacy in the United States of America

In the United States, there exists a considerable degree of variability in the regulation of surrogacy among the various individual states, thus engendering a complex and multifaceted regulatory landscape that reflects a wide range of legal, cultural and ethical approaches. The absence of federal legislation that uniformly regulates this practice has resulted in the devolution of the issue to state legislatures. This state of affairs gives rise to a triad of conditions: those characterised by a high degree of permissiveness, those marked by a restrictive character, and those devoid of any explicit regulatory provisions on the matter.

In the state of California, a leading proponent of surrogacy legislation, the legal framework is distinguished by its sophistication and inclusivity. The California Family Code permits both gestational and traditional surrogacy, although the former is preferred to avoid legal disputes related to the surrogate mother's genetic link. It is imperative to note that surrogacy contracts are legally recognised and must be formally documented prior to the commencement of the pregnancy. Furthermore, the Californian system permits a prenatal ruling that assigns parental responsibility to the intended parents even before the child is born. This mechanism serves to reduce legal uncertainties and to guarantee the protection of the rights of all parties involved, most particularly those of children born through surrogacy.

Particularly famous is the case *Buzzanca v. Buzzanca*,[69] in which the California Court of Appeal held that intended parents can be recognised as legal parents even when there is no direct genetic link to the child, reinforcing the principle of voluntariness in surrogate parenting.

In Illinois, surrogacy is regulated by the Gestational Surrogacy Act,[70] which attempts to provide a detailed regulatory framework protecting both the position of the intended parents and the surrogate mother. The Act stipulates that both parties must be represented by legal counsel and that the contract must explicitly delineate the terms of compensation, medical expenses and any necessary medical procedures. Furthermore, the law permits the issuance of a prenatal administrative order, thereby granting parental responsibility, provided that all the stipulated legal requirements are met. In the absence of such consent, it may be necessary to resort to legal guardianship or other procedures, such as adoption, in order to obtain recognition of parental responsibility.

Illinois does not recognise traditional surrogacy through ordinary procedures and requires that there be a genetic link between at least one of the intended parents and the child. Illinois is a state that also recognises the legitimacy of arrangements of a commercial nature, carried out by single, LGBTQ + couples. Consequently, it has become a popular destination for so-called procreative tourism.

In the state of New York, legislation was passed in 2021, namely the Child-Parent Security Act,[71] with the result that surrogacy was made legal. The new regulations permit gestational surrogacy, but maintain the prohibition on traditional surrogacy.

---

[69] *Buzzanca v. Buzzanca* (1998) is the case of a couple that had entered into a gestational surrogacy contract and divorced after fertilisation of the egg, but before the child was born. Neither of the intended parents wanted to be given parental responsibility for the child on the assumption that there was no genetic link between them and the child. The lower court had ruled that neither the surrogate mother nor the intended parents had parental responsibility for the child because there was no genetic connection between them. However, the California Court of Appeal, in its well-known decision of 10 March 1998 (*In re Marriage of Buzzanca*, 72 Cal. Rptr. 2d 280 [Cal. Ct. App. 1998]), held that intent to parent is sufficient to establish legal parenthood, even in the absence of a genetic link, as this best serves the interests of the child. Available at: https://law.justia.com/cases/california/court-of-appeal/4th/61/1410.html; "Even though neither Luanne [Buzzanca] nor John [Buzzanca] are biologically related to Jaycee, they are still her lawful parents given their initiating role as the intended parents in her conception and birth. And, while the absence of a biological connection is what makes this case extraordinary, this court is hardly without statutory basis and legal precedent in so deciding. Indeed, in both the most famous child custody case of all time, fn. 19 and in our Supreme Court's Johnson v. Calvert decision, the court looked to intent to parent as the ultimate basis of its decision. fn. 20 Fortunately, as the Johnson court also noted, intent to parent "'correlate[s] significantly' "with a child's best interests. (Johnson v. Calvert, supra, 5 Cal.4th at p. 94, quoting Schultz, 1990, p. 397.) That is far more than can be said for a model of the law that renders a child a legal orphan". For a reconstruction of the Court's reasoning see also Schultz (1990).

[70] Gestational Surrogacy Act (2015) Illinois Compiled Statutes. Available at: https://www.ilga.gov/legislation/ilcs/ilcs3.asp?ActID=2111.

[71] Child-Parent Security Act (2021) New York State Department of Health. Available at: https://www.health.ny.gov/vital_records/child_parent_security_act/.

The law introduces a series of rigorous requirements[72] with the aim of safeguarding the interests of the mother surrogate. In addition to this, the legislation formally acknowledges the surrogate's entitlement to health, life and health insurance, which is to be provided by the intended parents. Furthermore, the law ensures the surrogate's right to compensation for legal expenses. Furthermore, she possesses the right to terminate the pregnancy, to make all decisions relating to her own health and that of the conceived child or the pregnancy independently, and to receive compensation for surrogacy that must be deposited in escrow with an independent escrow agent. The website of the New York State Department of Health even indicates that the cost of a surrogacy contract ranges from $60,000 to $150,000.[73]

The Child-Parent Security Act represents a significant change from the past, when both commercial and altruistic surrogacy were prohibited.

In contradistinction to the preceding example, states such as Michigan adopt a markedly more restrictive approach. State law, as stipulated by the Surrogate Parenting Act,[74] explicitly prohibits surrogate parenting. Offenders can face criminal penalties of up to $50,000 and a prison sentence of up to five years. Furthermore, the legal status of surrogacy contracts is such that they are considered to be null and void, thus serving as a significant deterrent to those who wish to engage in this practice. In addition to this, the law stipulates that the court shall award custody of the child on the basis of an exclusive assessment of the best interest of the child.[75]

---

[72] New York State Legislature (2021) Family Court Act, Art. 5-C, Part 6, § 581–403. Available at: https://www.nysenate.gov/legislation/laws/FCT/581-403.

[73] New York State Department of Health (2024) *Child-Parent Security Act*. Available at: https://www.health.ny.gov/vital_records/child_parent_security_act/.

[74] Surrogate Parenting Act (1988) *MCL §722.851–863*. Available at: https://law.justia.com/codes/michigan/chapter-722/statute-act-199-of-1988/.

[75] Section 722.23 of the Michigan Compiled Laws identifies the criteria for assessing the best interests of the child in custody disputes. These include: (a) The love, affection, and other emotional ties existing between the parties involved and the child; (b) The capacity and disposition of the parties involved to give the child love, affection, and guidance and to continue the education and raising of the child in his or her religion or creed, if any; (c) The capacity and disposition of the parties involved to provide the child with food, clothing, medical care or other remedial care recognized and permitted under the laws of this state in place of medical care, and other material needs; (d) The length of time the child has lived in a stable, satisfactory environment, and the desirability of maintaining continuity; (e) The permanence, as a family unit, of the existing or proposed custodial home or homes; (f) The moral fitness of the parties involved; (g) The mental and physical health of the parties involved; (h) The home, school, and community record of the child; (i) The reasonable preference of the child, if the court considers the child to be of sufficient age to express preference; (j) The willingness and ability of each of the parties to facilitate and encourage a close and continuing parent-child relationship between the child and the other parent or the child and the parents. A court may not consider negatively for the purposes of this factor any reasonable action taken by a parent to protect a child or that parent from sexual assault or domestic violence by the child's other parent; (k) Domestic violence, regardless of whether the violence was directed against or witnessed by the child; (l) Any other factor considered by the court to be relevant to a particular child custody dispute. See: *MCL §722.23*. Available at: https://www.legislature.mi.gov/Laws/MCL?objectName=MCL-722-23.

Another significant example is Nevada, a state with highly permissive legislation, where commercial gestational surrogacy (to the exclusion of traditional surrogacy) is legal and regulated by the Nevada Revised Statutes.[76] These provides for binding contracts between intended parents, the surrogate mother and any gamete donors through which the latter waive all rights and duties to the child for the benefit of the intended parents, who will instead acquire parental responsibility. The law stipulates that the intended parents must be named on the child's birth certificate, thus obviating the need for further legal proceedings and greatly simplifying the postnatal process. It is important to note the stipulation[77] within the surrogacy contract that the surrogate mother is obligated to comply with all medical examinations, treatments, and monitoring procedures recommended by the physician responsible for the care of the gestational mother during the pregnancy. This obligation extends to the surrogate mother refraining from any activity that is deemed by the parent, intended parents, or the physician providing care to be potentially detrimental to the pregnancy and the future health of the unborn child. The state of Nevada is distinguished by its progressive policies, which include provisions for surrogacy that are inclusive of single parents and same-sex couples, thereby mitigating the risk of discriminatory practices.

The phenomenon of 'reproductive tourism' is encouraged by regulatory fragmentation in the United States, as it attracts international intended parents to permissive states such as California and Nevada. This predicament has given rise to a series of ethical and legal dilemmas concerning the potential economic exploitation of surrogate mothers and the absence of uniform standards that would ensure equivalent rights across all states (Hofman 2009).

The regulatory framework surrounding surrogacy in the United States is characterised by a heterogeneity of approaches, reflecting a unique combination of liberal and restrictive elements. While certain states have enacted advanced and comprehensive legal frameworks, the absence of uniform federal regulation gives rise to concerns regarding the potential for inequality and the exploitation of surrogate mothers. This situation necessitates a more profound reflection on the equilibrium between individual liberties, human rights, and ethical principles.

2.11 Bioethical Principles and Surrogacy

After having introduced the legal-philosophical issues underlying the bioethical discussion on surrogacy, mentioned the evolution of the concepts of parenthood and motherhood, and quickly reviewed the ways in which surrogacy is regulated on the international scene, it is appropriate to get to the heart of the matter through an

---

[76] Nevada Revised Statutes (NRS 126.500–126.810). Available at: https://www.leg.state.nv.us/division/legal/lawlibrary/nrs/NRS-126.html#NRS126Sec021.

[77] Nevada Revised Statutes (NRS sec. 126.750). Available at: https://www.leg.state.nv.us/division/legal/lawlibrary/nrs/NRS-126.html#NRS126Sec021.

analysis that relates the fundamental principles of bioethics (Gillon 1994) historically identified in the principle of autonomy, beneficence, non-maleficence and justice (Beauchamp and Childress 2001), with the essential features of the practice.

The objective of this study is to ascertain the ethical acceptability of surrogacy, with a particular focus on the limits and safeguards that should be in place for the involved parties.

In the discourse on surrogacy, fundamental principles of bioethics are implicated in a complex manner. The principle of autonomy is frequently cited as a defence of women's right to self-determination regarding their own bodies, including the capacity to consent to pregnancy on behalf of others. However, this freedom must be balanced with the principles of beneficence and non-maleficence, which dictate that harm to the surrogate mother and the born child must be avoided and, on the contrary, the greatest possible benefit to them must be provided, all consistent with the principle of justice.

One of the fundamental principles that upholds the ethical admissibility of surrogacy is the principle of autonomy, which posits that every individual possesses the right to self-determination and the freedom to make decisions regarding their own body.

The right to self-determination[78] as a fundamental right to express one's personality both in the intimate and in the social context and to express oneself through one's own free and independent decisions (Grasso 2018, p. 159; Mangiameli 2009, p. 1) is protected by Article 8 ECHR,[79] which enshrines respect for private and family life.

Self-determination, indeed, presupposes the highest expression of freedom in the head of a conscious subject and is a cardinal principle on which doctrine and jurisprudence base the right to dispose of one's own body,[80] with all its attendant limitations.[81]

---

[78] On the principle of self-determination see Gusmai (2019); Mangiameli (2011); Antonini (2012).

[79] Council of Europe (1950) Convention for the Protection of Human Rights and Fundamental Freedoms (European Convention on Human Rights), Rome, 4 November 1950, Art. 2. Available at: https://www.echr.coe.int/documents/convention_eng.pdf.

[80] Articles 1, 2 and 3 of the Charter of Fundamental Rights of the European Union" (para. 1), specifies: "every person has the right to know his or her health condition and to be informed in a manner that is complete, up-to-date and comprehensible to him or her with regard to the diagnosis, prognosis, benefits and risks of diagnostic tests and indicated health treatments, as well as with regard to possible alternatives and the consequences of refusing health treatment and diagnostic tests or of foregoing them." Even, we read in the text, "he may refuse in whole or in part to receive the information or indicate family members or a person he trusts to receive it and to give consent on his behalf if the patient so wishes." In this case, "the refusal or renunciation of information and the possible designation of a person in charge shall be recorded in the medical record and in the electronic health record" (para. 3). In Italy, for example, these principles have been applied through Law 219/2017 on informed consent and advance treatment provisions (DAT) and have been defined the logical landing place of informed consent (Rossi and Foglia 2014, p. 668). On the novelties introduced by Law No. 219/2017, see Baldini (2018, p. 97). On the meaning of the right to information under Article 21 of the italian Constitution, see Loiodice (1971, p. 472).

[81] There are several limits imposed on the right to dispose of one's body. These include the prohibition of buying and selling organs (Radin 1996), of extreme bodily modifications (Habermas 2003), and of the possibility of experimenting on oneself (Jonas 1979).

From these derives the principle of autonomy—the exact content of which is widely debated in doctrine (Nelson 2013)—underpinning the recognition of a large proportion of fundamental human rights also in the context of health protection.

In this process of recognition, science plays a key role, as stated by Gusmai (2019), by changing the natural conditions of freedom (Jasanoff 2011, p.1). Scientists thus become the new 'architects' of the perimeter of human life, i.e. those who can, through research and experimentation, write the 'palimpsest of life'[82] far beyond the 'natural history' narrated for millennia only by law and religion (Bauman 1992).[83]

According to Emily Jackson, the principle of autonomy is rooted in the idea that, provided third parties are not harmed, each individual should have the right to pursue his or her own life project according to his or her own beliefs and convictions (Jackson 2001).[84]

In order for the principle of autonomy to be truly valid, it is necessary for there to be two indispensable prerequisites, namely authenticity and awareness (Nelson 2013). The decision must be authentic in the sense that it belongs to the individual and must be made in absolute freedom and without any coercion; it must also be conscious in the sense that it is based on an understanding of the possible consequences.

This healthcare principle is closely associated with the doctrine of so-called informed consent, which stipulates that patients must consent to any proposed healthcare treatment after being informed of all possible consequences[85] and being given the opportunity to decide what can and cannot be done to their body.

The right to self-determination is an inescapable element of surrogacy, both in relation to the surrogate mother's willingness to carry out a reproductive project that is not reduced to the mere bodily biological female element but also involves the willingness to make others parents by submitting to a specific human relationship such as that of pregnancy (Pezzini 2017), and in relation to the would-be parents who must consciously accept that their desire for parenthood is fulfilled through a third party.

Allowing surrogacy practices would therefore mean protecting the principle of autonomy and self-determination even in the name of moral pluralism (Pennings 2002).

This assumption is often criticised because the principle of autonomy is rooted in liberalism and while it requires the state not to interfere with the free decisions of individuals, it also requires it to take action to enable all individuals to make these decisions freely and fairly. Hence the concept of *reproductive justice*[86] which

---

[82] For an in-depth study of 'natural history' before the advent of biology, see Foucault (1970).

[83] Bauman recalls how, in the pre-modern phase (prior to the rise of legal positivism), it was religion that constructed the meaning of human life and, consequently, influenced the very content of freedom rights, including the right to self-determination.

[84] Autonomy is also defined as 'the prerogative of the individual to live her own life, in accordance with her own values and desires: to live by her own lights'.

[85] For an overview of the theories opposing the idea that informed consent can be equated with the principle of autonomy, see Dodds (2000).

[86] For a discussion of the concept of reproductive justice see Ehrenreich (2008).

theorises an approach to reproductive rights and reproductive health that goes beyond mere access to health services to include a broader perspective that recognises the intersections between different social, economic and political factors that influence people's ability to make free and informed decisions about their reproductive lives.

The concept of reproductive justice—closely linked to the principle of autonomy—basically theorises three rights: a) The right to have children, according to which individuals should have the right to decide whether, when and how many children to have, without pressure or coercion. This includes access to high quality reproductive health information and services; b) The right not to have children, according to which individuals should have access to safe and legal contraceptive methods, as well as safe and legal abortion if they so wish; c) The right to raise children in safety and with dignity, according to which individuals should have the support they need to raise their children in safe and healthy environments, with access to adequate resources such as education, health care and housing.[87]

Underlying this concept is the idea that, in order to truly guarantee autonomy of choice with regard to the reproductive issue, the state must intervene to limit external interference in decision-making. External interference includes various factors for which the state itself is responsible.

For instance, the existence of legislation providing for parental leave at state expense is an element that might influence a woman's choice to carry a pregnancy. Some women, who are more vulnerable socially and economically, may be influenced in their choice to carry a pregnancy by the social stigma attached to its possible absence, or if the stigma attached to the choice to carry a pregnancy on behalf of others or to take advantage of a pregnancy carried out by others, thus leading to an impairment of their autonomy.

The state, therefore, has the task of 'level the playing field' (Roberts 1997, p.23) within which the decision is made in order to truly ensure the autonomy of choice.

Consequently, the notion of autonomy has been the focus of efforts by numerous bioethicists to redefine it, with the objective of encompassing the reality that individuals are situated within both their individuality and their social dimension. The concept of 'relational autonomy', as understood by Catriona Mackenzie and Natalie Stoljar (2000, p. 4), is defined as an 'umbrella term' under which a series of perspectives based on certain shared convictions converge.

The prevailing perspective is that human beings are inherently social creatures, with their identities being forged within the intricate tapestry of social interactions and influenced by a myriad of social factors, including but not limited to race, class, gender and ethnicity. This conception of autonomy has been the subject of various criticisms.

Firstly, the concept of autonomy per se and the concept of relational autonomy do not necessarily exclude each other; indeed, the latter can be considered to be perfectly compatible with the former (Nelson 2013, p. 23). Furthermore, as

[87] For further discussion, see also Ross and Solinger (2017).

Nelson asserts, the conceptualisation of relational autonomy does not contribute to the identification or comprehension of autonomy. Should this be the case, the notion of autonomy would be more closely aligned with that of relationship than with that of person. This would imply that an individual could be considered truly autonomous only if they fell within certain types of relationships; otherwise, their autonomy would be undermined inexorably. A final critique of the notion of relational autonomy is offered, which challenges the paternalistic conception of autonomy. This conception posits the ability to periodically assess the autonomy of decisions, distinguishing those that are truly autonomous from those that are not.

While on the one hand critics of liberalism have theorised a poorer and more restrictive idea of autonomy, on the other hand a broader and richer conception of reproductive autonomy could lead to a more accurate and normatively desirable description (Jackson 2001, p. 293). In contrast, various feminist theories on the point hold that women's decision-making autonomy in certain contexts is severely limited if not entirely absent.[88]

From the debate just mentioned, a nuanced and contextualised concept of autonomy emerges that is not based on the social dimension but must take it into account (Callahan and Roberts 1996).

With regard to the approach to the concept of autonomy, the debate can be summarised as follows: some contend that an individual's decision to sign a contract in order to become a surrogate cannot be disregarded; others argue that there is empirical evidence to suggest that such decisions are rarely truly autonomous.

A considerable number of studies have concentrated on the effects of commercial surrogacy. These studies have sought to empirically analyse the conditions of women who have decided to sign a surrogacy contract in relation to the legislation in force in the country under consideration.[89]

A number of studies have been analysed by Karen Busby and Delaney Vun (2010), who have indicated that there appear to be particular differences in the reasons why a woman chooses to become a surrogate in countries of the Northern Hemisphere, such as the United States, Canada or Great Britain, or in any case the more industrialised countries, as opposed to those in the Southern Hemisphere or the Third World, such as India and Thailand.

The analysis of these studies suggests that, with a few exceptions, women who enter surrogacy contracts in countries such as the United States do so of their own volition, without psychological coercion or desperation for economic reasons. Nonetheless, the aforementioned studies demonstrated that surrogate mothers expected to be remunerated for their services in every instance. However, the

---

[88] Some feminist theories claim that even giving consent to infertility treatments may in some contexts entail a risk of social stigma by virtue of a particular pressure with respect to parenthood. See on this point Callahan and Roberts (1996, p. 1227).

[89] See for example: Horsey (2004, p. 5); Baron et al. (2024); Smerdon (2008); Pande (2011).

economic aspect was rarely cited as the primary motivation for surrogate mothers to enter into surrogacy contracts.[90]

It would therefore seem that the main stated motivations are the desire to help other people have children, the idea that surrogacy is a kind of 'calling' (Busby and Vun 2010) or the simple desire to be pregnant again.

On the contrary, in the countries of the southern hemisphere, it would seem to emerge that economic reasons preponderate over all others, also by virtue of the disparity in economic value between the counter-performances. In India, for instance, the average fee for a surrogate mother was around five times India's average annual salary, thus having a preponderant influence on the decision to go ahead with the practice. In both contexts, however, several elements emerged that pointed to a greater complexity of motivations leading to the choice of surrogate mothers, especially of a social nature.

However, it should be noted that the validity of the data may be questionable, given that the surrogate mothers interviewed in these studies may have been inclined to prioritise social acceptability and personal fulfilment, particularly in empirical studies based on direct interviews. Consequently, there might have been a reluctance to emphasise the economic aspect, although this factor may be predominant in some countries.

It is imperative to acknowledge the inherent interconnectedness between the principle of autonomy and the imperative to safeguard the dignity of the human being. This notion occupies a central position within the discourse on bioethics, as it pertains directly to the intrinsic value of each individual. It is of paramount importance to recognise that no individual should be subjected to the commodification or exploitation of their person. The protection of the principle of autonomy and the right to self-determination is inextricably linked to the protection of an individual's dignity, even in circumstances where the individual has made choices that may be considered by some to be against their own best interests. This is particularly salient in cases where the individual in question is particularly vulnerable (Shalev 1989).

In order to safeguard the dignity of the individual, it is imperative that the decision to procreate is made in a truly autonomous manner. However, in order to ensure the autonomy of the decision-making process (Purdy 1989), it is essential to provide individuals with all the relevant information in a comprehensible format. Furthermore, it is crucial to minimise the influence of external factors on those seeking to enter into surrogacy practices, particularly in cases where the primary criterion for determining the ethical acceptability of the practice is its altruistic nature, thereby classifying surrogacy as a gift.

The protection of the surrogate mother's autonomy of decision and free self-determination is a cardinal principle on which to base the ethical admissibility of surrogacy. However, this principle requires a thorough evaluation by the legislator,

[90] This could be because in countries like the United States, the liberalist and capitalist conception of society and the economy could lead women to conceive of surrogacy as real work.

precisely with respect to the silent and hidden elements that can generate a preponderant influence on the choice to offer oneself as a surrogate mother. The relevance of such social and economic aspects is probably inversely proportional to the autonomy of the choice, which is why it is of fundamental importance to identify criteria that can ensure that this principle is respected.

Closely linked to the principle of autonomy we find two other principles that are essential in the analysis of the relationship between scientific and technological progress and the individual's freedom of self-determination, both of which form the basis of the bioethical discussion.

As James Childress and Tom Beauchamp established in their 1979 publication Principles of Biomedical Ethics, the principles of beneficence (the greatest good for the patient) and non-maleficence (inflicting no harm) are recognised as fundamental values of health ethics and the basis of bioethics.

The principle of beneficence, which can be defined as the obligation to act for the good of the patient, can be further delineated into two meanings. Firstly, there is positive beneficence, which can be defined as the general duty to promote the good. Secondly, there is the principle of utility, which prescribes choosing the action that produces the greatest positive result between costs and benefits. The latter also includes the prevention of harm and, when possible, its removal. It is therefore regarded as an indispensable extension of positive beneficence in order to allow for the balancing of harms and benefits. The principles of beneficence encompass the defence of the rights of others, the prevention of harm, the elimination of harmful conditions, the provision of assistance to the disabled, and the duty to assist those in need of help.

Paired with this principle, although distinct, is the principle of non-maleficence, which prescribes, like the Hippocratic precept, not to harm (*neminem laedere, primum non nocere*) and not to harm others. The notion of maleficence is interpreted in the biomedical field primarily in terms of harm, not only physical harm, but also including the possibility of non-observable harm. The principle of non-maleficence justifies the rules of practice that prohibit killing, inflicting pain or suffering, causing a state of incapacity, offending and depriving others of relevant goods.

The principle of beneficence, therefore, entails the need for the scientific and technical progress introduced and applied to be of benefit to all parties involved and the principle of non-maleficence the need for the scientific treatment or practice introduced not to harm the parties.

In an era characterised by the advancement of scientific knowledge that promises to broaden the scope of personal autonomy, it is imperative that the exercise of these freedoms be accompanied by the acknowledgement of previously established rights. Consequently, the augmentation of these decision-making capabilities must not result in the infringement of the rights of other individuals (Balistrieri 2007). The exercise of certain freedoms must be of benefit to the parties involved and, in any case, must not harm anyone.

In any case, the general principles of bioethics must be considered as penultimate or '*prima facie*' principles which are generally valid, 'to a relative extent, until each of them collides with one of the others and forces us to choose which of them to satisfy first' (Ross 1930).

This is precisely why Article 26 of the *Universal Declaration on Bioethics and Human Rights*,[91] adopted by the UNESCO General Conference on 19 October 2005, considers the principles of bioethics to be 'complementary and interdependent. Each principle must be considered in the context of the other principles, to an extent appropriate and relevant to the circumstances.'

In the case of surrogacy, there are typically three parties directly involved: the surrogate mother, the intended parents (or parent) and the conceived child.

The principles of beneficence and non-maleficence, to be balanced with that of autonomy, must therefore take into account the interests and rights of all three parties.

Intentional parents, who commission surrogacy and intend to raise the child born through this practice, may have to pay significant sums of money without being able to exercise any control or rights over the surrogate mother or the manner in which the pregnancy is carried out and may therefore be subject to particular forms of stress or suffering due to the distance from their future child (Golboni et al. 2020). At the same time, intended parents might suffer the fear of social judgement associated with the use of this type of procedure to be counterbalanced, almost always, by the advantages associated with surrogacy through which the ultimate desire to become parents can be fulfilled (MacCallum 2003).

The surrogate mother, on the other hand, will have to bear the risks of pregnancy with all the well-known consequences in terms of quality of life; the risk of social stigma and ostracism (often from her own family) that may even lead her to abandon her social environment during pregnancy. Of particular relevance are the possible consequences based on the mother-child relationship and separation after childbirth as one of the deepest and most complex relationships in human life. The fact that—and this is perhaps the most relevant element—in most cases[92] the surrogate mother has no rights over the delivered child and is obliged to detach herself from it can lead to possible psychological consequences.[93] Obviously, the surrogate mother's perception and existence of benefits or harms derives from the protections afforded by the various legislative systems, with different results depending on the regulatory framework applied, exacerbated by the fact that the studies were conducted in high-income countries as opposed to low-income countries (Jadva et al. 2003; Lamba et al. 2018; Hemalal and Librach 2020).

[91] Art. 26, Universal Declaration on Bioethics and Human Rights, adopted by UNESCO on 19 October 2005. Available at: https://www.unesco.org/en/legal-affairs/universal-declaration-bioethics-and-human-rights?hub=387.

[92] This depends on the legislation in force in the state where gestation for others is implemented. See for further discussion Ellenbogen et al. (2021).

[93] On the issues faced by gestational mothers see Rozée et al. (2020), Riddle (2022), Hodson et al. (2019), Bagcchi (2014), Agnafors (2014).

Some authors, in favour of the practice of surrogacy, compare it to *nannying*, arguing that there is no relevant difference between a prenatal nanny (surrogate mother) and a postnatal nanny (Nisand 2010) there is no evidence that surrogacy involves the exploitation of the person (Blyth 1994; Ciccarelli and Beckman 2005).

In this case, too, the assessment of the convenience of the path is a matter of choice—on the freedom, awareness and information of which, as we have previously observed, there is debate—and a benefit, which for some is understood as economic, for others as essentially psychological, i.e. linked to the gratification of the altruistic gesture in itself.

In the case of the relationship between the surrogate mother and the intended parents, it is customary to observe the presence of a contract or some form of agreement that, at the very least, demonstrates the synallagmatic satisfaction of interests. However, the same cannot be said with respect to the conditions of the unborn child. The central issue in the academic debate and jurisprudential production is the necessity to protect the child born of surrogacy as an individual who will blamelessly suffer a special condition. A wide-ranging literature has developed for the protection of this individual, for whom there is a so-called *harm principle* (Mill 2008). This literature includes works by Trezza (2020), Olivito (2018), Danna (2017), Di Mauro (2017), Muraro (2016), Carone (2016), Corti (2000) and Pisapia (1959). The child born of surrogacy is usually attributed certain 'harm' when learning of its true origins or the difficulty of knowing or having contact with its biological mother (Mitra 2018; Montanari Vergallo et al. 2018).

Some developmental psychologists have highlighted the importance of prenatal bonding and early attachment for the well-being of the child (Feldman 2007). According to several studies, separation immediately after birth, which is typical in surrogacy contracts, can affect the emotional development of the newborn (Bowlby 1969), leading to anxiety problems, attachment problems and difficulties in managing emotions later in life (Revarthen 2001; Simmons and Tighe 2005). Even some studies in perinatal psychology indicate that the foetus is sensitive to the mother's emotional states during pregnancy (Van den Bergh 2014; Glover 2015). Other scholars, on the other hand, argue that there is no scientific evidence to show that the unborn child may have a higher risk of illness or a worse life in the event of immediate removal from the birth mother (Mercer 2006). The same applies to the ability of same-sex couples or singles to adequately raise children (Montanari Vergallo 2019) conceived by means of these techniques, in respect of whom early studies are showing that there are no significant differences with opposite-sex parents (Pennings 2011; Jadva et al. 2019).

In any event, despite the absence of consensus on the health issues of children born through surrogacy (Caporale et al. 2016; Carone 2016) and the current limitation of data collection (Jadva 2020; Zadeh 2018) to such an extent that meaningful scientific conclusions are not yet possible, the primary responsibility of the legislator, whether national or international, is to ensure the provision of due protection for the only parties not involved in the decision to come into existence.

The principle of justice, one of the four pillars of bioethics as elucidated by Beauchamp and Childress, stipulates that the distribution of resources must be equitable and proportional, whilst simultaneously upholding the right of every individual to access the highest attainable level of care.[94] This principle is firmly embedded in the realm of distributive ethics and occupies a pivotal role in contemporary ethical discourse. It reinforces the concept of fairness and impartiality in the distribution of resources and access to medical benefits, ensuring their equitable distribution among all parties involved.

The principle under discussion can be traced back to the contractualist and utilitarian tradition, as well as the theories of justice developed by prominent thinkers such as John Rawls and Amartya Sen. In his seminal work "A Theory of Justice" (2020, pp. 3–6), Rawls puts forward a concept of justice as fairness based on the idea of an original social contract. His famous 'original position' beyond the 'veil of ignorance' requires structuring institutions in such a way that inequalities are only acceptable if they improve the condition of the disadvantaged. This approach has profoundly influenced bioethics, inspiring health distribution criteria that privilege the most vulnerable.

Utilitarian theories, in contrast, emphasise the maximisation of overall welfare. In the philosophical tradition espoused by Jeremy Bentham and John Stuart Mill, the concept of justice is predicated on the principle of maximising benefits for the greatest number of people, even when this may necessitate certain sacrifices by some individuals (see Mill 1861, pp. 85–89). This model has been implemented in public health systems, particularly in emergency situations where health resources are limited (Ferrara 2023).

Nevertheless, a prevalent critique of this standpoint is that a utilitarian approach may, under certain circumstances, result in the neglect of the most vulnerable, thereby giving rise to substantial ethical dilemmas.

The principle of justice in bioethics is expanded further in the context of global inequalities. Amartya Sen contests the notion of justice as being confined to the assertion of abstract principles, advocating instead for its contextualisation according to individuals' actual ability to access fundamental goods, including health (Sen 2009). This approach underscores the pivotal role of public policies and the imperative for international solidarity in ensuring an equitable distribution of health resources.

---

94 "Justice requires that benefits and burdens be distributed fairly, without exploitation or favouritism. Beauchamp and Childress identify several criteria for determining fair distribution: to each an equal share: each person receives an equal share of the available resources; to each according to need: resources are allocated according to individual needs; to each according to effort: distribution is based on a person's level of effort or dedication; to each according to contribution resources are distributed according to the contribution made by each person; to each according to merit: allocation is based on individual merit; to each according to free market exchanges: distribution is determined by free market dynamics; The authors emphasise that none of these criteria, taken individually, can constitute a comprehensive theory of justice. Therefore, it is necessary to balance and specify these principles on the basis of concrete situations, emphasising the importance of ensuring equal opportunities" (Beauchamp and Childress, 2013, p. 228).

In the context of surrogacy, this principle necessitates a profound reflection on the interests and rights of the surrogate mother, the child, and the intended parents. This reflection must encompass not only the guarantee of fair access to parenthood, but also the protection of the rights and dignity of the women who agree to carry a pregnancy on behalf of others, and ultimately of the children deprived from birth of the bond with their biological mother.

The fundamental principle of justice is predicated on the notion that the decision to become a surrogate mother should be made in a truly autonomous manner and not be subject to the influence of economic or social disadvantage, particularly in contexts where social and economic inequalities have the capacity to exert a significant influence on decision-making. In such circumstances, there is a genuine risk that surrogacy may become a form of exploitation, whereby less affluent women are coerced into selling their reproductive capacity in exchange for financial compensation. This phenomenon is observed in both the context of commercial surrogacy and altruistic surrogacy, wherein surrogate mothers are provided with substantial financial compensation in the form of reimbursement of expenses or loss of earnings. In this regard, Laura Palazzani (2020) underscores the significance of a regulated approach to surrogacy, emphasising that commercial surrogacy poses a threat to the principles of justice and fairness, particularly when involving economically disadvantaged women who may lack genuine autonomy in decision-making. According to Elizabeth Anderson, when a woman's body becomes a means of generating income, her dignity and autonomy risk being compromised, which is a clear violation of the principle of justice (Anderson 1993).

In any case, in evaluations related to surrogacy, the issue of justice is also crucial in order to reach conclusions on the ethical admissibility of the practice and any limits that could or should be imposed.

Concomitantly, it is imperative to consider the best interests of the child, who must be accorded the utmost protection.

The crux of the matter pertains to the delicate balancing of the various rights involved, a critical aspect that must be addressed to ascertain the ethical acceptability of surrogacy. Despite the theoretical limitations in postulating a legitimate right to parenthood, which is predicated on the capacity to demand state intervention through the coercion of third parties to attain its fulfilment, it is imperative to recognise the significance of the parental project in the context of personal sphere and private life fulfilment, as articulated in Article 8 of the European Convention on Human Rights.

Whilst it cannot be discounted that there are women who, for purely philanthropic purposes, elect to carry a pregnancy on behalf of others, it must also be acknowledged that in a significant number of cases, women are motivated by purely economic factors, which violate human dignity. In order to assess the ethical permissibility of surrogacy practices, it is necessary to consider the gender, racial, economic and other forms of oppression present in modern society, as well as the experiences of the most marginalised and vulnerable communities. The aim is to limit factors that affect people's ability to choose freely and to remove barriers that prevent them from exercising their rights.

2.12 The *Logique du Fait Accompli* and the Best Interest of the Child

As we have seen above, surrogacy practices have direct implications for 3 different 'parties', the intended parents, the surrogate mother and the child.

If the ethical admissibility of surrogacy is primarily based on respect for the individual's autonomy and self-determination—and this applies both to the surrogate mother and the intended parents—a different matter applies to the unborn child.

In fact, for self-evident reasons, the unborn child does not participate in any way in the decision and its autonomy and self-determination does not come into play at all. For this reason, both doctrine and jurisprudence have paid particular attention to the condition of the child born of surrogacy by resolving the issue of legal recognition of the parental responsibility relationship between the child and the intended couple by going beyond the 'natural' function of childbirth, on the basis of the *logique du fait accompli* and the *best interest of the child.*

The necessity to safeguard the paramount interests of children is not only derived from the aforementioned points, but also from the escalation in international surrogacy practices, which has engendered the establishment of a substantial reproduction market.

The best interests of the child are interpreted as requiring the national authorities to cooperate with the intended parents, even if the intended parents, according to the national authorities themselves, have acted contrary to the law as well as the interests of the child and the surrogate mother by using goods and services from an illegal or foreign reproductive market. In instances where intended parents travel abroad in order to access a foreign reproductive market, and subsequently return to their home country with their newborn child, national authorities are confronted with a complex dilemma that intersects with both family law and immigration law.

These questions are often answered by case law, which tends to apply what is called la *logique du fait accompli* (Fabre-Magnan 2013). That is to say, the principle that as soon as the birth of a child becomes a *fait accompli*, even if the law considers it illegal that conception was preceded by the purchase of gametes from an anonymous donor or may result from the possible exploitation of a surrogate mother, granting the would-be parents' request for recognition is considered the best way to protect the child's interest.

The basic idea is that it is in the child's best interest to be brought up by those who have strongly desired it. Among other things, studies would show that there is no evidence to suggest that there are any substantial differences in the psycho-emotional development of the child born of surrogacy (Jadva 2012; Golombok 2017; Zadeh 2018). Nevertheless, it should be borne in mind that several states—in particular those that also prohibit the practice as contrary to public order—consider it legitimate to refuse automatic recognition of the validity of foreign birth certificates within their own country even if this may conflict with the right of every human being to an identity.[95]

Also the European Court of Human Rights in a recent judgment,[96] as well as in a well-known opinion requested by the French Court of Cassation,[97] stated that the right of every child to respect for his or her private life under Art. 8 of the European Convention on Human Rights entails that the domestic law of member states must provide for ways in which to recognise the filiation relationship between the child and the intended parent, who is the legal parent of the child on the basis of a valid certificate issued abroad.[98] Similarly, the Court has held that the choice of the means to be used to enable the recognition of the child-parent-child relationship falls within the margin of appreciation of the States and that therefore such

---

[95] The right of every human being to an identity has been enshrined as part of the guarantees afforded by Article 8 of the European Convention on Human Rights by several rulings of the European Court of Human Rights, most notably *Mennesson v. France*, no. 65192/11, *Labassee v. France*, no. 65941/11, and *K.K. and Others v. Denmark*, no. 25212/21. According to the Court, respect for private life includes the ability of every individual to establish the elements of their personal identity, which encompasses filiation. When filiation is at stake, the Court considers it to affect a fundamental aspect of personal identity. In the case of minors born abroad through surrogacy arrangements, the lack of recognition in domestic law of the legal bond with the biological father was held to seriously impair their right to private life, raising serious concerns as to the compatibility of such a situation with the best interests of the child, which must guide all decisions concerning them.

[96] In the recent case C v. Italy (Appeal No. 47196/21), the Edu Court reconstructed the jurisprudential evolution on the subject of the recognition of the parental relationship between the intended parents and the child born from surrogacy, stressing that the lack of legal recognition of the bond between the child and the intended parent can have a negative impact on various aspects of the child's private life, creating a situation of legal uncertainty regarding the child's identity within society. The Court cited two important pronouncements of the Italian Supreme Court in United Sections (no. 12193 of 8 May 2019 and no.38162 of 30 December 2022) in which the principle had been reaffirmed "according to which the measure of a foreign judge by which the filiation relationship between a child born abroad through GPA and a person who has no biological relationship with the same cannot be transcribed in the Italian civil status registers" and that "the child born through surrogacy has a fundamental right to the recognition, also legal, of the bond created by virtue of the emotional relationship established and experienced with the person who shared the parental plan", a right guaranteed in Italy by the "adoption procedure in particular cases" pursuant to art. 44, paragraph 1 (d), of Law No. 184 of 1983, the constitutionality of which was declared unconstitutional by the well-known sentence No. 79/2022 of the Italian Constitutional Court, insofar as it does not ensure that the same relationship of kinship is created between the adoptee and the adopter's family as with the other types of adoption (*trans. by the author*).

[97] European Court of Human Rights (ECHR), Advisory Opinion concerning the recognition in domestic law of a legal parent-child relationship between a child born through a gestational surrogacy arrangement abroad and the intended mother, Requested by the French Court of Cassation (Request no. P16-2018-001), 10 April 2019, available at: https://hudoc.echr.coe.int/fre#{%22itemid%22:[%22003-6380464-8364383%22]}.

[98] "The child's right to respect for private life within the meaning of Article 8 of the Convention requires that domestic law provide a possibility of recognition of a legal parent-child relationship with the intended mother, designated in the birth certificate legally established abroad as the 'legal mother'" (ECHR, Advisory Opinion, 2019).

recognition need not necessarily take place through the recognition of the foreign birth certificate in the State registry but may also take place through a different procedure, provided that its timely and effective implementation is guaranteed, in the child's best interests.[99]

Indeed, as stated in the case law of certain states, the recognition of parenthood cannot be entrusted to an automatic instrument, such as the recognition of the validity of the foreign birth certificate within the State, because the establishment of parenthood requires an evaluation of concreteness that postulates the finding of the child's pre-eminent interest in continuing, in the legal guise of status, a relationship of care and affection that, already in fact, takes the form of a parental relationship and that "a different solution would lead to basing the acquisition of parenthood solely on the choice of the adults, rather than on an affective relationship already in fact established and consolidated".[100]

In view of the reasons that have been analysed, the interest of the child born of surrogacy must be protected by states, even in cases where the practice of surrogacy is regarded as a universal offence by those states, and even if the legitimate intention of those states is to discourage reproductive tourism and international surrogacy practices.

Indeed, the child is a third party who will suffer the consequences of the choices made by others blamelessly, and it is to the child that the greatest caution must be directed.

2.13 Surrogacy and Neoliberalism, Biocapitalism and the Feminisation of Labour

The advent of biotechnological developments in recent decades has precipitated the emergence of novel neo-liberalist conceptions of the commodity, a phenomenon that has ensued following the dissolution of the Fordist labour system.

The human body has begun to acquire an extrinsic value linked to the possibilities granted by science to use and capitalise on the products of the human body and to enhance the generative capacity of the biological product. In the neoliberal conception, stem cells, gametes, umbilical cords, tissues, and so forth, are regarded as a new product, namely 'bio-capital'.[101]

---

[99] "The child's right to respect for private life within the meaning of Article 8 of the Convention does not require such recognition to take the form of entry in the register of births, marriages and deaths of the details of the birth certificate legally established abroad; another means, such as adoption of the child by the intended mother, may be used provided that the procedure laid down by domestic law ensures that it can be implemented promptly and effectively, in accordance with the child's best interests" (ECHR, Advisory Opinion, 2019).

[100] Italian Court of Cassation, United Sections, Judgment No. 38,162 of 30 December 2022 (*trans. ny the author*). Available at: https://www.cortedicassazione.it/documenti/38162_30-12-2022.pdf.

[101] Term introduced by Codeluppi (2008). See also Helmreich (2008).

The externalisation of relational, communicative, bodily skills in the form of work have allowed the introduction of a concept of feminisation of work (Marazzi 1999; Casalini 2018), precarious, flexible work previously devoid of dichotomous value compared to the Marxist conception of work that distinguished between technical and inert capital and the—living—activity carried out by the worker.

"The twentieth century injects the production process into the body, circulates organs, blood and cell lines outside the body itself" (Cooper and Waldby 2014) giving rise to a new transnational market whose difficulty of regulation threatens the fundamental rights of all stakeholders.

In the context of the new liberalist economy, surrogacy is assigned a notably elevated economic value, thus meriting rigorous investigation and analysis. Consequently, surrogacy is transformed into a commodified service, wherein the ability to generate life is regarded as an economic commodity. In this context, surrogacy, while representing an economic opportunity for some women, risks perpetuating inequality and injustice, especially when it involves women from disadvantaged socio-economic backgrounds. This scenario gives rise to a number of significant bioethical questions, as the risk of exploitation and violation of human dignity is real and tangible.

In a similar vein, in order to discourage the black market, to recognise the possibility of parenthood for those who wish to become parents, and above all to protect the rights, identities and future of children born through surrogacy, in cases where it can be effectively ascertained that the risk of exploitation of women and violation of their dignity will be excluded, it is necessary to identify criteria and parameters at an international level that can standardise the approach to the practice of surrogacy, thus overcoming the critical issues that have emerged in connection with reproductive tourism.

In view of the various elements analysed to date, the difficulties encountered by the legislator when deciding how to regulate surrogacy are clearly evident. The various ethical approaches adopted, and the difficulties encountered, are evident from the lack of consensus within and between the disciplines, both internationally and at the European level.

It is evident that a number of states permit commercial surrogacy and, through the intermediation of authorised agencies, render surrogacy analogous to a eugenic practice by allowing users to select the phenotype of both the gamete donors and the surrogate mother.[102]

Others, on the other hand, repudiate all forms of surrogacy, punishing anyone who 'carries out, organises, or publicises gestation for others and trade in gametes

[102] See for example https://success-maternita-surrogata.it/?gad_source=1&gclid=Cj0KCQiA7se8BhCAARIsAKnF3rwnXeaHlWQzme4xZBz7qkswPg1QAsmmpaWazmGjTeKyukCYQN-nkj8aAoPlEALw_wcB; and https://fiv-et.it/?utm_source=google&utm_medium=cpc&utm_campaign=20316935453&utm_term=uteri%20in%20rent&gad_source=1&gclid=Cj0KCQiA7se8BhCAARIsAKnF3rwa2AGQt3svd7avsymaudmA8AP3dTm1ifSzwsgOfosLO9BqcZIOD7kaAvpnEALw_wcB.

or embryos with imprisonment of three months to two years and a fine of EUR 600,000 to EUR 1 million'[103] even if committed abroad.

In between, there is a myriad of different and controversial disciplines, which allow surrogacy for altruistic purposes with subjective and objective requirements that vary from state to state, but without, in truth, being able to respond effectively to the need to safeguard the dignity of the human beings involved by ensuring that the choice to offer one's body to carry a pregnancy to term on behalf of others is truly an autonomous choice not influenced by external factors other than the will to do good to others.

In order to establish an ethically sustainable surrogacy model, it may be useful to take a cue again from the reflections of the International Bioethics Committee of UNESCO[104] on the subject.

The IBC methodically examines the arguments both for and against surrogacy. In a multitude of instances, women who elect to proceed with a pregnancy on behalf of others are often 'forced' to do so[105] as a consequence of the precarious circumstances to which they are exposed, characterised by vulnerabilities of a social, economic and cultural nature. This predicament invariably renders them susceptible to the risk of exploitation by intermediary agencies.

Furthermore, there are significant concerns regarding the reliability of the informed consent provided by women who may lack the capacity to comprehend the emotional implications of the decision to terminate the pregnancy, despite the emotional connection established with the unborn child. Furthermore, the mother's lifestyle and behaviour during pregnancy have been demonstrated to exert a direct influence on the child, thereby giving rise to a potential conflict of interest between the surrogate mother and the intended parents. This conflict may manifest in the form of attempts by the intended parents to exert pressure on the surrogate mother or to unduly condition her autonomy of choice leading to psychological problems for the surrogate mother.[106]

Various concerns also arise with respect to the position of intended parents, both with respect to the possibility of selecting embryos after pre-implantation diagnosis and the characteristics of donors, trespassing into a sort of choice of the 'best product', and with respect to the suffering that may result from the

[103] Art. 12, para. 6, Law No. 40 of 19 February 2004, *Norme in materia di procreazione medically assistita* (Law on Medically Assisted Reproduction) (Italy). Available at: https://www.normattiva.it/urires/N2Ls?urn:nir:stato:decreto.presidente.della.repubblica:2004;40~art12!vig=#:~:text=Whoever%20realizes%20a%20process%20involved.

[104] International Bioethics Committee (IBC) (2019) Report of the IBC on Assisted Reproductive Technologies (ART) and parenthood. UNESCO. Available at: https://unesdoc.unesco.org/ark:/48223/pf0000367957.

[105] VI.31, 155 p.30, International Bioethics Committee (IBC) (2019) Report of the IBC on Assisted Reproductive Technologies (ART) and parenthood. UNESCO. Available at: https://unesdoc.unesco.org/ark:/48223/pf0000367957.

[106] World Health Organization (2009) Mental health aspects of women's reproductive health: a global review of the literature. WHO, Geneva. Available at: https://iris.who.int/bitstream/handle/10665/43846/9789241563567_eng.pdf.

knowledge that surrogacy may represent the last chance to become parents, leading to relational problems with the surrogate mother due to anxiety about the outcome of the pregnancy.[107]

A further issue dealt with by the IBC is that of the possible alteration of the concept of family as identified by Article 16 of the Universal Declaration of Human Rights,[108] in cases where the surrogate mother is a close relative of the intended parents, if so-called *doubling* situations (aunt-mother, sister-mother, grandmother-mother) could be created, risking an impairment of the child's interest, as stated by the European Court of Human Rights.[109]

Contrary to these perspectives, others argue that surrogacy may in some cases be the last chance for some women to become mothers, for instance in cases of infertility caused by illness. Some utilitarian philosophers see gestation as a tradable commodity, but call for the necessary legal regulation to protect the human rights of the parties involved, including children and surrogate mothers, and prevent their exploitation. However, it is pointed out that altruistic surrogacy would risk increasing the cross-border exploitation of women.

The Report of the IBC conducts a thorough analysis of the ethical issues related to human dignity and the practice of surrogacy, emphasising the centrality of these issues within the context of human rights. Human dignity, recognised as an intrinsic value that is the same for all and inalienable, implies unconditional respect for every individual, regardless of sex, gender identity, age, health status, political views or religion. This fundamental principle proscribes any form of exploitation of the human body. Consequently, the sale of cells or body parts is rejected, as is any payment to a woman to carry a pregnancy on behalf of others. These practices are considered incompatible with respect for human dignity.[110]

The practice of commercial surrogacy gives rise to a number of ethical concerns, particularly with regard to the potential exploitation of economically disadvantaged women who may be persuaded to participate due to financial pressures. Moreover, the pregnant woman is exposed to significant health risks without any direct benefits, in addition to the trauma resulting from the psycho-physical bonding with the foetus and the subsequent separation. Surrogacy contracts may also

[107] Robertson S (2018) Infertility: Social impact. Medical Life Sciences News. Available at: https://www.news-medical.net/health/Infertility-Social-Impact.aspx.

[108] The Universal Declaration of Human Rights (UDHR), Art. 16, sect. 3, "The family is the natural and fundamental nucleus of society and is entitled to protection by society and the State". Available at: https://www.un.org/en/about-us/universal-declaration-of-human-rights.

[109] In the well-known *Frette v. France* ruling of 2002, the Court affirmed the principle that "it is not about giving a child to a family, but a family to the child", https://hudoc.echr.coe.int/fre#{%22itemid%22:[%22001-60168%22]}.

[110] For this reason, "all committee members reject commercial surrogacy". International Bioethics Committee (IBC) (2019) Report of the IBC on Assisted Reproductive Technologies (ART) and parenthood. UNESCO. sec. 163. Available at: https://unesdoc.unesco.org/ark:/48223/pf0000367957.

entail the risk of control over the surrogate's body and lifestyle, imposing health checks and, in some cases, even termination of the pregnancy due to genetic disorders or malformations not accepted by the intended parents.

The regulatory approaches employed by individual states vary significantly. Some explicitly prohibit it, others accept it under specific regulated conditions, while still others tacitly tolerate it. The IBC has rejected the latter position on the basis that it is too risky due to the high probability of exploitation associated with the absence of regulation. A thorough examination of the document drafted by the IBC reveals the presence of three primary positions. The first rejects surrogacy outright because of the risks associated with the exploitation of women, the principle of the best interest of the child and the negative impact on the family institution. The second position asserts that altruistic surrogacy is permissible under the condition that the rights of the child, the autonomy and well-being of the surrogate, and the conscious involvement of all parties are guaranteed. A third position asserts the acceptability of altruistic surrogacy in specific cases, while simultaneously expressing significant reservations regarding the feasibility of meeting the requisite conditions in practice.

For IBC members who advocate altruistic surrogacy, there are several key conditions that must be met. Firstly, the existence of a close family or relational bond between the surrogate mother and the intended parents is necessary to ensure an autonomous decision. Secondly, the financial neutrality of the act is paramount, meaning that reimbursement of expenses is the only acceptable outcome. Thirdly, surrogacy should only be considered as a last resort if no alternative option exists for having a child. Furthermore, the principle of the child's best interests must always prevail, regardless of the position of states on surrogacy. Indeed, the European Court of Human Rights has emphasised in several rulings that, even in states where the practice is prohibited, children born through surrogacy are entitled to an identity, parents and citizenship. In conclusion, the report which acknowledges the numerous ethical dilemmas connected with surrogacy, promotes a judicious approach founded upon the safeguarding of human dignity, the rights of the women involved, and, most significantly, the best interests of the child.

2.14 An Ethically Sustainable Model for Surrogacy, the Woman as an End and Not as a Means

In the light of the foregoing paragraphs, there are no fixed points on which the academic and scientific community seem to agree when it comes to surrogacy.

According to some schools of thought, the surrogate mothers' right to self-determination is to be considered prevalent over the need to protect their human dignity and to exclude the risk of commodification and exploitation of women's bodies. According to others, on the other hand, surrogacy is a way to exploit women from third-world countries for the benefit of first-world countries (Gupta 2006, 2012; Rudrappa 2015). Furthermore, surrogacy is regarded as a criminal act that should be prosecuted, even when it is deemed to be contrary to the best interests of the child.

The element that appears to have garnered the most support—also by virtue of the explicit prohibitions on the commodification of the human body contained in, among others, the Oviedo Convention[111] and the Charter of Fundamental Rights of the European Union[112]—is the exclusion of the ethical admissibility of commercial surrogacy. This is defined as a pregnancy carried to term by a woman for others in exchange for financial compensation with the objective of generating profit.

Also the National Bioethics Committee with a motion on surrogacy for money[113] and the European Parliament in the Annual Report on Human Rights and Democracy in the World 2014[114] have expressed themselves recognising in the performance of surrogacy the compromising of the dignity of the human being, the commodification of the body and reproductive functions for financial gain, which mainly involves vulnerable women in developing countries.

---

[111] Convention for the Protection of Human Rights and Dignity of the Human Being with regard to the Application of Biology and Medicine: Convention on Human Rights and Biomedicine (1997) Oviedo. Chapter VII—Prohibition of Profit and Use of a Part of the Human Body, Article 21—Prohibition of Profit, "The human body and its parts shall not, as such, be a source of profit". Available at: https://rm.coe.int/168007cf98.

[112] Charter of Fundamental Rights of the European Union (2000/C 364/01), OJ C 364, 18.12.2000, Art.3 the integrity of the person, "the prohibition of making the human body and its parts as such a source of financial gain". Available at: https://www.europarl.europa.eu/charter/pdf/text_it.pdf.

[113] *Comitato Nazionale di Bioetica (CNB) Mozione sulla maternità surrogate a titolo oneroso 2016* (Italy) [National Bioethics Committee, Motion on surrogacy for remuneration]. Available at: https://bioetica.governo.it/media/4867/m17_2016_maternita-surrogata-a-titolo-oneroso.pdf.
Within the aforementioned motion, a dissenting opinion is also indicated that 'the CNB preferred to issue an unappealable condemnation, which closes the discourse before it even begins. Establishing that "surrogacy is a contract detrimental to the dignity of the woman and the child" means denying that there is a human fabric around the birth of those children, of investments, thoughts, desires, feelings, first and foremost on the part of the gestating mother. That is, it means denying subjectivity to women, to consider them once again as 'mute' bodies, the object of prescriptions, to give birth or not to give birth, according to wills other than their own" (*trans. by the author*).

[114] European Parliament, Motion for a Resolution on the Annual Report on Human Rights and Democracy in the World in 2014 and the European Union's policy on the matter, (2015/2229 (INI)), 17 December 2015. Available at: https://www.europarl.europa.eu/doceo/document/A-8-2015-0344_EN.html. The European Parliament in its resolution "condemns the practice of surrogacy, which undermines the human dignity of women as their bodies and reproductive functions are used as a commodity; considers that the practice of surrogacy involving reproductive exploitation and the use of the human body for financial or other gain, particularly in the case of vulnerable women in developing countries, should be prohibited and treated as an urgent issue in human rights instruments". Available at: https://www.europarl.europa.eu/doceo/document/A-8-2015-0344_EN.html.

Bearing in mind the *logique du fait accompli* according to which surrogacy is often to be considered a fact from which there is no turning back, in order to avoid the risk of commodification of a woman's body and reproductive functions, even the scholars most critical of the ethical admissibility of the practice have opened the door to altruistic surrogacy on condition that it is adequately regulated according to criteria that guarantee its altruistic purpose through the exclusion of consideration and profit and consequently with the diminution of the risk of infringement to human dignity.

Many bioethicists have assessed as acceptable—excluding the payment of a fee for the gestational 'service'—the reimbursement of expenses incurred by the surrogate mother or, in some cases, of the loss of profit associated with the pregnancy,[115] believing that this element was sufficient to exclude or minimise the risk of exploitation and commercialisation.

It can be argued that, in order to exclude the risk of exploitation of the human body and commodification of the reproductive function, it is not sufficient to exclude payment as a consideration but as reimbursement, compensation or compensation. It is instead necessary to provide regulations that ensure that the woman abandons the role of *means* to become the *end* of surrogacy herself.

In fact, a classic argument used by scholars against surrogacy (Palazzani 2020; Frati et al. 2021)[116] refers to Kantian moral theory, according to which "the human being cannot be used simply as a means by anyone, (not even by any other rational being) [God], but must at the same time always be used as an end" (Kant 1998, § 38), otherwise the inherent dignity of the human being would be violated.[117]

A particular interpretation of Kantian moral principles, surrogacy that is truly and absolutely altruistic could be approved even by the Königsberg philosopher himself. In order to establish an ethically sustainable model of altruistic surrogacy, it is first necessary to clarify the concept of altruism.

August Comte, before coining the concept of 'altruism', highlights the need to place the collective good above personal interests as a fundamental character of positive morality.[118] With *Vivre pour autrui*[119] (living for others) Comte indicates a

[115] Both in the sense of loss of income due to the interruption of existing employment and in the sense of loss of opportunities due to the impossibility of looking for and finding work.

[116] "The Kantian principle, to which the National Bioethics Commission (CNB) has often referred in recent times, according to which, and by virtue of which, each one of us is an end in itself, and cannot be used as a medium to achieve external ends or the interests of third parties, also provides that each one of us is a body that performs certain actions and achieves certain ends, again in accordance with the above maxim" (*trans by the author*). See also Adorno (2012).

[117] "Humanity itself is a dignity" (Kant 1998, § 38).

[118] "*La prépondérance de la sociabilité sur la personnalité constitue le caractère essentiel de la morale positive*" [The predominance of sociability over individuality constitutes the essential character of positive morality], (*trans. by the author*). Comte (1853) Vol. IV, Leçon 47: Sur l'étude sociale, p. 697.

[119] "*Vivre pour autrui constitue donc la loi fondamentale de l'humanité, tant dans sa destinée privée que publique*" [Living for others thus constitutes the fundamental law of humanity, both in its private and public destiny], (*trans. by the author*). Comte (1851–1854) Vol. I, Chapter II: De la sociabilité humaine, p.547.

fundamental law of humanity by introducing the term *altruism*[120] to describe a central moral principle that privileges the welfare of others over individual selfishness.

A harmonious society is based on altruistic interaction between individuals. Altruistic action for Comte is essential for the progress of society in that acting for the good of others is tantamount to acting for the common good, altruism for this reason is understood as moral behaviour. The notion of altruism is seen as a means to overcome social divisions and to foster collective solidarity, underpinned by a global vision of an ordered society based on relationships of interdependence. According to Comte, acting out of altruism and solidarity means acting in fulfilment of moral duties without a reward or form of compensation, but on the contrary, sacrificing one's personal interests.[121] Solidarity, considered as the set of altruistic actions that within society contribute to the collective wellbeing, to be authentic, cannot be commodified or subject to material compensation. For Comte, the notion of solidarity, if it were to be compensated, would consequently lose its moral significance, transforming into a self-serving endeavour.

It can be argued that altruism is defined by the sacrifice of one's own interests for the benefit of others. Consequently, any form of compensation for this sacrifice could potentially lead to the dissolution of altruism itself. Once the meaning of altruism has been identified, the question arises as to whether altruistic action, as stated by Comte, is actually moral action.

In order to verify whether altruistic action can be considered a moral action, reference should be made to *the premier moral theory* (Kant 1996, p. vii–xxvi).

Kant's endeavour was to establish a universal morality, applicable to all human beings, that transcends the experiences of the sensible world and the *arbitrium brutum* (Kant 1997, p.13) and that, through the concept of free will, enables the identification of maxims of behaviour that have the potential to become universal laws, i.e. applicable to all human beings without exception. From this perspective, Kant considers moral laws to be imperatives that prescribe obligations for us, positive or negative, to respect, which we cannot in any way escape. These laws are therefore categorical, i.e. they identify the fundamental criteria on the basis of which we construct our maxims of behaviour, which by virtue of this become duties for us.

The representation of an action considered necessary not by virtue of a secondary end or purpose, but directly as such, is in itself capable of creating a categorical imperative, i.e. an imperative to which a duty is directly linked within

---

[120] "*Le mot altruisme, que je crois devoir introduire pour désigner sommairement cet état de choses, constitue une expression directe du grand principe positiviste de vivre pour autrui*" [the word altruism, which I believe I must introduce to succinctly designate this condition, constitutes a direct expression of the great positivist principle of living for others] (*trans. by the author*) Comte (1851–1854) Vol. I. Chapter IV: Théorie de la Sociabilité, p. 611.

[121] "*L'homme ne peut devenir pleinement homme qu'en se sacrifiant aux autres. C'est la loi fondamentale de la morale positive*" [Man can only fully become man by sacrificing himself for others. This is the fundamental law of positive morality] (*trans. by the author*) Comte (1851–1854) Vol. I, Chapter II, p. 549.

us. The founding criterion of the possibility of the existence of a categorical imperative within us is inextricably linked to our internal freedom.

And it is precisely the internal incentive of duty that for Kant is the differentiating element in the identification of what is moral: "for considering the action in terms of moral laws, no special law would be required for it" (Kant 1997, [6:223] p.16). It is not the action itself that constitutes the fundamental element in determining what is considered moral and what is not, but rather, it is the principle on which the maxim employed by the subject in determining its own actions or inactions is based.

In order to define altruistic action as moral action, according to Kantian precepts, it is necessary to assert that altruistic action can conform to a maxim of behaviour capable of being subsumed as a universal law, considered by the agent as a categorical imperative.

Similarly, while the definition of a maxim of behaviour is a metaphysical activity, performed simply through the use of reason, the exercise of free will requires human beings to perform external actions. This necessarily determines that human beings also act and relate to each other on the basis of other assumptions and different incentives.

It can therefore be posited that the role of the legal legislator is to create incentives for action that conform to maxims of conduct deemed moral; alternatively, as in the case of surrogacy, the legal legislator may have the negative duty of prohibiting actions that are contrary to moral duties and permitting those that conform to moral duties. Irrespective of one's personal conception of what is moral and what is not,[122] in accordance with the theories just identified—in respect of which, given their complexity, it is not claimed that a complete overview can be offered in a few lines—if altruistic action is considered a moral action (understood in the Kantian sense), altruistic surrogacy (understood in the Comtian sense) can not only be considered ethically permissible, but can even be regarded as a moral action.

In the event of a surrogate mother acting in fulfilment of a moral duty, the status of surrogacy changes, moving from being a 'means' for the good of others to being defined as an 'end' for its own sake, categorised as a good for the good in itself, or a categorical imperative for the agent.

Therefore, in order to state that surrogacy is an ethically permissible practice, it is necessary to state that the internal incentive for surrogate mothers' action is exclusively the altruistic purpose, perceived as a moral duty by the latter. Even if it is possible to state that the requirement for the ethical admissibility of surrogacy is the existence of an internal incentive for the action of an altruistic type. However, considering that human beings do not always act in accordance with their internal incentives but are also influenced by the presence of external incentives for the action, it is not possible to affirm, *sic et simpliciter*, its legality.

[122] Kant (1997, Part. I, Book I, chap.I) believed that even in a world of purely rational beings (such as angels) there could be disagreement about what is good, not because angels have selfish inclinations, but because good is not an immediate objective reality, but something that requires rational moral legislation.

The incentive to act, in fact, is not knowable outside the agent and consequently cannot be used as a legal parameter to discriminate between cases in which surrogacy is ethically acceptable and cases in which it is not. Instead, it will be necessary for the legislature to identify legal criteria that ensure that the free will of the agent and the corresponding action are in conformity with moral duties.

In practice, the legislator will have to identify a number of requirements that ensure, with the greatest possible degree of probability, the altruistic purpose of surrogacy. Only then could one speak of altruistic surrogacy.

One could imagine a National Centre for Altruistic Gestation, similar to the National Transplant Centre, which would oversee the processes necessary for the practice. A directory could be created where women intending to carry a child for another person could register to fulfil their altruistic purpose. Registration requirements could be carefully identified and assessed directly by the institutions to protect both surrogate mothers (e.g. a certain age limit, having already had a pregnancy, and the absence of transmissible diseases or genetic disorders) and intended parents (e.g. infertility issues, age requirements, income, and the presence of at least two people as intended parents).

The National Centre for Altruistic Gestation could facilitate the matching of requests from intentional parents with gestational mothers. This could be done through bilateral or multilateral agreements with other states or through international organisations.[123] The centre would guarantee the anonymity of all parties involved. This would prevent pressure and/or coercion from one another and the pursuit of any eugenic intent.

Furthermore, if the parental plan were recognised as constitutional dignity (on the basis of Articles 2 and 3 of the Constitution and 7 and 8 ECHR), the national health services could cover the expenses necessary to perform the practice, guaranteeing that the gestational act would be completely free of charge. This would also guarantee the authenticity of the gestational mother's altruistic and solidaristic intent (the internal incentive). On the other hand, this would enable individuals with fewer financial resources to access the practice, ensuring parity and equality for intended parents, who are currently predominantly wealthy individuals or couples.

Although the process should be institutionalised by assigning the surrogate mother to the intended parents based on clinical compatibility, exceptions could be made in cases where the gestational mother is a close relative of the intended parents, assuming this is permitted, to guarantee the altruism and solidarity of the practice. Careful consideration should also be given to whether the gestational mother should have the right to keep the child after birth, weighing up the potential

[123] Like Eurotransplant is a non-profit service organization which facilitates patient-oriented allocation and cross border exchange of deceased donor organs. Eurotransplant provides services to transplant centers and their associated tissue typing laboratories and donor hospitals in its member states. Available at: https://www.eurotransplant.org/about-eurotransplant/eurotransplants-aims/.

psychological harm of forced separation from the child against the harm to the intended parents associated with the failure of the surrogacy arrangement, particularly when cryopreserved gametes are used for fertilisation.

The previously put forward argument and consequent suggestions are not without their weaknesses. The main one might be the idea that the sacrifice associated with the altruistic or solidarity act is represented exclusively by the pregnancy itself, rather than including the associated economic expenditure. Therefore, even if the gestational mother is reimbursed for out-of-pocket expenses, the altruistic and solidarity purpose, and consequently the ethical admissibility of the practice, may remain uncertain. One might also agree with this, since strict parameters would need to be identified to ensure that the reimbursement of expenses does not represent an external incentive to gestation for others, thereby rendering the altruistic purpose futile.

In any event, in light of the globalised practice of access, which enables intended parents of children born through GPA to obtain recognition of the parental relationship, even if the birth took place through a practice that is contrary to the law of the intended parents' country, it is advisable to identify directives at a supranational level, in order to control a phenomenon that, far from being carried out purely for altruistic or solidarity purposes, in some cases even explicitly, often seriously violate the dignity and rights of the human beings involved, especially women.

References

Aach J, Lunshof J, Iyer E, Church GM (2017) Addressing the ethical issues raised by synthetic human entities with embryo-like features. eLife 6: e20674

Adorno R (2012) Bioetica y dignidad de la persona. Tecnos, Madrid

Agacinski S (2013) Corps en miettes. Flammarion, Paris

Agnafors M (2014) The harm argument against surrogacy revisited: two versions not to be forgotten. Med Health Care Philos 17(3):357–363

Aguilera-Castrejon A, Oldak B, Shani T, Ghanem N, Itzkovich C, Slomovich S, Tarazi S, Bayerl J, Chugaeva V, Ayyash M, et al. (2021) Ex utero mouse embryogenesis from pre-gastrulation to late organogenesis. Nature 593:119–124

Anderson E (1993) Value in ethics and economics. Harvard University Press, Cambridge, MA

Annas GJ (1988) Death without dignity for commercial surrogacy: the case of Baby M. The Hastings Center Rep 18(2):21–24

Antonini L (2012) Autodeterminazione nel sistema dei diritti costituzionali. In: D'Agostino F (ed) Un diritto di spessore costituzionale? Giuffrè, Milano

Aristotle (1943) Generation of Animals. In: Peck AL (trans). Loeb Classical Library. Harvard University Press, Cambridge, MA

Bagcchi S (2014) Mothers who turn to surrogacy to support their families face ostracism, study shows. BMJ 348:g3257

Baldini G (2018) Prime riflessioni a margine della legge 219/17. Bio Law J 2:97

Balistrieri M (2007) La clonazione: tra libertà di ricerca e natura umana. In: Baldini G, Soldano M (eds) Tecnologie riproduttive e tutela della persona: verso un comune diritto europeo per la bioetica. Firenze University Press, Firenze, p 210

Baron T, Svingen E, Leyva R (2024) Surrogacy and adoption: an empirical investigation of public moral attitudes. J Bioeth Inq 21(4):671–681

Bauman Z (1992) Mortality, immortality and other life strategies. Polity Press, Cambridge

Beauchamp TL, Childress JF (2001) Principles of biomedical ethics, 5th edn. Oxford University Press, New York
Behjati-Ardakani Z, Akhondi MM, Mahmoodzadeh H, Hosseini SH (2016) An evaluation of the historical importance of fertility and its reflection in ancient mythology. J Reproduct Infertility 17:2–9
Blyth W (1994) I wanted to be interesting. I wanted to be able to say I've done something with my life: interviews with surrogate mothers in Britain. J Reprod Infant Psychol 12:189–198
Bowlby J (1969) Attachment and loss: volume I. Attachment. Basic Books, New York
Brandão P, Garrido N (2022) Commercial surrogacy: an overview. Revista Brasileira de Ginecologia E Obstetrícia 44(12):1141–1158
Brunet L, Carruthers J, Davaki K, King D, Marzo C, McCandless J (2013) A comparative study on the regime of surrogacy in EU member states. European Parliament, Brussels
Busby K, Vun D (2010) Revisiting The Handmaid's Tail: Feminist Theory Meets Empirical Research on Surrogate Mothers Can J Fam L 26(13)
Cahill LS (1988) The ethics of surrogate motherhood: biology, freedom, and moral obligation. Law Med Health Care: Publ Am Soc Law Med 16(1–2):65–71
Callahan JC, Roberts DE (1996) A feminist social justice approach to reproduction-assisting technologies: a case study on the limits of liberal theory. Ky Law J 84:1197–1227
Caporale L, Veronesi U, Mancini E, Flamigni C (2016) Maternità surrogata: profili etici. Future Sci Ethics 1:80
Carone N (2016) In origine è il dono. Mimesis, Milano
Casalini L (2018) Il femminismo e le sfide del neoliberismo. DeriveApprodi, Roma
Chen JY (2013) Reproductive donation: practice, policy, and bioethics. Yale J Biol Med 86(3):434–435
Chini C (2016) Maternità surrogata: nodi critici tra logica del dono e preminente interesse del minore. Bio Law J 1:169–177
Ciccarelli JC, Beckman LJ (2005) Navigating rough waters: an overview of psychological aspects of surrogacy. J Soc Issues 61:21–43
Cicero (2008) On duties (De Officiis). Griffin MT, Atkins EM (trans. and eds.) Oxford University Press, Oxford
Codeluppi G (2008) Biocapitale. Verso lo sfruttamento integrale di corpi, cervelli ed emozioni. Bollati Boringhieri, Torino
Comte A (1851–1854) Système de politique positive. ou, Traité de sociologie, instituant la religion de l'humanité. Carilian-Goeury et V. Dalmont, Paris
Comte A (1853) L'étude sociale, in Système de politique positive. Carilian-Goeury et V. Dalmont, Paris
Cooper M, Waldby C (2014) Clinical labor: tissue donors and research subjects in the global bioeconomy. Duke University Press, Durham
Corti I (2000) La maternità per sostituzione. Giuffrè, Milano
Danna D (2017) Fare un figlio per altri è giusto (Falso!). Laterza, Roma-Bari
de Beauvoir S (2010) The second sex. In: Borde C, Malovany-Chevallier S (trans). Knopf, New York
de Miguel Beriain I (2017) Patenting human embryonic stem cells in the European union context: an updated analysis of a complex issue. In: Pham P, Rosemann A (eds) Safety, ethics and regulations. Stem cells in clinical applications. Springer, Cham pp 263–273
Den Bergh BRH V, Mulder EJH, Mennes M, Glover V (2014) The influence of maternal stress on fetal development: a critical review. Neurosci Biobehav Rev 43:17–34
Derbyshire SW, Bockmann JC (2020) Reconsidering fetal pain. J Med Ethics 46:3–6
Di Mauro E (2017) Epigenetica, il DNA che impara. Istruzioni per l'uso del patrimonio genetico. EUT Edizioni Università di Trieste, Trieste
Dodds S (2000) Choice and control in feminist bioethics. In: Mackenzie C, Stoljar N (eds) Relational autonomy: feminist perspectives on autonomy, agency, and the social self. Oxford University Press, Oxford, pp 213–235

Ehrenreich N (2008) Introduction. In: Ehrenreich N (ed) The Reproductive Rights Reader. New York University Press, New York, pp 1–14
Ellenbogen A, Feldberg D, Lokshin V (2021) Surrogacy – a worldwide demand. Implementation and ethical considerations. Gynecol Reproduct Endocrinol Metabol 2(2):066–073
Fabre-Magnan M (2013) La gestation pour autrui: fictions et réalités. Fayard, Paris
Feldman R (2007) Parent-infant synchrony: biological foundations and developmental outcomes. Curr Dir Psychol Sci 16(6):340–345
Feldman EA (2018) Baby M turns 30: the law and policy of surrogate motherhood. Am J Law Med 44(1):7–22
Fenton-Glynn C (2016) Outsourcing ethical dilemmas: regulating international surrogacy arrangements. Med Law Rev 24(1):59–75
Ferrara A (2023) The ethical triage dilemma: who should receive medical care first; is this the right question? Ratio Juris 36(2):178–190
Foucault M (1970) The order of things: an archaeology of the human sciences. Tavistock Publications, London
Frati P, La Russa R, Santurro A, Fineschi B, Di Paolo M, Scopetti M, Turillazzi E, Fineschi V (2021) Bioethical issues and legal frameworks of surrogacy: a global perspective about the right to health and dignity. Eur J Obstet Gynecol Reprod Biol 258:1–8
Gheaus A (2024) Against private surrogacy: a child-centred view. In: Gheaus A and Straehle C (eds) Debating surrogacy. Oxford University Press, New York
Gillon R (1994) Medical ethics: four principles plus attention to scope. BMJ 309:184
Glover V (2015) Prenatal stress and its effects on the fetus and the child: possible underlying biological mechanisms. Adv Neurobiol 10:269–283
Golboni F, Jalali A, Dinmohammadi M, Taghizadeh Z, Nouri P, Salahsoor MR (2020) Iranian model of decision making to use surrogacy: a grounded theory study. Health Care Women Inter 41(7):853–865
Golombok S, Ilioi E, Blake L, Roman G, Jadva V (2017) A longitudinal study of families formed through reproductive donation: parent-adolescent relationships and adolescent adjustment at age 14. Dev Psychol 53:1966–1977
Grasso AG (2018) Per Un'Interpretazione Costituzionalmente Orientata Del Divieto Di Maternità Surrogata. TCRS - Teoria e Critica Della Regolazione Sociale 2:153–190
Guerra-Palmero MJ (2017) Contra la llamada gestación subrogada. Derechos humanos y justicia global versus bioética neoliberal. Gac Sanit 31(6):535–538
Gupta JA (2006) Toward transnational feminism. Some reflections and concerns in relation to the globalization of reproductive technologies. Eur J Womens Stud 13:23–38
Gupta JA (2012) Reproductive biocrossing: Indian egg donors and surrogates in the globalized fertility market. Int J Fem Approaches Bioeth 5:25–51
Gusmai A (2019) Il diritto all'autodeterminazione: una libertà "perimetrata" dal sapere scientifico? Dirittifondamentali.it 1:5
Habermas J (2003) The future of human nature. Polity Press, Cambridge
Hammond-Browning N, Williams NJ (2020) Developing an international registry for uterus transplantation (IRUTx): promises and challenges. Hum Reprod 35:2643–2649
Heidegger M (1947) Letter on humanism. In: Capuzzi FA, Gray JG (eds) Basic writings. Harper & Row, New York, pp 217–269
Helmreich S (2008) Species of biocapital. Sci Cult 17(4):463–478
Hemalal S, Librach CL (2020) "Not my child to give away": a qualitative analysis of gestational surrogates' experiences. Women Birth 33(3):e256–e265
Hibino Y, Shimazono Y (2013) Becoming a surrogate online: 'message board' surrogacy in Thailand. Asian Bioethics Review 5(3):255–269
Hippocrates (1931) Nature of women (De Natura Muliebri). In: Potter P H (ed) Vol. X, Loeb Classical Library. Harvard University Press, Cambridge, MA
Hodson N, Townley L, Earp BD (2019) Removing harmful options: the law and ethics of international commercial surrogacy. Med Law Rev 27(4):597–622

Hofman DL (2009) Mama's baby, daddy's maybe: a state-by-state survey of surrogacy laws and their disparate gender impact. William Mitchell Law Rev 35(2):449–468

Horn C (2020) Gestation and ectogenesis: self-determination for pregnant people ahead of artificial wombs. J Med Ethics 46:787–788

Horsey K (2024) The future of surrogacy: a review of current global trends and national landscapes. Reprod Biomed Online 48(5)

Hyun I, Munsie M, Pera MF, Rivron NC, Rossant J (2020) Toward guidelines for research on human embryo models formed from stem cells. Stem Cell Rep 14(2):169–174

Irigaray L (1985) Speculum of the other woman. In: Gill GC (trans). Cornell University Press, Ithaca, NY

Jackson E (2001) Regulating reproduction: law, technology and autonomy. Hart Publishing, Oxford

Jadva V (2012) Subrogacía en el Reino Unido: experiencia de padres, niños y madres por encargo. In: Esteinou R (ed) La nueva generación social de familias. Tecnologías de reproducción asistida y temas contemporáneos. Centro de Investigaciones y Estudios Superiores en Antropología Social. Mexico, pp 75–90

Jadva V (2020) Postdelivery adjustment of gestational carriers, parents, and their children. Fertil Steril 113(5):903–907

Jadva V, Gamble N, Prosser H, Imrie S (2019) Parents' relationship with their surrogate in cross-border and domestic surrogacy arrangements: comparison by sexual orientation and location. Fertil Steril 111:562–570

Jadva V, Murray C, Lycett E, MacCallum F, Golombok S (2003) Surrogacy: the experiences of surrogate mothers. Hum Reprod 18(10):2196–2204

Jasanoff S (2011) Introduction: rewriting life, reframing rights. In: Jasanoff S (ed) Reframing rights: bioconstitutionalism in the genetic age. MIT Press, Cambridge, MA, pp 1–24

Jonas H (1979) The imperative of responsibility: in search of an ethics for the technological age. University of Chicago Press, Chicago

Kane E (1988) Birth mother: the story of America's first legal surrogate mother. Harcourt, New York

Kant I (1996) The metaphysics of morals. In: Denis L (ed), Gregor M (trans). Cambridge University Press, Cambridge, MA

Kant I (1997) Critique of practical reason. In: Gregor M (trans). Cambridge University Press, Cambridge, MA

Kant I (1998) Groundwork of the metaphysics of morals. In: Gregor M, Timmeman J (eds and trans). Cambridge University Press, Cambridge, MA

Kendal ES (2022) Form, function, perception, and reception: visual bioethics and the artificial womb. Yale J Biol Med 95:371–377

Kennedy S (2020) Willing mothers: ectogenesis and the role of gestational motherhood. J Med Ethics 46:320–327

Kirk GS, Raven JE, Schofield M (1963) The presocratic philosophers: a critical history with a selection of texts. Cambridge University Press, Cambridge, MA

Knight G (2020) Gestation, equality and freedom: ectogenesis as a political perspective. J Med Ethics 46:76–82

Kristeva J (1987) Tales of love. In: Roudiez LS (trans). Columbia University Press, New York

Lam RX (2024) Rethinking 'family': a call for conceptual amelioration. Bioethics 38(7):705–713

Lamba N, Jadva V, Kadam K, Golombok S (2018) The psychological wellbeing and prenatal bonding of gestational surrogates. Hum Reprod 33(4):646–653

Locke J (1980 [1690]) Second treatise of government. In: McPherson CB (ed). Hackett Publishing Company, Indianapolis

Loiodice A (1971) Informazione (diritto alla). In: Enciclopedia del Diritto, vol XXI. Giuffrè, Milano, p 472

MacCallum F, Lycett E, Murray C, Jadva V, Golombok S (2003) Surrogacy: the experience of commissioning couples. Hum Reprod 18(6):1334–1342

Mackenzie C, Stoljar N (2000) Introduction: autonomy reconfigured. In: Mackenzie C, Stoljar N (eds) Relational autonomy: feminist perspectives on autonomy, agency and the social self. Oxford University Press, Oxford, pp 1–29

Mangiameli S (2009) Autodeterminazione: diritto di spessore costituzionale?, Relazione tenuta al IV Laboratorio Sublacense su «La comunità familiare e le scelte di fine vita». Forum di Quaderni Costituzionali 1–25

Mangiameli S (2011) Autodeterminazione: diritto di spessore costituzionale? In: Navarini C (ed) Autonomy and Self-determination. Profili etici, bioetici e giuridici. Roma, p 82–94

Marazzi C (1999) Il posto dei calzini. La svolta linguistica dell'economia e i suoi risvolti sulla politica. Bollati Boringhieri, Torino

May T (2009) Bioethics in a liberal society: the political framework of bioethics decision making. Johns Hopkins University Press, Baltimore

Mercer JR (2006) Understanding attachment: parenting, child care, and emotional development. Praeger, Westport

Merleau-Ponty M (2012) Phenomenology of perception. In: Landes DA (trans). Routledge, New York

Mill JS (1861) Utilitarianism. Parker S, Bourn L, Crisp R (ed) (1997) Utilitarianism by J.S. Mill. Oxford University Press, Oxford, pp 85–89

Mill JS (2008) Utilitarianism. In: Crisp R (ed). Oxford University Press, Oxford

Mitra P (2018) Invisible women in reproductive technologies: critical reflections. Indian J Med Ethics 3(2):113–119

Montanari Vergallo G (2019) A child of two mothers: what about the father? Italian overview. Acta Biomed 90(3):319–325

Montanari Vergallo G, Marinelli E, di Luca NM, Zaami S (2018) Gamete donation: are children entitled to know their genetic origins? A comparison of opposing views. The Italian state of affairs. Eur J Health Law

Muraro L (2016) L'anima del corpo. Contro l'utero in affitto. Vita e Pensiero, Milano

Murdoch L (2014) Australian couple leaves down syndrome baby with Thai surrogate. Sydney Morning Herald, 1 Aug 2014

Nelson E (2013) Law, policy and reproductive autonomy. Hart Publishing, Oxford

Nisand I (2010) Grossesse pour autrui: pour le cas par cas. Gynécol Obstét Fertil 38(3):226–229

Okesanya OJ, et al. (2024). Ectogenesis: understanding opportunities, implications, concerns, and ways forward. Int J Surg Glob Health 7(1):e0398

Olivito E (2018) Di alcuni fraintendimenti intorno alla maternità surrogata. Il giudice soggetto alla legge e l'interpretazione para-costituzionale. Rivista Associazione Italiana dei Costituzionalisti 2

Palazzani L (2020) Reproductive technologies and the global bioethics debate: a philosophical analysis of the Report on ART and Parenthood of the International Bioethics Committee of UNESCO. Phenomenol Mind 19:138–149

Pande A (2011) Transnational commercial surrogacy in India: gifts for global sisters? Reprod Biomed Online 23(5):618–620

Partridge EA, Davey MG, Hornick MA, et al. (2017) An extra-uterine system to physiologically support the extreme premature lamb. Nat Commun 8:15112

Pennings G (2002) Reproductive tourism as moral pluralism in motion. J Med Ethics 28(6):337–341

Pennings G (2011) Evaluating the welfare of the child in same-sex families. Hum Reprod 26(7):1609–1615

Pezzini B (2017) Nascere da un corpo di donna. Costituzionalismo.it 1:217

Piersanti V, Consalvo F, Signore F, Del Rio A, Zaami S (2021) Surrogacy and "procreative tourism": what does the future hold from the ethical and legal perspectives? Medicine (Kaunas) 57(1):47
Pisapia GD (1959) Adulterio artificiale? Rivista Italiana di Diritto e Procedura Penale
Plato (1997) Timaeus. In: Cooper JM, Zeyl DJ (trans). Plato: Complete Works. Hackett Publishing, Indianapolis, pp 1224–1291
Poli L (2015) Maternità surrogata e diritti umani: una pratica controversa che necessita di una regolamentazione internazionale? Biolaw J 3:7–28
Purdy LM (1989) Surrogate mothering: exploitation or empowerment? Bioethics 3(1):18–34
Quaas AM, Penning G (2018) The current status of oocyte banks: domestic and international perspectives. Fertil Steril 110(7):12–3–1208
Radin MJ (1996) Contested commodities: the trouble with trade in sex, children, body parts, and other things. Harvard University Press, Cambridge, MA
Raposo VL (2017) The new Portuguese law on surrogacy – the story of how a promising law does not really regulate surrogacy arrangements. JBRA Assist Reprod 21(3):230–239
Rawls J (2020) A theory of justice, revised edn. Harvard University Press, Cambridge, MA
Revarthen C (2001) Infant Intersubjectivity: research, theory, and clinical applications. J Child Psychol Psychiatr 42(1):3–48
Richards M, Pennings G, Appleby JB (2012) Reproductive donation: practice, policy, and bioethics. Cambridge University Press, Cambridge, MA
Riddle MP (2022) The psychological impact of surrogacy on the families of gestational surrogates: implications for clinical practice. J Psychosomatic Obstet Gynecol 43(2):122–127
Roberts D (1997) Killing the black body: race, reproduction, and the meaning of liberty. Pantheon Books, New York
Romanis EC (2020) Artificial womb technology and clinical translation: innovative treatment or medical research? Bioethics 34:392–402
Ross L, Solinger R (2017) Reproductive justice: an introduction. University of California Press, Oakland, CA
Ross WD (1930) The right and the good. Clarendon Press, Oxford, pp 19–36
Rossi S, Foglia M (2014) Testamento biologico. In: Digesto delle discipline privatistiche. Sezione Civile, Aggiornamento IX. UTET, Torino, pp 668
Rousseau JJ (1979) Emile, or on education. In: Bloom A (trans). Basic Books, New York
Rozée V, Unisa S (eds) (2016) Assisted reproductive technologies in the Global South and North: issues, challenges and the future. Routledge, London
Rozée V, Unisa S, de La Rochebrochard E (2020) The social paradoxes of commercial surrogacy in developing countries: India before the new law of 2018. BMC Women's Health 20(1):234
Rudrappa S (2015) Discounted life: the process of global surrogacy in India. New York University Press, New York
Sahoo T, Gulla KM (2019) Artificial placenta: miles to go before I sleep .... Am J Obstet Gynecol 221:368–369
Schroeder D (2002) Ethical issues in human reproduction. Palgrave Macmillan, Basingstoke
Schultz N (1990) Reproductive technology and intent-based parenthood: an opportunity for gender neutrality. Wis Law Rev 1990:297–339
Segers S (2021) The path towards ectogenesis: looking beyond the technical challenges. BMC Med Ethics 22:59
Segers S, Pennings G, Mertes H (2020) The ethics of ectogenesis-aided foetal treatment. Bioethics 34:364–370
Sen A (2009) The idea of justice. Allen Lane, London
Seneca (2014) Consolation to Helvia. In: Fantham E (trans.), Seneca: Selected Philosophical Letters and Consolations. Oxford University Press, Oxford
Sgorbati B (2016) Maternità surrogata, dignità della donna e interesse del minore. BioLaw J 2:111–129

Shahbazi MN, Zernicka-Goetz M (2018) Deconstructing and reconstructing the early mammalian embryo. Nat Cell Biol 20(8):878–887
Shalev C (1989) The ethics of surrogacy: women's rights, women's bodies. Hastings Cent Rep 19(1):31–37
Simmons R, Tighe SM (2005) The Impact of Surrogacy on the Child: a Review of Psychological Research. J Child Fam Stud 14(2):155–169
Smerdon UR (2008) Crossing bodies, crossing borders: international surrogacy between the United States and India. Cumb Law Rev 39:15
Stasi A (2017) Protection for children born through assisted reproductive technologies act, B.E. 2558: the changing profile of surrogacy in Thailand. Clin Med Insights Reprod Health, Dec 20
Stratman C (2023) Ectogestation and the good Samaritan argument. J Law Biosci 10:lsad 012
Trezza R (2020) Maternità surrogata: ordine pubblico o best interest of the child? Federalismi.it 22:278–308
Tumanishvili GG, Poli M (2017) Fertilisation in artificial womb: legal and bioethical issues. GESJ: Educ Sci Psychol 3(45):14
van Niekerk A, van Zyl L (1995) The ethics of surrogacy: women's reproductive labour. J Med Ethics 21(6):345–349
Villalba A, Rueda J, de Miguel Beriain Í (2023) Synthetic embryos: a new venue in ethical research. Reproduction 165(4):V1–V3
Vitale AR (2018) Rilievi biogiuridici su onerosità e gratuità della maternità surrogata. Rivista Scientifica di Diritto Civile, Sociale, Religioso e Laico (RSCSRL)
Whiteman H (2014) Surrogate mom vows to take care of ill twin 'abandoned' by parents. CNN Wire, 4 Aug 2014
Whittaker A (2016) From "Mung Ming" to "Baby Gammy": a local history of assisted reproduction in Thailand. Reprod Biomed Soc Online 2:71–78
Zadeh S, Ilioi EC, Jadva V, Golombok S (2018) The perspectives of adolescents conceived using surrogacy, egg or sperm donation. Hum Reprod 33(6):1099–1106

Chapter 3
Between Euthanasia and Assisted Suicide: Is There an Ethics of the 'Good' Death?

> If one excludes the paths permitted by scientific knowledge, capable of ploughing the tragic path that can lead a person to put an early end to his or her life, any attempt to legalise the path of death would be a futile pleonasm. For the law, indeed, death, understood as the person's ultimate and supreme choice, should not matter. No legal system, not even the most oppressive, would in fact be able to deter a subject from the intention to end his time. So much so that the criminal legislature does not punish suicide, having noted the intimidating ineffectiveness of the punishment imposed on those who, in their own souls, have tragically matured the intention to end their own life.[1]

---

[1] Gusmai (2019) (*trans. By the author*). By absurd hyperbole, not even the recourse to Orwellian psychopolice within Jeremy Bentham's Panopticon would be able to prevent men from finding, by the most unthinkable means, ways to kill themselves. For such an 'evasion', history has amply demonstrated that everyone possesses Gige's ring: like the bovine in Candaule's service, the person can make himself invisible by 'turning the bezel' where the gem of his will is fixed. The reference, as can be guessed, is to the famous myth of Gige narrated by Plato in The Republic (2016, book II). More complex, on the other hand, are the cases in which the subject is unable, by himself, to realise his will. This is the hypothesis of the person in a condition of terminal or incurable illness 'armoured' by his own body, who needs to be helped in his suicidal intention. Since, in fact, the constitutional system must distinguish "letting oneself die" (refusal of therapeutic treatment protected by art. 32 of the Constitution) from "giving oneself death" (suicide) or "helping oneself to die" (aid to suicide) or "letting oneself be killed" (consenting murder), the risk of incurring in the violation of the principle of equality for different treatment of subjects in the same situation of suffering is very high. In fact, only 'if a person's survival is linked to some form of pharmacological or mechanical therapy, the patient may (indeed has the constitutionally guaranteed right to) ask for it to be interrupted and thus end his life and his suffering; but if he has the 'terrible misfortune' of not seeing his life linked to any therapy, this possibility is precluded, since to end his life he needs the active intervention of a doctor who prescribes or administers a lethal drug'. Thus Tripodina (2018) On the differences between 'letting die' and 'helping to die', for all, D'Aloia (1998).

A. Ferrara, *Bioethical Reflections on the Border between Life and Death*, European Union and its Neighbours in a Globalized World 32,
https://doi.org/10.1007/978-3-032-09985-3_3

3.1 The Desire for Death at the Origin of Humanity

Quaeris quod sit ad libertatem iter? quaelibet in corpore tuo vena (Seneca 1928, III.15).

Just as there is no doubt that death belongs to nature, it is also irrefutable that developments in medicine have made dying "increasingly governable by man", since death itself "belongs to his life, and therefore falls within the autonomy of each person's choices" (Rodotà 2012).[2]

The concept of death, and suicide in particular, has been a subject of philosophical discussion since ancient Greece and the dawn of human history. Plato in the Phaedo tells us about the most famous suicide in classical philosophy, that of Socrates. During an intense dialogue with Cebetes and Simmia, Socrates discusses the concept of the death of the body versus the immortality of the soul. Socrates, condemned to die by his own hand, states that the true philosopher should not fear death, but neither should he seek it through suicide since suicide is an ungodly act as the life of human beings belongs to the Gods, good and wise, and that only the latter can decide when to end it.[3] At the same time, Socrates justifies his decision to take his own life because only through the splitting of soul and body will the rational soul, purified of the influence of the corporeal, be able to free itself from the prison of life and know the truth.[4]

Plato in the *Laws* on the one hand expresses contempt for those who, through inertia, cowardice and weakness, decide to die by suicide without serious justification, stating that they should be buried in isolation, without a headstone and

[2] On euthanasia as an "ethical and not legal choice", see Casavola (2013, p. 23). Reference is made to the well-known European Court of Human Rights (ECtHR) (2011) *Haas v. Switzerland*, Application No. 31322/07, Judgment of 20 January 2011. Available at: https://hudoc.echr.coe.int/eng?i=001-102940.

[3] It does not seem at all illogical that one should not take one's life before a god has put him in the necessity of doing so, as in this, for example, in which I find myself today (Plato 1990, 6b-6c).

[4] There is like a path that leads us in the right direction, but as long as we have a body and our soul is confused to such an ugliness, we will never come to possess what we desire, which is, then, what we call truth. And not only does our body cause us endless discomfort by the very fact that we must, of course, nourish it, but when it becomes ill, new hindrances arise that distract us from our search for truth; and then again, loves, desires, fears, fallacious visions of all kinds, countless vanities, do nothing but distract us (that is the right word) so that as long as we are at its mercy, we cannot concentrate on anything. And so do wars, discords, fights, it is the body that gives birth to them with its passions. The lust for possession, that is the cause of all wars, and if we strive for wealth, it is the body whose slaves we are. Hence the fact that we no longer find time to devote ourselves to philosophy. And the worst of it is that, even if we manage, for a moment, to get rid of it and turn our minds to something, we are immediately diverted from it by its importunate intrusion, which confuses us, distracts us, bewilders us, to the point of making us incapable, by now, of distinguishing the truth. Therefore, it is clear that if we want to attain pure knowledge of anything, we must detach ourselves from the body and contemplate with the soul alone things in themselves. Only then, it seems, will we have what we desire and claim to love: wisdom, but after we are dead and certainly not while we are alive, as all this discourse is intended to show (Plato 1990, VII–XI).

without a name to distinguish their grave.[5] In the *Republic*, with a collectivist vision typical of the time, justifying the death of those who are hopelessly ill, whose cure would not be able to restore total health and therefore could no longer be useful to society (Plato 2016, 307d–e).

The *Stagirite*, on the other hand, by virtue of his view of man as a social man, as a political animal, regards suicide as an unjust act against the community that is deprived of a citizen useful for its purposes (Aristotle 2009, 1138a5–15).

A different approach, which would later be adopted by the Renaissance and humanism, was proposed by the Epicureans and Stoics. They decoupled the issue of suicide from social and religious ethics, placing it in an anthropological and existential context (Hutchinson 1994, p. vi). The precariousness of the human condition in its individually and morally relevant reality can determine that one's own death becomes an act of freedom, that is, as an act of salvation from the constraint imposed by fate, human injustice or naturalistic necessity.[6] The pursuit of pleasure and the absence of pain (ataraxia) are the ultimate goals in life; therefore voluntary death can be an acceptable choice if it avoids unbearable suffering. However, suicide must not be indiscriminate, since a life lived in accordance with philosophy can guarantee serenity even amidst hardship. Death in any case should not be feared because "where we are, there is no death, where there is death, we are no more" (Epicurus 1974).

The Stoic view, founded by Zeno of Cizio, opens to a life lived in accordance with nature, and if it becomes unbearable due to illness or loss of reason, suicide is a rational choice (Laërtius 2008). By affirming that "the door is open" (Epictetus 1925, I.24.20) for those who can no longer live in harmony with reason[5] Epictetus wants to affirm the concept of freedom to act, of accepting life's difficulties as an opportunity for action to overcome them.

Cicero, in the *Tusculanae Disputationes*, while recognising that death can sometimes be an honourable choice, believes that man must fulfil the duties of life as long as possible:[7] "he who has the greater number of things conforming to nature has the duty to remain alive; he who has or believes himself destined to have the greater number of things contrary to nature has the duty to leave life. From this it is clear that the wise man sometimes has the duty to go out of life while being happy and the foolish man to stay alive while being unhappy" (Cicero 1927a, III.60, b).

---

[5] Plato refers to one who decides to commit suicide without being condemned by the city, without being compelled to do so by some distressing case or having committed some ignominy that has no remedy to make life impossible (Plato 1926).

[6] "Necessity is a bad thing, but there is no necessity to live under necessity" (Epicurus 1983b, p. 215).

[7] The divinity that rules in us forbids us to leave here without its command; but when it is the god himself who provides a just cause—as happened then to Socrates, now to Cato and often to many others—there is no doubt, for Hercules, that the wise man joyfully departed from this darkness into that light. However, he did not break the chains of the prison—since the law forbids this—but went out as if he had been called and freed not by a magistrate or a legitimate authority, but by God himself. For, as the philosopher himself says, the whole life of philosophers is a preparation for death (Cicero 1927a, I.74, b).

Even Seneca, one of the most famous proponents of philosophical suicide, regarded the ability to end one's own life as a mark of wisdom and freedom, considering death to be nature's greatest gift (Seneca 1920, Vol. II, Epi. 70 § 14). He states that voluntary death is acceptable when it preserves the individual's dignity and frees them from unbearable suffering. This is why the wise man must not passively endure life, but have the courage to end it when it is no longer worth living. To die well is to avoid the danger of living badly (Seneca 1920, Vol. II, Epi. 70 § 6). Seneca does not extol suicide as an act in itself, but he does acknowledge it as a rational choice aimed at defending the fundamental principles and values of existence. His own death, to avoid condemnation by Nero, is an emblematic example of his philosophy. The wise man must be useful to the state; however, rather than compromising his moral integrity, he must also be prepared to sacrifice his life. Seneca's vision anticipates some modern secular bioethical conceptions of the end of life, which emphasise not the sacredness and intangibility of life, but the importance of self-determination in relation to one's own existence.

Seneca therefore advocates complete availability to life, comparing it to goods such as wealth, honours, and affections. He states that the wise man must be ready to relinquish these when fate demands them or when he deems it reasonable (Trombetti Budriesi 2013, pp. 393–397). However, he believes that suffering and pain are not good reasons to take one's own life, as someone who kills themselves because they cannot endure pain is weak and cowardly. Conversely, the knowledge that one's particular existential condition will prevent one from performing all those actions that constitute the reason for life is a good reason to take one's own life, since it is foolish to live to suffer (Seneca 1920, Vol. I, Epi. 58 § 36).

3.2 The Christian Perspective and the Condemnation of Voluntary Death

Nemo sua sponte debet occidere se ipsum (Augustine 1957, I.20).

The Christian tradition has always taken a position clearly opposed to suicide and euthanasia, considering human life as an inviolable and inalienable divine gift. This perspective is based on a theological conception of life and death, which finds its clearest expression in the Fathers of the Church and the scholastic philosophers, particularly St Augustine and St Thomas Aquinas.

Already in the early centuries of Christianity, suicide was considered an act contrary to the divine will and therefore morally unacceptable. St Augustine, in his *Confessions* and *De Civitate Dei*, explicitly condemns suicide, opposing the Stoic view that voluntary death can be a rational and noble choice, since no one has the right to take his or her own life, since it belongs to God.

Augustine also criticises the idea that suicide can be justified in the name of honour or escape from suffering, considering it rather a sin of pride and despair (Augustine 2014, I.19).

In the Middle Ages, the Christian condemnation of suicide and euthanasia found philosophical systematisation with St Thomas Aquinas, who developed three main arguments against suicide. The first argument qualifies suicide as contrary to natural law, since the instinct of preservation is one of the fundamental inclinations of the human being, and taking one's own life would be contrary to this natural law; the second argument, taking up the Aristotelian conception, is based on the assumption that suicide would be an offence against society, of which every individual is a part and to which suicide would cause harm by depriving him of a useful member for social purposes; the third is based on the idea that suicide is an infringement of God's will, since only God, who gave life, has the right to take it, not human beings. (Aquinas 1920, II–II.64.5).

Thomas considers life to be an inalienable good and believes that even the refusal of treatment aimed at survival can be morally problematic if not motivated by proportionate reasons.

At the same time, St Thomas elaborates the *principle of the double effect*—referring in particular to murder in self-defence—according to which it is possible to identify a set of ethical and philosophical criteria for determining whether it is morally acceptable to perform an action, legitimate in itself, from which consequences may arise that one would be morally bound to avoid. This dichotomous approach that distinguishes between intention and unintended expectation identifies three fundamental characteristics for evaluating the action: (a) the nature of the action in itself must be good or at least neutral; (b) the agent intends to pursue the good intent and not the bad intent, which is to be considered neither a means nor an end in itself; (c) the good intent must prevail over the bad consequence on the basis of sufficiently serious circumstances and the agent must exercise due diligence to minimise the effects of his action (Cavanaugh 2006, p. 36).

This principle, rejected by consequentialists who instead identify the consequences of an action as the way to assess its morality rather than its rightness, is taken up in bioethics by those who consider the fundamental principles of bioethics (autonomy, beneficence, non-maleficence, justice) as *prima facie* penultimate principles (Ross 1930, pp. 19–36) i.e. generally valid, but only until they come into conflict with each other and oblige us to establish which one should be fulfilled with priority.[8]

[8] This principle has also been incorporated into Article 26 of the Universal Declaration on Bioethics and Human Rights, adopted by the UNESCO General Conference on 19 October 2005, which considers the principles of bioethics to be "complementary and interdependent. Each principle must be considered in the context of the other principles, to an extent appropriate and relevant to the circumstances" (UNESCO (2005) Universal Declaration on Bioethics and Human Rights. Adopted on 19 October 2005 by the General Conference of UNESCO. Available at: https://unesdoc.unesco.org/ark:/48223/pf0000146180.

The principle that life is a gift from God, and therefore inviolable, is a cardinal principle of Christian doctrine, which has survived for centuries, as it is founded on the Holy Scriptures that explicitly affirm the sacred value of human life, in the commandment “Thou shalt not kill” (The Holy Bible, Exodus, 1989 20:13). This commandment is interpreted not only as a prohibition against murder, but also as a moral obligation to respect and preserve life in all its phases, which man cannot dispose of arbitrarily. Even suffering, in Christian thought, sometimes takes on a positive, redemptive value and therefore should not be avoided at all costs, but welcomed as part of the mystery of life and God’s will (Paul II 1995). The application of the principle of the double effect, however, even according to the Christian view, which, of course, does not necessarily require suffering, opens up the compassionate search for the alleviation of human pain, even if this entails, for charitable purposes, shortening the life of the sick person. This is why modern expressions of Christianity (Francis 2022, catechesis 11), while affirming that death can never be chosen but only expected, admit the possibility of accompanying others in dying without, however, provoking death or helping the human being to commit suicide.

Euthanasia, understood as an act aimed at ending the life of a sick person, by virtue of his or her suffering, is seen by Christian doctrine as a violation of this principle.[9]

Already in the earliest philosophy, the two main opposing orientations developed, on the one hand desiring death, and in particular suicide, does not represent a disvalue, indeed in some cases death by one’s own hand is the only virtuous choice left for the individual. Life is a good that belongs to the human being who has the right to dispose of it in accordance with his values, indeed in some cases he must dispose of it to demonstrate consistency with the principles applied during life. The only limit, in a collectivist view, is the common good, the collective good that serves—until individualist principles take hold—as the supreme interest over the individual.

On the opposite side is a conception whereby existence acquires an aura of sacredness; the product of a superior will, a gift of inestimable value that human beings cannot dispose of without seriously violating the foundation of the relationship with God, which only allows the suffering of existence to be mitigated without renouncing life.

The dichotomy between these two conceptions marks the contemporary debate on the end of life, pitting supporters of the availability of human life against those who consider it an unavailable good.

[9] “Whatever the motive and means, direct euthanasia consists in ending the life of handicapped, sick or dying persons. It is morally unacceptable” (Catechism of the Catholic Church 1997, §2277).

3.3 Reflections on Suicide in Contemporary Thought

> It would be no crime in me to divert the Nile or Danube from its course, were I able to effect such purposes. Where then is the crime of turning a few ounces of blood from their natural channels? (Hume 1985).

The modern and contemporary philosophical debate on the end of life has developed a myriad of different perspectives to the treatment of which an encyclopaedic work would perhaps not be sufficient.

In this section, we will briefly touch upon some of the most relevant ideas argued in contemporary philosophy in order to have further food for thought on the end of life.

One of the most original perspectives on suicide is theorised by Kant who argues the unavailability of human life, not because it belongs to God, but because of the concept of the irreducibility of life to a merely material element.[10] Suicide is not contrary to the will of God, the interests of society or the natural will of man, but is contrary to the human being itself and its pure or *noumenal* rationality. Kant opposes the justification of suicide by considering it immoral, not by virtue of the application of heteronomous principles, but precisely by virtue of the autonomy and free will that Kant recognises in the human being (Kant 2003, p. 1). Life, in this perspective, is an absolute value because it is a necessary condition for the exercise of morality and the rational autonomy of the individual. For this reason, suicide can be considered morally unacceptable, since it implies the self-destruction of that very rationality that is the foundation of human dignity (Kant 1998, p. 47).

On the other hand, Kantian man must act according to inescapable moral principles and duties founded on reason and not according to inclinations and aversions founded on passions. Moral action, defined as action based on a maxim of behaviour capable of becoming a universal law, can never be reconciled with suicidal action that annihilates itself.

Unlike Hegel, he conceives of life and death as dialectical moments in the development of the Absolute Spirit, both of which are unavailable to the human being (Hegel 1999, § 70–71). Death is not merely a biological cessation, but a necessary transition for the realisation of the universal ethical idea. In this sense, individual life is not an end in itself, but a moment in the broader realisation of objective rationality: consequently, the decision on one's own death cannot be seen in merely subjective terms, but must be placed in the context of the ethical community (Hegel 1977, pp. 289–295). Death and life, for Hegel, are not arbitrarily and reductively interchangeable dimensions, but coexist within a single reality, that of the human subject who if, on the one hand, he cannot dispose of his own death as something extrinsic to be procured and inflicted on his body; at the same time, suicidal death implies a dimension of will and self-determination that cannot

---

[10] "Man cannot dispose over himself because he is not a thing; he is not his own property, to say that he is would be self-contradictory (Kant 1984, p. 189).

be denied or ignored, if it is true that "I have these limbs and my life only in so far as I will it; the animal cannot mutilate or destroy itself, but the human being can" (Hegel 2003, 78).

Of particular interest are the conclusions that David Hume draws in his essay 'Of Suicide' (Merrill 1999), in which he attempts to refute the idea of the sacredness of life and the moral condemnation of suicide. Hume's main argument that suicide is not a transgression of God's will be as follows. God established the general and immutable laws of nature and created the material and animal worlds (including human beings), endowing them with senses, passions, memory and judgement. Existence involves the continuous relationship between the material and animal worlds, and the constant interplay of their powers and faculties, so that man's actions constantly alter matter, which in turn directs and directs man's powers and faculties. If suicide is considered immoral because it contradicts the natural flow of events, then it would also be immoral to intervene and save a person's life, as this would oppose nature taking its course. Conversely, suicide is part of the evolution of human nature and therefore conforms to it insofar as it responds to the human interest and duty to free oneself from an unbearable existence.

A radically different perspective is that proposed by Nietzsche, who, rejecting Christian and Kantian morality, exalts the will to power as the criterion for affirming life according to self-determined values. His conception of death is closely linked to individual freedom and the ability to choose one's own destiny. Nietzsche, in stating that "he who has a reason to live can endure almost anything" (Nietzsche 1966, p. 157) affirms the concept that what counts is the quality of life lived, not its mere biological preservation. In his pessimism of force, he sees in birth the inevitability of death that follows, which allows every human being who comes into the world both to experience his own finitude and the serenity associated with the end of existence, without hoping to go beyond it.[11]

In Arthur Schopenhauer's thought, suicide represents a paradoxical gesture: although it appears as a denial of life, it is not, according to the philosopher, a true renunciation of the will to live. The suicide, in fact, does not reject existence as such, but only the particular conditions in which it manifests itself for him, namely those dominated by pain and suffering. Understood in this way, suicide is not an act of metaphysical liberation, but an extreme—and still willful—form of rebellion against individual discomfort. Unlike asceticism, which extinguishes the will at its root and leads to peace, suicide remains within the cycle of the will, itself an expression of the will that permeates every aspect of being. Hence Schopenhauer's ambivalent position: he does not morally condemn suicide, as the Christian tradition does, but considers it insufficient to break man's bond with the suffering of the world (Schopenhauer 1969, 1974).

[11] "Death is a cessation from the impression of the senses, the tyranny of the passions, the errors of the mind, and the servitude of the body" (Marcus Aurelius 1902, p. 65; VI.28).

Jean-Paul Sartre approaches the theme of suicide not from a moral perspective, but from an existential and logical perspective, consistent with his conception of human freedom as an open-ended and never-ending project (Sartre 2003, p. 487). Since every action acquires meaning only over time, through the way it is reworked by the subject in the future, suicide—which cuts short the temporality of existence—is, paradoxically, an act without meaning. If the present does not possess autonomous meaning, but is consigned to the future to receive retroactive qualification, as Sartre suggests, then suicide, being final and definitive, eludes this interpretative possibility. The subject, by dying, renounces the possibility of recontextualising his gesture, which makes suicide a 'radical absurdity', that is, the extreme gesture that not only fails to give meaning to life, but also sanctions its total vacuity. Sartre observes that only a religious vision—one that postulates an afterlife capable of giving meaning to sacrifice—can somehow justify suicide as a meaningful act. However, he rejects such 'ontological faith', denying that there is a higher plane from which life could derive value. In this framework, suicide does not represent the extreme expression of human freedom, but rather its annihilation: a gesture that interrupts the very possibility of the project and, therefore, of freedom. Thus, instead of resolving the absurdity of existence, suicide radicalises it, transforming itself into an existential scandal that deprives man not only of life, but also of the power to signify it.

Unlike Sartre, who saw suicide as the ultimate manifestation of the absurd, Camus believed that suicide liberates man from the absurdity that shapes his existence. Dying means resolving the absurdity generated by birth in such a way as to zero out any further experiential possibilities. In The Myth of Sisyphus,[12] Camus argues that the universe does not offer any predetermined meaning, and this is precisely why the human being lives in a condition of absurdity: a contrast between the need for meaning and the silence of the world. Faced with this fracture, suicide might seem a 'logical' solution. However, for Camus, committing suicide is a mistake, because it means surrendering, closing down any possibility of experience, giving up the fight.

On the contrary, the man Camus admires is the one who rejects both physical suicide and 'philosophical suicide': that is, blind adherence to religions, ideologies or absolute truths that delude one into thinking they give life meaning. Man does not live because he gives meaning to life, but because before thinking, the body wants to live. This biological, unreflective impulse also resists despair and forms the basis of the revolt against the absurd. Whoever commits suicide betrays this profound and original force, which drives one to exist even without hope. The 'absurd man', on the other hand, accepts the non-sense of existence, but decides to live anyway, without hope but with lucidity, trying to enjoy everyday experiences. This is why Camus

[12] Sisyphus, according to Greek mythology, was a cunning and deceitful king who defied the gods several times: he betrayed divine secrets, chained Death to prevent men from dying, and tricked Hades into returning to the world of the living. As an eternal punishment, the gods condemned him to push a huge boulder up a mountain: every time he reached the top, the stone rolled back down into the valley, forcing him to start again. His condemnation thus consisted of endless, aimless toil (Camus 2000, p. 7).

proposes a ‘Homeric’ ethic, similar to that of the ancient Greeks: to live as much as possible, to have as many experiences as one can, without worrying about finding a definitive meaning. In this sense, he who commits suicide deprives himself of the only thing he has: the possibility of living again (Flores d’Arcais 2010, p. 7).

The symbolic figure of this position is Sisyphus: forced to push a boulder up a mountain for eternity, but capable, according to Camus, of being happy precisely in his struggle, because he has made his condition his own, without illusions and without resignation.

Philosophical speculation around the subject of death wish and suicide has always been flourishing; death has always been one of the most discussed topics as it is among the most elusive of human nature.

The current debate on the subject of the end of life, however, has its origin in the progress of medicine, which has today extended the possibilities of treatment and is now able to keep human beings alive for longer and longer, sometimes in precarious conditions or in great suffering.[13] The extension of the possibilities conferred by medical science (Gusmai 2019, p. 5) has led to new situations in which the instruments through which one can exercise one’s autonomy have changed their content and the very meaning of the concept of autonomy and freedom of choice.

These new possibilities have consequently led to the need for an evolution of the discussion at the academic, political and social level with the intention of establishing whether, and especially where, it is necessary to place the new limits to the right of self-determination and individual autonomy.

The fundamental issues and questions that legal theorists and scholars have been trying to answer for decades are various; whether the right to self-determination and individual autonomy should be recognised absolutely or whether they should be limited within certain parameters; whether the State’s duty of protection towards the weakest and most vulnerable individuals is expressed in a simple duty to verify the autonomy of the choice and the absence of external influences, or whether it can go so far as to assess the motivations for requesting assistance in dying; whether and how the consent given in dying should be assessed, and whether in fact the legalisation of euthanasia practices may over time produce in society a kind of predisposition to medically assisted dying and lead to the embarking on an unstoppable slippery slope.

In the following paragraphs, no attempt will be made to provide an answer to these questions, as to assume to be able to offer an exhaustive answer would amount to an act of undue intellectual ambition, given the depth and complexity of the philosophical debate on the subject. However, an attempt will be made to provide food for thought to help readers form their own convictions on the subject, by reconstructing the evolution of the jurisprudential and doctrinal debate among some of the main European countries.

---

[13] Comitato Nazionale per la Bioetica (2019) *Riflessioni bioetiche sul suicidio medicalmente assistito* [National Committee of Bioethics (2019) Bioethical Reflections on Medically Assisted Suicide], (Italy), Rome, 18 July 2019. Available at: http://www.bioetica.governo.it/media/3787/parere-su-suicidio-assistito-inglese.pdf.

3.4 The Good Death and the Medically Assisted Death

When talking about the end of life, a further fundamental distinction is appropriate, that between euthanasia and assisted suicide.

Euthanasia is defined as the deliberate and intentional act of causing the death of another person, typically a patient, at their request, often by a physician or healthcare professional. If death occurs as a result of the administration of a lethal drug to the patient, it is called active euthanasia; if, on the other hand, the action of the health care provider consists of the interruption of medical treatment that can keep the patient alive, it is called passive euthanasia.

According to the interpretation provided by the European Association of Palliative Care (EAPC), euthanasia is active by definition as it is defined as "the intentional killing of a person, carried out by a physician through the administration of medication, following the person's voluntary and conscious request" (Materstvedt et al. 2003). On the contrary, when we speak, according to some people improperly, of passive euthanasia, we are only talking about the restriction of treatments that lead to the death of the patient. For this reason, speaking of passive euthanasia risks constituting a contradiction in terms since the determinant of the event of death is the illness, not the suspension of treatment (Orsi et al. 2015). According to some scholars, therefore, it would make no sense to make such a distinction since, essentially, passive euthanasia does not exist. In some cases, one also speaks of indirect euthanasia when the doctor administers drugs that do not have the direct consequence of causing death but the primary objective of alleviating suffering, even though he knows that as a side effect these could accelerate the patient's death. At the same time, well-established scientific evidence shows that the discontinuation of many traditional treatments can result in a prolongation of survival (Maltoni et al. 2009) suggesting that definitional issues require contextualisation and more precise assessments to be made on a case-by-case basis.

The aforementioned distinction from a legal point of view, apart from the defining element, is not insignificant if one takes into account that the former conduct (active euthanasia) is illegal in most EU member states while the latter (passive euthanasia) actually corresponds to the exercise of a patient's genuine right to refuse any medical treatment.

In the academic debate, Rachels (1975) has pointed out that the distinction between active and passive euthanasia is morally inconsistent: if the intent is to alleviate suffering, there is no difference between 'letting die' and 'procuring death' actively, since in both cases the goal is the cessation of suffering.

Suicide assistance, on the other hand, consists of the provision of instruments, usually of a medical nature, that enable the patient to self-administer the lethal drug, thereby bringing about their own death.

The distinction between assisted suicide and euthanasia, as we will explore in more detail in the course of this chapter, is particularly relevant since, according to a part of the doctrine, it is precisely this distinction that distinguishes the cases in which it is ethically permissible—under certain conditions—to obtain help in dying from those cases in which it is not.

The autonomous performance of the action by the patient, would interrupt the direct causal relationship between the third action and death, thereby acknowledging the institutions involved and simultaneously ensuring the preservation of the patient's will until the ultimate moment.

Colloquially, the term euthanasia is often used to refer to both practices and this is probably due to its etymological origin.

The etymological origin of the word euthanasia immediately unmasks its current meaning: εὖ (eu), meaning 'good', 'good', 'just' and θάνατος (thánatos), meaning 'death' convey the idea of a just, good, positive death to be opposed to a bad, unjust death. The idea, which originates in its essential connotations in the philosophy we mentioned in the previous paragraphs, is that death, under certain conditions can take on a positive, liberating, cathartic meaning for the human being and is therefore worthy of being desired. Regardless of the ways in which it is pursued and achieved.

This overturning of 'ordinary' values, however, requires the fulfilment of a series of conditions that justify the pursuit of an objective that could be considered, as St. Thomas Aquinas argued, contrary to natural law and the inclination of every being to preserve its own existence.

In the modern debate, on the other hand, we generally refer to Medically Assisted Death as both doctrine and European jurisprudence, albeit with various points of divergence, have identified among the requirements admitting the legitimacy of the practice accompanying a good death the need for it to take place through the participation or under the close supervision of health or medical personnel.

On the legal philosophical level, two main orientations have developed, according to an approach defined as "strategic dichotomous" (Fornero 2020), on the one hand the supporters of a subjectivist ethics (Steinbock and Norcross 1994; Foot 2001) that excludes the existence of universal and objective values to which to conform but claims that it is the individual who attributes value or disvalue to the existential conditions that affect him. For this reason, the right to claim recognition is based on the freely exercised subjective will, regardless of the content of the claim.

In opposition to this conception, there are theories that maintain that the exercise of freedom alone is not capable of founding the legitimacy of the claim to a right. If the request for euthanasia or assisted suicide is based on a condition of suffering, it would be the condition of suffering that is the reason for the choice and not the exercise of freedom as such and therefore the will would in any case be influenced by other contingent conditions (Pessina 2007; Gensabella Furnari 2008; D'Agostino 2018).

This view, moreover, takes into account the fact that the exercise of freedoms and wills must always be subject to the minimum ethical limit of the freedom and will of others, such that individual freedom must also find limitations in the rule of law.

The objectivist view of existence is therefore based on the natural recognition of a value in the coexistence of human beings, implicitly recognised in the relationships from which social duties derive for individuals. From this perspective, the right to assisted dying is not considered a purely private activity, but rather one with a public dimension and social value (Palazzani 2020).

Such conclusions could also be reached with regard to the role of physicians, which, beyond the principles of Hippocrates, is considered to be protecting health and curing illness, rather than denying health by facilitating death. The goal of medicine is to cure illness, with death being the worst possible outcome. For this reason, some authors argue that assuming medicine can instead facilitate death would contradict the fundamental principles of medical ethics. However, the development of medical technology has led to situations where science can keep individuals alive despite there being no hope of a cure or recovery. This is why it is also the doctor's duty to avoid obstinately and unreasonably continuing treatment, in order to make efficient use of healthcare resources.

However, the specific situations that occur nowadays thanks to medical advances, evolving at the same time with the idea that illness can be considered not only as pain of the body but also as a synonym for suffering of the soul, could, according to a certain view, make the interruption of suffering—even through death—understood as the overcoming of illness.

The philosophical discussion is right in the middle between these two theories. The first of these affirms the existence of a right to die based on the protection of human dignity and the responsibility of the individual, duly informed, to self-determine even through the request to die. The second, in contrast, refuses this right, opening only to solutions in which death is the result—based on the relationship of care between doctor and patient—of the exercise of the right to refuse any health treatment and therefore that third parties can act on one's body against one's consent.

Having dealt with the salient elements of the debate, which we will go into in greater detail below, in the following paragraphs we will analyse what has happened in the Netherlands and Belgium, among the first countries in the world to regulate euthanasia and assisted suicide, and then verify the different positions and theories proposed by the legislature and national jurisprudence in the southern Mediterranean countries with a strong Catholic influence—such as Italy—with a final reference to the indications received from the European Court of Human Rights.

In order to provide the tools to reason about such a complex issue, it is often useful to flank theoretical speculation with the analysis of concrete cases from which useful insights can be gleaned.

In order to facilitate an understanding of the current state of the academic debate on the matter, we will proceed by examining some of the most prominent cases that have occurred in a number of EU countries. We will then analyse the doctrinal and academic debate that has developed around these cases, bringing together the most significant lines of thought. This will enable us to gain an overview of the academic debate on the subject. In conclusion, an attempt will be made to propose a personal point of view for consideration, in conjunction with the other positions that will be argued in the core of the chapter.

3.5 First Cases of Euthanasia in Europe: The Netherlands and Belgium

The first countries in which euthanasia was discussed in Europe are the Netherlands and Belgium, which are probably the most 'avant-garde' states—at least in Europe—in terms of legislation on euthanasia. As early as 2002, the Netherlands regulated the requirements and modalities of euthanasia, and over the past two decades they have been developing the content of euthanasia also thanks to the possibility of verifying the practical outcomes of its application.

In the 1980s, the Dutch Criminal Code provided a legal framework punishing the murder of consenting persons and aiding and abetting suicide.[14] As early as 1973[15] the non-punishability of aiding and abetting suicide by virtue of Article 40[16] of the criminal code began to be affirmed in jurisprudence.[17] The debate grew still further, also involving the institutions, and exploded following the famous *Postma van Boven* case,[18] a trailblazer case for a series of pronouncements, which basically tended increasingly to exclude the punishability of euthanasia practices under certain conditions. In the Dutch experience, as in most European countries, it was Jurisprudence in a constant dialectical relationship with Parliament that took the first steps towards the legalisation of euthanasia.[19] With the passage of time, the

---

[14] Sections 293 and 294 of the Dutch Criminal Code punished murder of the consenting person and aiding and abetting suicide. Government of the Netherlands (2005) Dutch Criminal Code, Book II, Sections 293–294. Ministry of Justice, The Hague. English translation available at: https://wetten.overheid.nl.

[15] The origin of the debate on euthanasia as a reaction to futile treatment and the progress of science can be traced back to the publication of a book in which several photographs of terminally ill patients subjected to medical interventions, even experimental ones, for the preservation of life were shown (van der Berg 1969; Illich 1975; Kübler-Ross 1975).

[16] Article 40 of the criminal code provides in the case of a conflict of duties that "A person who commits an act to which he is compelled by force majeure shall not be punished" (*trans. by the author*). Government of the Netherlands (2005) Dutch Criminal Code, Article 40. Ministry of Justice, The Hague. English translation available at: https://wetten.overheid.nl.

[17] For a comprehensive analysis of the issue from a criminal law perspective, (Griffiths, Bood and Weyers 1988).

[18] The famous case of Dr. *Postma*, who had given her incurably cancer-stricken mother a lethal injection, shook people all over the Netherlands by virtue of the particularly light sentence (1 week in prison) pronounced against her. The verdict for the first time set criteria for when euthanasia was considered acceptable by doctors, who wrote a letter to the Dutch Minister of Justice following the verdict in which they admitted that euthanasia was widely practised in the Netherlands.

[19] "A triangular confrontation between the government, the medical order and the judiciary aimed at defining a procedure for announcing and reporting cases of euthanasia has begun. In practice the doctors undertake to bring out from the 'underground' the cases of euthanasia in fact practised; the government, for its part, undertakes to work with the judiciary to limit the exercise of criminal prosecution or in any case to recommend to judges the imposition of light penalties. The Minister of Justice can in fact urge the judiciary to apply the law according to certain criteria, since the public prosecutor acts on the instructions of the executive. The judges accept the

decisions of the courts[20] have also oriented public opinion by identifying certain procedural justification criteria to exclude the doctor's punishability: the patient must be terminally ill, must be afflicted by unbearable physical or mental suffering, and must have requested euthanasia. (Cimbalo 2003) The person performing a euthanasia procedure must be a doctor and the patient's death must be imminent (Ricci Ascoli 2002).

The evolution of the debate—which in a society with a consociative system such as the Dutch one required the involvement of the various stakeholders in order to adopt widely shared decisions (Cimbalo 1989)—led the Netherlands, as the first country in Europe, to provide through the enactment of the Dutch End of Life and Assisted Suicide Act,[21] for the exclusion of the punishability of a doctor who, under certain conditions, assisted one of his patients to commit suicide.

The Act of 12 April 2001 (Wtl) in fact reformed the Dutch penal code by formally introducing a procedural justification for the conduct of a doctor who performs a euthanasia procedure.

To date, the Dutch rules provide for the exclusion of punishability of the doctor who has performed euthanasia if the latter has complied with the following 'criteria of diligence':[22] (a) he is convinced that the request is voluntary and well-considered; (b) he is convinced that the patient is suffering intolerable suffering and that there is no prospect of improvement; (c) he has informed the patient of his condition and of the various alternatives to euthanasia; (d) he has come to the conclusion with the patient that there is no alternative in the light of his condition; (e) he has consulted at least one other independent physician who has given a written opinion on the existence of the diligence criteria in the preceding points; (f) he has ended the patient's life with due care and through medical treatment.

The Dutch framework also provides for the establishment of regional euthanasia review commissions (RTEs) to verify *ex post* the regularity of euthanasia execution procedures.

---

compromise in order to help develop criteria to regulate a phenomenon that escapes, as a practical behaviour and as far as it remains unknown, the regulatory function of law. The parties are aware that the practice of euthanasia is widespread and therefore, rather than ignore the phenomenon, it is preferred to deal with it pragmatically, in order to prevent abuses" (*trans. by the author*) (Cimbalo, 2003, p. 9).

[20] In reality, the courts are only the last step in a process of 'negotiation' between government, parliament, judges, doctors' associations, and associations that support the legalisation of euthanasia. This should not come as a surprise, since it constitutes one of the characteristic features of the consociative system, which, even in the criminal field, uses the co-determination of measures in order to build the widest possible social consensus on the content of the norm. (Vinciguerra and Ricci Ascoli, 1997).

[21] *Wet toetsing levensbeëindiging op verzoek en hulp bij zelfdoding* [Act on Termination of Life on Demand and Suicide Assistance] Netherlands (2020) Available at: https://wetten.overheid.nl/BWBR0012410/2020-03-19.

[22] Art. 2(1), *Wet toetsing levensbeëindiging op verzoek en hulp bij zelfdoding* [Act on Termination of Life on Demand and Suicide Assistance] Netherlands (2020) Available at: https://wetten.overheid.nl/BWBR0012410/2020-03-19.

The Dutch experience is often used by scholars sceptical of the legalisation of euthanasia as an illustrative case to demonstrate the validity of the 'slippery slope' argument according to which a certain initial action or decision, apparently harmless or justifiable, will inevitably (or with high probability) lead to a chain of increasingly problematic or morally unacceptable events. In the case of euthanasia, the slippery slope argument would support the idea that even the provision of specific cases and stringent requirements in which to admit the non-punishability of medical personnel practising euthanasia or aiding suicide will tend to expand more and more to include more and more cases.

The slippery slope argument implies that if one considers a certain conduct (x), which is ethically permissible, to be acceptable, this will in time also lead to accepting a certain conduct (y), which is ethically impermissible, whether there is a logical or conceptual connection between the two conducts or whether there is an empirical or causal connection. The fallacy imputed to the proponents of the slippery slope theory is related to logical vagueness or false normative inevitability.

In any case, the Dutch experience—as we will elaborate on in relation to the 'Koffie' case—could in some respects empirically demonstrate the slippery slope effect.

Specifically, already in 2005, following the publication of the so-called "Groningen protocol", (Verhagen and Sauer 2005) the punishability of euthanasia practices performed on infants under the age of 12 months was in fact limited. The well-known article by Eduard Verhagen and Pieter Sauer started from the statistic that in the Netherlands, of the approximately 200,000 children born each year, about 1000 died within the first year of life, and of these 1000, about 600 died by virtue of 'medical decisions relating to the end of life;[23] this despite the fact that the performance of euthanasia practices on children under the age of 12 was prohibited and without any control. Verhagen and Sauer, on the other hand, identified a series of conditions[24] and procedures that doctors and paediatricians could have adopted to justify the implementation of euthanasia practices on minors of 12 months, suffering from incurable diseases, in cases where "death would be more humane than continued life" (Verhagen and Sauer 2005, p. 960).

The special feature of the Groningen Protocol is that although it was not initially incorporated into any legal source, its adoption as a guideline of national value by the Dutch Association for Paediatric Care resulted in no criminal proceedings

[23] Medical decisions relating to the end of life are understood to be the choice of doctors and paediatricians to interrupt or not to initiate at all the administration of medical treatment (especially intensive care) that would be able to keep the infant alive (Verhagen and Sauer, 2005, p. 959).

[24] Among the requirements in the Groningen Protocol for performing euthanasia practices on minors are: The diagnosis and prognosis of the illness must be certain. Unbearable suffering with no hope of improvement must be present. The diagnosis, prognosis and presence of unbearable suffering must be confirmed by at least one additional independent physician. Both parents must give informed consent to the implementation of the procedure. The procedure must be performed in accordance with generally recognised clinical standards (Verhagen and Sauer, 2005, p. 961).

being initiated as a consequence of its application until 2015.[25] In 2016, however, following a review of the protocol—carried out by the Royal Dutch Medical Association and the Netherlands Health Organization for Research and Development—the Ministry of Security and Justice and the Ministry of Health, Welfare and Sport approved a regulation establishing a committee for the assessment of reported cases of late termination of pregnancy and termination of life in infants[26] gave legal value to the procedures and requirements originally set out in the protocol,[27] effectively legalising euthanasia for children up to 12 months old.

The only age group that remained protected until 1 February 2024 was children between the ages of 1 and 12. Previously defined as a "grey area"[28] as it was difficult to distinguish between doctors practising palliative sedation to alleviate the suffering of young people and those actively ending their lives. As of 1 February 2024, the Dutch Ministry of Health has extended the Regulation on Late Termination and End of Life of Infants[29] also to children between 1 and 12 years of age in order to help terminally ill children with no hope of improvement and in unbearable suffering.

In 2019, the Dutch government commissioned a study to ascertain what the consequences and social reactions would be in the event of the enactment of a regulation providing for the possibility of so-called euthanasia *for completed life*.[30] That is to say, the right to die is also granted to people who do not suffer from

---

[25] European Institute of Bioethics (2015) Euthanasia of Newborns and the Groningen Protocol. The Dossiers of the European Institute of Bioethics, Issue 3. Available at: https://www.ieb-eib.org/ancien-site/pdf/20150204-groningen-eng.pdf.

[26] *Ministerie van Veiligheid en Justitie and Ministerie van Volksgezondheid, Welzijn en Sport* (2015) *Regeling van 11 december 2015, kenmerk 885614–145412-PG, houdende instelling van een commissie voor de beoordeling van gemelde gevallen van late zwangerschapsafbreking en levensbeëindiging bij pasgeborenen* [Ministry of Security and Justice and Ministry of Health, Welfare and Sport (2015). Regulation of 11 December 2015, reference 885614–145412-PG, establishing a committee for the assessment of reported cases of late pregnancy termination and termination of life in newborns]. Available at: https://zoek.officielebekendmakingen.nl/stcrt-2016-3145.html.

[27] For a more detailed discussion of the debate on the so-called 'Groningen Protocol' see (Wach, 2020; Cuttini et al, 2009 Francis, 2016; Tedesco, 2017).

[28] Hugo de Jonge, Minister of Health, stated in a letter to the Dutch Parliament that "There is a 'grey area' between doctors giving palliative sedation to relieve the suffering of these young people, and actively terminating their lives. In a small number of cases, palliative care isn't sufficient. Because of that, some children suffer unnecessarily without any hope of improvement", https://www.dutchnews.nl/news/2020/10/dutch-parliament-to-discuss-possible-new-laws-to-help-suffering-children-to-die/.

[29] *Ministerie van Veiligheid en Justitie and Ministerie van Volksgezondheid, Welzijn en Sport* (2021) *Wijziging regeling beoordelingscommissie late zwangerschapafbreking en levensbeeindiging pasgeborenen (LZA/LP) naar aanleiding van de levensbeeindiging van kinderen van 1–12 jaar* [Ministry of Security and Justice and Ministry of Health, Welfare and Sport (2021) Amendment of the Regulation on the Control Commission for Late Abortion and End-of-Life of Babies (LZA/LP) resulting in the End of Life of Children between 1 and 12 years]. Available at: https://wetten.overheid.nl/stcrt-2021-48254.html.

[30] The project commissioned by the Dutch government assumes that there is a large part of the population that cannot access euthanasia because their suffering is not medically based. This is the case of elderly individuals who consider their life path to be completed. ZonMw (2021)

any particular pathology, but simply to people who consider their life course to be complete. In view of the high level of consensus that this possibility seems to have received, a bill is currently being debated in Parliament that would tend to allow elderly people over 75 without any pathology the possibility of freely taking their leave of life and receiving help in dying.[31]

In addition, there is currently a heated debate on the cases of euthanasia—performed on patients suffering from mental illness and no longer capable of understanding and wanting—governed by Article 2(2) of the above-mentioned Wtl. According to Dutch law, in fact, if the patient is over the age of sixteen and is currently not capable of understanding but, before reaching this state, has been deemed capable of fully assessing his or her own interests and has drawn up a written declaration with a view to requesting euthanasia, the doctor may take this request into account by terminating the patient's life. The most striking case is the so-called Koffie case (Rozemond 2021), which we shall deal with specifically in a later Sect. 3.10 in which a doctor performed euthanasia on his own patient, suffering from Alzheimer's disease, without the latter's knowledge, by administering a sedative in her coffee, as well as against her will; or rather, considering the will currently manifested to be irrelevant, but on the basis of the request drawn up in writing by the patient before she fell ill and was considered incapacitated. It was precisely for this reason that the Euthanasia Code 2022,[32] revised the procedures in order to make them even more specific, especially in cases of euthanasia resulting from advance requests.

Euthanasia has also entered the legal system in Belgium as a procedural justification. Belgian law defines euthanasia as the act, performed by a third party, which intentionally ends the life of a person at the latter's request,[33] and excludes the punishability of the doctor who performs it if the following conditions are met (1) the patient is an adult or an emancipated minor, capable or a minor endowed with the capacity of discernment and is conscious at the time of his or her request;

Kennissynthese Ouderen en het zelfgekozen levenseinde [Knowledge synthesis on older adults and voluntary end-of-life decisions]. Available at: https://www.zonmw.nl/nl/onderzoek-resultaten/subsidie-en-inzichten-voor-gemeenten/programmas/project-detail/preventieprogramma-4/kennissynthese-ouderen-en-het-zelfgekozen-levenseinde/verslagen/. Accessed on 26 June 2025.

[31] *Tweede Kamer der Staten-Generaal* (2024) *Agenda commissievergadering, Voorstel van wet van het lid Podt houdende toetsing van levenseindebegeleiding van ouderen op verzoek en tot wijziging van het Wetboek van Strafrecht, de Wet op de beroepen in de individuele gezondheidszorg en enkele andere wetten* (*Wet toetsing levenseindebegeleiding van ouderen op verzoek*) (TK 35,534) [Bill proposed by MP Podt on the evaluation of end-of-life orientation for the elderly upon request, and amending the Penal Code, the Individual Healthcare Professions Act, and various other laws] item ID 2024A09470. Available at: https://www.tweedekamer.nl/debat_en_vergadering/commissievergaderingen/details?id=2024A09470.

[32] Euthanasia Code (2022) Euthanasia Code: Providing clarity and support in euthanasia practice. Regional Euthanasia Review Committees (*Euthanasiecommissie*), Utrecht. Available at: https://www.euthanasiecommissie.nl/binaries/euthanasiecommissie/documenten/publicaties/ec-2022/ec-2022/7/5/RTE_EuthaCode2022_English.pdf.

[33] Art.2, *Loi relative à l'euthanasie* (2002) [Belgian Euthanasia Act] Consolidated version as of 23 March 2020. Available at: https://eol.law.dal.ca/wp-content/uploads/2015/06/Law-of-28-May-2002-on-Euthanasia-as-amended ... pdf.

(2) the request is made voluntarily, thoughtfully and repeatedly and is not the result of external pressure; (3) the patient, adult or emancipated minor, is in a desperate medical situation and reports constant and unbearable physical or mental suffering that cannot be alleviated and that results from an accidental or serious and incurable pathological condition; (4) a minor patient with the capacity of discernment is in a hopeless medical situation with constant and unbearable physical suffering that cannot be alleviated and may lead to death within a short period of time, and which results from an accidental illness or a serious and incurable pathological condition; (5) complies with the conditions and procedures stipulated in this Act.[34]

The Belgian legislature has provided for a series of procedural formalities to ensure a certain degree of control over the execution of euthanasia practices; the patient must be informed in detail of his condition and his life expectancy, the opinion of another doctor must be sought in order to assess the incurability of the illness and the unbearable suffering associated with it, and the persistence of the patient's wish to end his life must be ascertained through a series of interviews reasonably spaced out in time. Furthermore, the legislation of both Belgium and the Netherlands allows for the registration of a written declaration through which an individual may request euthanasia in advance in the event of future illness that results in unbearable suffering, incapacity, or unconsciousness due to an irreversible clinical condition.[35] Compliance with the procedure is also subject to verification by a federal control and evaluation commission, which may—if it finds doubts as to compliance with the law—inform the public prosecutor's office at the end of its activities.[36]

Belgium, like the Netherlands, has regulated in great detail the requirements for being granted aid to die, but despite this, since 2002, the tendency to expand the number of cases covered by the specific procedural justification seems to have been steadily growing.

In Belgium, too, the current discipline is the result of several reforms, probably the most controversial being the one of 13 February 2014, following which the euthanasia practice performed on a minor, capable of discernment, regardless of his or her age, became non-punishable, subject to additional requirements.[37]

---

[34] Art. 3, *Loi relative à l'euthanasie* (2002) [Belgian Euthanasia Act] Consolidated version as of 23 March 2020. Available at: https://eol.law.dal.ca/wp-content/uploads/2015/06/Law-of-28-May-2002-on-Euthanasia-as-amended ... pdf.

[35] Art. 4, *Loi relative à l'euthanasie* (2002) [Belgian Euthanasia Act] Consolidated version as of 23 March 2020. Available at: https://eol.law.dal.ca/wp-content/uploads/2015/06/Law-of-28-May-2002-on-Euthanasia-as-amended ... pdf.

[36] Art. 6–9, *Loi relative à l'euthanasie* (2002) [Belgian Euthanasia Act] Consolidated version as of 23 March 2020. Available at: https://eol.law.dal.ca/wp-content/uploads/2015/06/Law-of-28-May-2002-on-Euthanasia-as-amended ... pdf.

[37] "The suffering endured must be of a physical nature and death expected within a short period of time; it is necessary that the parents or legal representatives give their written consent and that a child psychologist or psychiatrist be consulted in order to ascertain the minor's capacity for discernment" in (*trans. by the author*) (Casonato, 2016). For a more in-depth discussion of euthanasia performed on minors see also: (Herremans and Genicot, 2016; Amato, 2016; Alfonzo, 2016).

On 23 March 2020, on the other hand, the indefinite validity of the written declaration through which one can request euthanasia for a future and possible time was extended, which no longer expires five years after the declaration.

In any case, legislative developments, hand in hand with the social changes of recent years, have led to a proportional increase in the number of cases in which euthanasia has been legitimately (and perhaps in some cases illegitimately) practised in the Netherlands[38] and Belgium (Siegel et al. 2014; Dierickx et al. 2015; Snijdewind et al. 2015) taking what some scholars consider to be a real slippery slope (Lerner and Caplan 2015; Lewis 2007; Walker 2001).

The legal evolution on the subject of euthanasia and assistance to suicide in any case shows a tendency to go beyond the regulatory boundaries with instances that increasingly push to extend the range of cases that can be brought within a discipline based on the same *ratio*. The range of cases in which it is possible to exclude the punishability of the doctor who practises euthanasia—despite the specificity of the discipline produced—seems to be in continuous expansion (Lerner and Caplan 2015) as it is founded on assumptions characterised by a high degree of subjectivity. The increase in the number of cases in which it is possible to request euthanasia practices, especially in cases in which the discriminating factor is based on the assessment of the patient's capacity to understand and will (an element that is difficult to place in time and can be attested with certainty and precision even by medical science), has given rise to a continuous debate[39] as well as some criminal proceedings against doctors who have practised euthanasia in cases bordering on legitimacy.[40] The experiences of Holland and Belgium, the salient features of which have just been sketched out, however, seem to provide useful indications as to whether from an empirical point of view the slippery slope argument may be well-founded. This point will be discussed in more detail in Sect. 3.10 where we will go into the merits of a well-known ruling of the Dutch Supreme Court.

It is evident that social instances can influence normative evolution, and vice versa. This interplay can lead to the acceleration of social progress, thereby legitimising the pursuit of specific objectives, including those pertaining to human rights. Indeed, it is appropriate to take into account the different interests at stake and the different facets that specific individual cases may present, while avoiding that the normalisation of such a way of taking leave of life fosters a resigned inclination to take leave of existence with a lightness disproportionate to the inestimable value of existence.

---

[38] Regional Euthanasia Review Committees (2025) Annual report 2024. *Euthanasiecommissie*, Utrecht. In 2024, euthanasia accounted for 5.8% of all deaths in the Netherlands, up from 5.4% in 2023. Available at: https://www.euthanasiecommissie.nl/ … /jaarverslag-2024.pdf.

[39] See also (Dresser 2017, pp. 5–6; Dresser 1995, pp. 32–38).

[40] See Hoge Raad (Supreme Court of the Netherlands), 2020a. Case No. 19/04910 CW. Available at: https://uitspraken.rechtspraak.nl/inziendocument?id=ECLI:NL:HR:2020:712.

3.6 Euthanasia in Southern Mediterranean Countries: The Italian Case

In order to provide an overview of how some Member States have regulated the end of life, with the aim of broadening the overview of the arguments used to justify the wide margin of appreciation that according to the ECtHR must be left to individual States, an attempt will be made to briefly summarise what has happened in recent years in three southern Mediterranean States with a strong Catholic influence, Italy, Spain and France.

Indeed, as we have seen above, among the schools of thought that tend to regard life as an unavailable good are those influenced by a Christian conception of the sacredness of life.

This may also be the reason why euthanasia practices remain prohibited in Italy and France, and there is currently no established discipline to facilitate access to medically assisted death.

In Spain, on the other hand, the first euthanasia law was only recently enacted, which allows for medicalised assisted death under certain conditions.

Despite the prevalence of civil law systems in most European countries, particularly in the southern Mediterranean region, there has been an increasing trend of judicial creation of legislation, particularly in areas of high social sensitivity, where legislative bodies are concerned about the potential political ramifications of their actions. This phenomenon is exemplified by Italy.

In fact, in Italy it was only after the Welby[41] and Englaro[42] cases that L.219/2017 was promulgated, thanks to which the right of any individual to

[41] Piergiorgio Welby was a man suffering from muscular dystrophy since his teenage years. In the last years of his life he was completely paralysed, communicated with a voice synthesiser and survived on an artificial ventilator. Despite full mental lucidity, his quality of life was severely compromised. He publicly and repeatedly asked for the right to die, i.e. to be allowed to stop the artificial ventilation that was keeping him alive, a request that had no clear legal basis in Italy at the time. In 2006, Welby wrote an open letter to the President of the Republic Giorgio Napolitano, in which he demanded recognition of his right to refuse medical treatment, arguing that his was a biologically assisted form of life, but no longer humanly sustainable. He said he wanted to die with dignity, not in technological slavery. The case concerned the right to refuse life-saving medical treatment, according to many jurists already guaranteed by the Constitution, and not specifically euthanasia. On 20 December 2006, the anaesthetist Mario Riccio, after verifying Welby's informed consent, interrupted mechanical ventilation and administered palliative sedation to accompany his death without suffering. Investigated Mario Riccio was later acquitted for respecting the patient's will in accordance with the discipline of informed consent.

[42] Eluana Englaro was a 22-year-old woman who, after a serious car accident, remained in a permanent vegetative state in which her body was kept alive in a state of absolute unconsciousness, fed by a nasogastric tube but without any artificial ventilation. Eluana's father waged a legal battle to obtain the interruption of artificial nutrition, which only succeeded in 2008 following a ruling by the Court of Cassation in which it was stated that in the absence of a current will it is legitimate to reconstruct a presumed will provided that it is based on serious, precise and concordant elements, including through the testimony of those who knew him.

refuse any health treatment, even life-saving treatment, was recognised and *advance treatment declarations* (DAT) were introduced into the legal system. At the same time, until the historic ruling of the Constitutional Court No. 242/2019[43] there was no jurisprudential precedent of reference that allowed access to any euthanasia procedure, which was punishable under Article 580 (instigation and assisting suicide) and 579 (murder of the consenting person) of the Criminal Code.

It was only with the aforementioned pronouncement in 2019 that the partial illegitimacy of Article 580 of the Criminal Code was sanctioned and the non-punishability of a person who provides assistance in dying was recognised when certain requirements are met.

Today, the Italian Parliament is moving, still slowly, towards the identification of a legal regulation on assisted suicide and euthanasia. Such a much debated issue, with such significant social implications, certainly requires a careful analysis of the assumptions and criteria that could theoretically allow the execution of a request for early termination of life[44] but at the same time requires swift action.

To remedy the legislature's inertia, a referendum question was submitted on 20 April 2021 to partially repeal Article 579 of the Criminal Code, which penalises the conduct of murder of a consenting person.[45] This question was subsequently declared inadmissible by the Constitutional Court pursuant to Article 75 of the Italian Constitution with ruling No. 50 of 2022.

During the eighteenth legislature, a unified bill was approved on first reading in the Chamber of Deputies, and subsequently passed to the Senate for consideration. It encompassed several bills introduced in Parliament from 2013[46] onwards. The aforementioned bill saw its approval process interrupted due to the fall of the

---

[43] Constitutional Court (Italy) (2019) Judgment No. 242 of 25 September 2019, published in *Gazzetta Ufficiale* No. 48 of 27 November 2019. Available at: https://www.cortecostituzionale.it/actionSchedaPronuncia.do?anno=2019&numero=242.

[44] The scholarly production following pronouncements No. 242/2019 and No. 207/2018 has been particularly flourishing. On the subject see, without claiming to be exhaustive: (Tamburini, 2020; Pizzetti, 2019; Adamo, 2020; Veronesi, 2019; Canestrari, 2019. See also (Vinciguerra, 2020; Zagrebelsk, 2020; Risicato, 2020; Bignami, 2018; Cupelli, 2018; Cupelli, 2019; Cupelli, 2020; Donini, 2020; Eusebi, 2018; Fiandaca, 2020; Catalano, 2020; Pellizzone, 2020).

[45] *Gazzetta Ufficiale della Repubblica Italiana* (2021) *Serie Generale No 95, 21 April 2021: Annuncio di una richiesta di referendum abrogativo riferito all'omicidio del consenziente* (codice 21A02408). (Italy) [Official Gazette of the Italian Republic (2021) General Series No. 95, 21 April 2021: Notice of a request for a abrogative referendum concerning the offence of consensual homicide]. Available at: https://www.gazzettaufficiale.it/eli/id/2021/04/21/21A02408/sg.

[46] *Senato della Repubblica Italiana, Disegno di legge n.104, Disposizioni in materia di morte volontaria medicalmente assistita* [Senate of the Republic (2022) Senate Bill No. 104. Provisions on Medically Assisted Voluntary Death]. Available at: https://www.senato.it/leg/19/BGT/Schede/FascicoloSchedeDDL/ebook/55281.pdf.

Italian government in October 2022.[47] A new proposal[48] with the same content was immediately re-proposed for consideration in the Senate during the current Legislature and therefore, in the near future, the Italian Parliament will certainly be faced with the need to pass legislation regulating euthanasia and/or assisted suicide—as was also done by Spain[49] with a special law approved on 18 March 2021[50]—in accordance with the principles expressed by the Constitutional Court in the above-mentioned rulings.

The bill currently pending for approval in the Senate regulates the conditions, limits, prerequisites and modalities for an individual to voluntarily and autonomously end his or her own life.[51] In order to request *medically assisted voluntary death*, the individual must be over 18 years of age, capable both of understanding and of making free, current and conscious decisions, fully informed and previously involved in a palliative care process; he or she must also be suffering from an irreversible pathology with a certain inauspicious outcome or be the bearer of an irreversible clinical condition that is the source of physical *and* psychological suffering that she or he finds intolerable.[52]

A discipline that affects the relationship between the right to life, the protection of human dignity and the freedom of self-determination, certainly requires a high level of attention and in-depth study on the part of those involved. The overturning of values required to admit medical assistance in dying, based on the principle of solidarity with the sick person, in fact requires a solid ethical justification as well as a specific regulation that regulates in detail the requirements for access and the methods of execution.

Below, albeit briefly, an attempt will be made to reconstruct the philosophical-legal argumentative process underlying the recognition of the appropriateness of

---

[47] *Senato della Repubblica Italiana, Disegno di legge n. 2553, 18ª Legislatura. Roma, 11 March 2022, Disposizioni in materia di morte volontaria medicalmente assistita* (Italy) Senate of the Republic (2022) Senate Bill Senate Act No. 2553 [Provisions on Medically Assisted Voluntary Death]. Available at: https://www.senato.it/service/PDF/PDFServer/BGT/01341458.pdf.

[48] *Senato della Repubblica Italiana, Disegno di legge n.104, Disposizioni in materia di morte volontaria medicalmente assistita* [Senate of the Republic (2022) Senate Bill No. 104. Provisions on Medically Assisted Voluntary Death]. Available at: https://www.senato.it/leg/19/BGT/Schede/FascicoloSchedeDDL/ebook/55281.pdf.

[49] For a reconstruction of the evolution of the processes that led Spain to the promulgation of the law regulating euthanasia, see Tigrino (2021).

[50] *Ley Orgánica 3/2021, de 24 de marzo, de regulación de la eutanasia* [Organic Law 3/2021 of 24 March on the regulation of euthanasia], Boletín Oficial del Estado, No. 72:34,041–34,075 (25 March 2021). Available at: https://www.boe.es/diario_boe/txt.php?id=BOE-A-2021-4628.

[51] *Senato della Repubblica Italiana, Disegno di legge n.104, Disposizioni in materia di morte volontaria medicalmente assistita* [Senate of the Republic (2022) Senate Bill No. 104. Provisions on Medically Assisted Voluntary Death] Art. 1. Available at: https://www.senato.it/leg/19/BGT/Schede/FascicoloSchedeDDL/ebook/55281.pdf.

[52] Art. 3(a). *Ley Orgánica 3/2021, de 24 de marzo, de regulación de la eutanasia* [Organic Law 3/2021 of 24 March on the regulation of euthanasia], Boletín Oficial del Estado, No. 72:34,041–34,075 (25 March 2021). Available at: https://www.boe.es/diario_boe/txt.php?id=BOE-A-2021-4628.

fully regulating aid to suicide and euthanasia. Starting from an examination of some principles affirmed in the well-known pronouncements of the Constitutional Court nos. 242/2019 and 207/2018, as well as commenting on some profiles of inadmissibility of the abrogative referendum found in judgement no. 50/2022, an attempt will be made to provide some useful food for thought for analysing the ethical issues under debate.

With pronouncements nos. 242/2019 and 207/2018[53] the Italian Constitutional Court intended to allow, if certain requirements are met, medical practices aimed at helping an individual to interrupt his or her life prematurely.[54] The need to protect the dignity of the sick person, the latter's right to self-determination as well as the solidaristic principles underlying the reasoning of the Constitutional Court[55] are the same that drove, as early as 2002 both the Netherlands and Belgium to promulgate, respectively, the Law on the interruption of life on request and assistance to suicide (Wet toetsing levensbeëindiging op verzoek en hulp bij zelfdoding)[56] and the Law on Euthanasia (*Loi relative à l'euthanasie*)[57].

The question of legitimacy raised by the Court of Assizes of Milan on the occasion of the well-known Cappato case,[58] concerned the verification of the constitutional legitimacy of Article 580 of the Criminal Code in the part in

[53] Constitutional Court, 2018. Pronounce No. 207 of 24 October 2018. Published in *Gazzetta Ufficiale* No. 46 of 21 November 2018. Available at: https://www.cortecostituzionale.it/actionSchedaPronuncia.do?anno=2018&numero=207.

[54] The Constitutional Court, in fact, in its judgment no. 242/2019 has sanctioned the partial unconstitutionality of Article 580 of the Criminal Code in the part in which it does not exclude the punishability of the conduct of aiding suicide 'if the would-be suicide is identified as a person (a) suffering from an irreversible pathology and (b) the source of physical or psychological suffering, which he finds absolutely intolerable, who is (c) kept alive by means of life-support treatment, but remains (d) capable of making free and conscious decisions (*trans. by the author*).

[55] See, Constitutional Court, Judgment No. 242 of 25 September 2019, published in G.U. 48 of 27.11.2019, https://www.cortecostituzionale.it/actionSchedaPronuncia.do?anno=2019&numero=242; and Constitutional Court, *Ordinance No. 207 of 24 October 2018*, in judgment on the constitutionality of Article 580 c.p. Published in *Gazzetta Ufficiale* No. 46, 21 November 2018. Available at: https://www.cortecostituzionale.it/actionSchedaPronuncia.do?anno=2018&numero=207.

[56] *Wet toetsing levensbeëindiging op verzoek en hulp bij zelfdoding* [Act on Termination of Life on Demand and Suicide Assistance] Netherlands (2020) Available at: https://wetten.overheid.nl/BWBR0012410/2020-03-19.

[57] *Loi relative à l'euthanasie* (2002) [Belgian Euthanasia Act]. Consolidated version as of 23 March 2020. Available at: https://eol.law.dal.ca/wp-content/uploads/2015/06/Law-of-28-May-2002-on-Euthanasia-as-amended … pdf.

[58] Fabiano Antoniani, known as Dj Fabo, was a young musician and producer from Milan who became blind and tetraplegic after a serious accident. Despite numerous attempts at rehabilitation and a great initial determination, in the following years he matured the will to end his own life, judging his condition unbearable and unworthy. In 2017, Marco Cappato—a member activist of the Luca Coscioni Association—accompanied Fabiano to a clinic in Switzerland to access assisted suicide, a legal practice in that country. Upon his return to Italy, Cappato self-reported that he had violated Article 580 of the Italian Criminal Code (incitement or aid to suicide), which also punishes those who facilitate the execution of suicide.

which it provided for the parity, also from the point of view of the applicable sentence framework, of the conduct of assisting and instigating suicide as well as with regard to the criminal relevance of the conduct of assisting suicide in cases where certain specific conditions were met.[59]

Although the Constitutional Court in Order no. 207/2018 had granted time to Parliament to take the necessary decisions referred in principle to its discretion[60] however identifying a series of criteria and principles[61] that could have guided the legislative activity elapsed approximately one year after the first pronouncement, the Constitutional Court found itself forced to intervene, again, moving within the "self-imposed bottleneck with Ordinance 207 of 2018" (Adamo 2020, p. 32), declaring the partial illegitimacy of Article 580 of the Criminal Code.[62]

The Court's position is that it is only possible to justify conduct in assist of a suicidal intention if the necessary conditions are met to determine the prevalence—based on the principle of solidarity—of the right to the protection of human dignity and the freedom of self-determination of the sick person over the general right to life of the individual and the duty of the State to protect its citizens, especially the most vulnerable.

---

[59] The conduct of incitement to suicide is that conduct which is characterised by being causally connected not with the execution of the suicidal intent but with the determination or reinforcement of the suicidal intent itself. Aiding and abetting suicide, on the other hand, consists in the conduct of others that is causally connected with the suicide of the facilitator.

[60] Constitutional Court, 2018. Ordinance no. 207 of 24 October 2018, published in *Gazzetta Ufficiale* no. 46, 1st special series, 21 November 2018.

[61] Constitutional Court, 2018. Ordinance no. 207 of 24 October 2018, published in *Gazzetta Ufficiale* no. 46, 1st special series, 21 November 2018. In the aforementioned ruling, the Court first justifies the *ratio of* art. 580 placed to protect above all "sick, depressed, psychologically fragile, or elderly and lonely persons, who could easily be induced to take a premature leave of life, if the legal system allowed anyone to cooperate even only in the execution of their suicide choice, perhaps for reasons of personal gain" (p. 6 of *cons.* in *rig.* to 6 *cons. in rig.*), then identifies 'situations unimaginable at the time when the incriminating rule was introduced, but brought under its sphere of application by developments in medical science and technology, often capable of snatching from death patients in an extremely compromised condition, but not of restoring to them sufficient vital functions' (p. to 8 *cons. in rig.*) and finally—after introducing a parallelism with L. 219 of 2017—affirms the principle according to which 'if a person who is kept alive by an artificial support treatment is considered by the legal system to be able, under certain conditions, to take the decision to end his or her existence by interrupting that treatment, it is hard to see why the same person should be considered to be in need of ironclad and indiscriminate protection against his or her own will when the decision to end his or her existence with the help of others is being discussed, as an alternative considered to be more dignified to the aforesaid interruption' (p. 9 *cons. in. rig.*) hoping for reforming parliamentary intervention in this regard (*trans. by the author*).

[62] The Italian constitutional Court has declared the illegitimacy of Article 580 of the Criminal Code "insofar as it does not exclude the punishability of a person who, in the manner provided for by Articles 1 and 2 of Law 22 December 2017, no. 219 (Rules on informed consent and advance treatment provisions) [. . .] facilitates the execution of the intention to commit suicide, independently and freely formed, of a person kept alive by life-support treatments and affected by an irreversible pathology, source of physical or psychological suffering that she considers intolerable, but fully capable of making free and conscious decisions, provided that these conditions and the modalities of execution have been verified by a public structure of the national health service, after obtaining the opinion of the territorially competent ethics committee" (*trans. by the author*).

The fundamental elements on which the pronouncement of partial unconstitutionality of Article 580 of the Criminal Code is based are essentially two. The first, linked to the questioning of the punishability of those "acts of assisting and abetting suicide which have not contributed to determining or strengthening the victim's intention".[63] The second, linked to the punitive treatment reserved for the conduct of incitement to suicide, from the point of view of the edictal framework, equal to the less serious conduct of assisting.

The analysis of the Court starts from the consideration according to which the *ratio* of the sanctioning provision for the conduct of assisting and abetting suicide has its origin in the need to protect the most vulnerable persons (depressed, sick, elderly) by creating a protective belt around them and preventing third parties from being able to cooperate with them in the execution or determination of the suicidal intent. The non-punishability of the suicide itself (e.g. in cases of attempted suicide), on the other hand, would exclude that the judgement of disvalue could be linked to the act of suicide as such, thus implying an implicit recognition of the greater weight of the protection of the individual's right to self-determination[64] over the general interest of the State in the health of its citizens.[65]

Having thus established the basis of the offending rule, the Court, in the first part of its decision, seems to categorically exclude the existence of a '*right to die*' also in the light of Article 2 ECHR, which enshrines as inviolable the right to life of the human being.[66]

At the same time, the Court seems to recognise a right to be assisted in carrying out one's own free determination even if it leads to death.

In fact, the Constitutional Court, on the basis of what was affirmed by the Supreme Court of Cassation[67] in the Englaro case, as well as the interpretation provided by the ECtHR of Art. 8 ECHR,[68] seems to affirm that "the right of each

---

[63] Constitutional Court, 2019. Judgment no. 242 of 22 November 2019, published in *Gazzetta Ufficiale* no. 47, 1st special series, 26 November 2019.

[64] Right enshrined, among others, in Article 8 ECHR as well as in Articles 2, 3(2) and 13 of the Constitution.

[65] Consistent with such a reconstruction, the rationale of Article 580 of the italian Criminal Code (which, moreover, already existed in the previous code of 1889, at Article 370) envisaged by the 1930 legislator, was intended to protect human life as an inalienable good, also and above all because of the interest that the community had in preserving the lives of its citizens, in a vision that, contrary to today's, placed the State and not the person at the centre of society's interests and, therefore, holder of the right to the life of its *citizens*.

[66] The Court often refers to the European Court of Human Rights' ruling No. 2346 of 29 April 2002, *Pretty vs. the United Kingdom,* in which the European Court of Human Rights explicitly states that "no right to die, by the hand of a third party or with the assistance of public authority, can be derived from Article 2 of the Convention".

[67] *Corte di Cassazione* [Court of Cassation] 2007. *Judgment no. 21748 of 16 October 2007*, published in *Gazzetta Ufficiale*, 1st special series, no. 43 of 15 October 2008.) https://www.robertobin.it/COST10/CassazioneEnglaro1.pdf.

[68] European Court of Human Rights (ECtHR), 2011. *Haas v. Switzerland*, Application no. 31322/07, Judgment of 20 January 2011. Available at: https://hudoc.echr.coe.int/eng?i=001-102940; in the same sense, European Court of Human Rights (ECtHR), 2012. *Koch v. Germany*, Application no. 497/09, Judgment of 19 July 2012. Available at: https://hudoc.echr.coe.int/eng?i=001-112868;

person to decide how and when his life should end, provided that he is a person capable of making a free decision and acting in accordance with that decision, is one of the aspects of the right to private life recognised by Article 8 ECHR".[69]

Therefore, although it would seem that the right to demand assistance to suicide from the State or in any case from third parties cannot be considered to exist, the right—recognised in Italy by L. 219/2017[70]—to knowingly refuse any health treatment, even if such a refusal leads to death, certainly derives from the Court's jurisprudence.

The Court thus seems, on the one hand, to conceive of the possibility of the individual adopting autonomous determinations leading to his or her death and, at the same time, and by virtue of the same principle, to consider the punishment of conduct aiding suicide to be justified on the basis of a duty to protect the weakest and most vulnerable persons.

After having apparently ruled out the constitutional illegitimacy of Article 580 of the Criminal Code, the Court, instead, concludes its analysis in the light of the provisions of Law 219/2017, which provides, as part of the therapeutic alliance between doctor and patient, the right of the individual to be able to refuse any therapeutic treatment (considering artificial nutrition and/or hydration as such) by virtue of the combined provisions of Articles 2, 13 and 32 of the italian Constitution, assuming a sort of right of the individual to let himself die.

An egalitarian and reasonable application of the *ratio* contained in Law 219/2017, according to the Court, would lead in certain circumstances[71] to consider recourse to assisted suicide as the only way to escape from an "artificial and no longer wanted maintenance in life and which he has the right to refuse, pursuant to Article 32, paragraph 2, of the Constitution".[72] According to the provisions of the so-called *Informed Consent* Act, in fact, the patient has the right to request the interruption of any medical treatment and to be subjected to deep sedation.[73] Such

European Court of Human Rights (ECtHR), 2013. *Gross v. Switzerland*, Application no. 67810/10, Judgment of 14 May 2013. Available at: https://hudoc.echr.coe.int/eng?i=001-119703.

[69] Constitutional Court, 2018. Ordinance no. 207 of 24 October 2018, published in *Gazzetta Ufficiale* no. 46, 1st special series, 21 November 2018.

[70] *Legge n. 219 del 22 dicembre 2017. Norme sul consenso informato e sulle disposizione anticipate di trattamento* (2017) Italy [Law No. 219 of 22 December 2017. Rules on informed consent and advance treatment arrangements]. Published in *Gazzetta Ufficiale* no. 12 of 16 January 2018.

[71] Where the person being facilitated is a "person (a) suffering from an irreversible disease and (b) causing physical or psychological suffering, which he or she finds absolutely intolerable, who is (c) kept alive by means of life-support treatment, but remains (d) capable of making free and conscious decisions" (*trans. by the author*).

[72] Constitutional Court (2018) Order no. 207 of 24 October 2018, published in *Gazzetta Ufficiale*, Serie Generale no. 46 of 21 November 2018, p. 8.

[73] The right to access to palliative care and pain therapy is guaranteed not only by Article 2 of Law no. 219 of 22 December 2017, but also by Law no. 38 of 15 March 2010, which aims to include in the essential levels of care also therapies capable of limiting as much as possible the suffering of the sick person precisely by virtue of the recognition of the principle of dignity of the human being.

a procedure could force the patient, in certain cases, to undergo a slower process, sometimes less corresponding to the personal concept of dignity in dying and certainly more fraught with suffering for loved ones.[74]

The reasoning is based on two main arguments: the first, according to which if the legal system recognises the right of the sick person to end his own life through the suspension of any medical treatment, even through active heteronomous conduct, at the same time it must recognise the right of the sick person to seek help from a third party in order to avoid reaching death through a slower process, which is considered contrary to his own idea of a dignified death; The second standpoint asserts that if the vulnerability of the sick person is not to be regarded as a limitation on the recognition of their right to terminate medical treatment that is likely to result in their death, it is not reasonable—nor preordained for the protection of another constitutionally significant interest[75]—to regard it as such when it is a matter of adopting a decision that will result in their death through the assistance of a third party.

By analogically adapting the *ratio* of the regulation provided for by Law 219 of 2017, the Judges limit the illegitimacy of Article 580 of the Criminal Code to the failure to provide for a cause of exclusion of punishability, or rather a so-called procedural justification,[76] for those who have carried out an activity auxiliary to the suicidal intent when the conditions previously identified occur,[77] similarly to what happens in the Dutch or Belgian discipline. The principles affirmed in arts. 1 and 2 of the *Informed Consent* Act[78] should therefore serve as a guide to determine how the medical verification of the existence of the conditions in the presence of which an assistance to terminate one's own existence may be required.

The arguments adopted by the Italian Constitutional Court are consistent with a vision that, while recognising an intrinsic value to existence, recognises that if the

[74] Constitutional Court (2018) Ordinance no. 207 of 24 October 2018, published in Gazzetta Ufficiale, Serie Generale no. 46 of 21 November 2018, p. 9.

[75] Constitutional Court (2018) Ordinance no. 207 of 24 October 2018, published in *Gazzetta Ufficiale*, Serie Generale no. 46 of 21 November 2018, p. 9.

[76] For a more in-depth study on the topic *see,* for all, (Sessa 2018).

[77] Constitutional Court (2019) Judgment no. 242 of 22 November 2019, published in *Gazzetta Ufficiale*, Serie Generale no. 47 of 27 November 2019, § 1.2.

[78] Articles 1 and 2 of L. 219 of 2017—in addition to containing an explicit reference to "Articles 2, 13 and 32 of the Constitution and Articles 1, 2 and 3 of the Charter of Fundamental Rights of the European Union" which provide for the protection of the "right to life, health, dignity and self-determination of the person"—by defining as health treatments also "artificial nutrition and hydration, as the administration, on medical prescription, of nutrients by means of medical devices" allowed the Court to hold by analogy that "if a person who is kept alive by an artificial support treatment is considered by the legal system to be capable, under certain conditions, to take the decision to end his own life through the interruption of such treatment, it is difficult to see why the same person should be deemed to be in need of strict and indiscriminate protection against his own will when the decision to end his own life with the help of others, as a more dignified alternative to such an interruption, is at issue" (*trans. by the author*) (Constitutional Court (2018) Order no. 207 of 24 October 2018, in *Gazzetta Ufficiale*, Serie Generale no. 46 of 21 November 2018, p. 9 cons. in rig.).

result of death is legitimately pursuable through the refusal of life-support treatment, it can only be pursued through assistance that anticipates the result if the slow onset of death is contrary to one's conception of a dignified death as well as a source of suffering for one's loved ones.

In fact, the bill currently pending before the Senate attempts to comply with the principles affirmed in the aforementioned judgments, among which, an essential element—and a *unicum* in the European regulatory panorama—is that the applicant is kept alive by life-supporting medical treatment,[79] the suspension of which would cause, anyway, his or her death.[80]

Precisely on this last point, two recent rulings of the Italian Constitutional Court, No 135 of 2024 and No 66 of 2025, have broadened the interpretation of what is defined as life-support treatment.

The above-mentioned pronouncements, in essence, justify the criterion according to which it is necessary for the patient to be subjected to life-support treatment in order to exclude the punishability of the auxiliary of suicidal intent.

The Court therefore defended its argument that while there is no doubt as to the non-punishability of a doctor who interrupts life-sustaining treatment in order to comply with a patient's request in accordance with the rules on informed consent, the same conclusion cannot but be reached where the interruption of medical treatment leads to death in a manner deemed by the patient to be contrary to his dignity. In such a case, therefore, conduct in assistance of suicide that anticipates the event of death is also admissible.

For this reason, the fact that the patient is kept alive by life-support treatment is essential to justify auxiliary conduct.

In conclusion, the Court clarified that life-sustaining treatment includes "those procedures that are normally carried out by medical personnel, the performance of which certainly requires special skills that are the subject of specific professional training, but which could be learned by family members or 'caregivers' who take charge of the patient's care"[81] thus extending the list of cases to those necessary to ensure the patient's vital functions, to the extent that their omission or interruption would foreseeably lead to the patient's death within a short period of time.[82]

---

[79] On this point, it is necessary to recall that Articles 1 and 2 of Law 219 of 2017 also define health treatments as 'artificial nutrition and hydration, as the administration, on medical prescription, of nutrients by means of medical devices'.

[80] *Senato della Repubblica Italiana, Disegno di legge n.104, Disposizioni in materia di morte volontaria medicalmente assistita* [Senate of the Republic (2022) Senate Bill No. 104. Provisions on Medically Assisted Voluntary Death]. Available at: https://www.senato.it/leg/19/BGT/Schede/FascicoloSchedeDDL/ebook/55281.pdf.

[81] Constitutional Court (2024) Judgment No. 135 of 9 July 2024, Constitutional Court of the Italian Republic, § 1.2, facts section. (*trans. by the author*) Available at: https://www.cortecostituzionale.it/actionSchedaPronuncia.do?param_ecli=ECLI:IT:COST:2024:135.

[82] See on this point the Trentini case, Available at: https://www.biodiritto.org/Biolaw-pedia/Giurisprudenza/Corte-d-assise-di-Massa-caso-Trentini-la-dipendenza-costante-da-cure-mediche-e-l-assistenza-permanente-nell-espletamento-di-una-funzione-organica-integrano-la-condizione-della-dipendenza-dai-trattamenti-di-sostegno-vitale-di-cui-alla-sent.-242-2019-de.

Finally, the Court clarified, but this could be deduced from a systematic interpretation of the ruling, that life-support treatment does not necessarily have to be started and then discontinued but that it must be necessary for the survival of the patient.

In any case, the bill, in addition to bringing back the individual requirements suggested by the constitutional jurisprudence, shifts part of the reasoning behind the declaration of partial constitutional illegitimacy of Article 580 of the Criminal Code in the moment in which it provides that the applicant's clinical condition must be such as to be able to lead to death even through the faculties provided by Law 219/2017 alone. In fact, stated the Court, "if one who is kept alive by an artificial support treatment is considered by the legal system to be able, under certain conditions, to take the decision to end his existence through the interruption of that treatment [through the faculties made available by L. 219/2017], it is hard to see why the same person should be deemed, conversely, in need of ironclad and indiscriminate protection against his or her own will when the decision to end his or her own existence with the help of others, as an alternative deemed more dignified to the aforesaid interruption, is being discussed".[83] The possibility of obtaining a medically assisted voluntary death therefore satisfies the need to protect the dignity of the person who does not wish to 'let himself die' by requesting the suspension of medical treatment for an indefinite period of time, amplifying his own suffering and that of his family members and harming his ideal of a dignified death.

Further food for thought, in particular with respect to the identification of the concept of vulnerability, can also be drawn from the declaration of inadmissibility of the proposed referendum to repeal Article 579 of the criminal code.[84]

Applying, in fact, the same reasoning operated by the Constitutional Court in relation to the conduct of instigation and assisting and abetting suicide, it is possible to affirm that also the incrimination of homicide of the consenting person is 'functional to the protection of the right to life, especially of the weakest and most vulnerable persons, whom the criminal law intends to protect from an extreme and irreparable choice.[85] The purpose of the rule would therefore be to protect persons experiencing difficulty and suffering when, for the execution of the suicide intention, conduct is required that "goes beyond the personal sphere of the person

---

[83] Constitutional Court (2018) Order No. 207 of 24 October 2018, Constitutional Court of the Italian Republic, p. 9, legal reasoning. (*trans. by the author*). Available at: https://www.cortecostituzionale.it/documenti/download/doc/recent_judgments/O207_2018_en.pdf.

[84] For further study, see also (Canestrari 2021; Donini 2016; Padovani 2019; Manna 2019; Marini & Cupelli 2019; Fornasari, Picotti & Vinciguerra 2019; D'Alessandro & Di Giovine 2020; Carnevale 1997).

[85] Constitutional Court (2018) Ordinance No. 207 of 24 October 2018, Constitutional Court of the Italian Republic, pt. 6, legal reasoning. Available at: https://www.cortecostituzionale.it/documenti/download/doc/recent_judgments/O207_2018_en.pdf; Constitutional Court (2019) *Judgment No. 242 of 22 November 2019,* Constitutional Court of the Italian Republic, pt. 2.2, legal reasoning. Available at: https://www.cortecostituzionale.it/documenti/download/doc/recent_judgments/S242_2019_en.pdf.

making it, triggering a *relatio ad alteros* in the face of which the need to respect the good of life comes into relief in its fullness".[86]

Furthermore, even if one considers the individual's right to decide how and when to end one's existence to exist, "this freedom, when it is oriented in the sense of ending one's existence, should in fact be ensured *usque ad vitae supremum exitum*: a view in which the execution of that extreme intention should remain reserved exclusively to the person concerned, so as to ensure the effectiveness of a possible reconsideration until the last moment".[87] The doctrine is divided on this point. According to some, it is essential to provide that the act of ending one's life should be *autonomous* and that therefore the last material conduct directly resulting in death should be performed by the applicant himself. Others, on the other hand, maintain that requiring the last act to be performed by the applicant would exclude all those cases in which the applicant is in a condition to be eligible for medically assisted death, but is in a condition of total immobility, often only able to communicate through the movement of his eyes, and thus giving rise to the paradox whereby the very person who would be most entitled to it would be prevented from dying.

The issue has problematic and in some respects paradoxical implications that could be resolved by the introduction of new technologies capable of combining instruments capable of injecting the lethal drug by mouth movement with the latest *eye-tracking* technologies. In this case, if the patient were unable to make any movement, but at least to communicate through *eye-tracking* systems—in view also of the fact that communication would be necessary in order to express consent anyway—the problem of administering the lethal drug autonomously would remain solely in the case of unconscious patients to whom euthanasia is performed on the basis of a previous request or patients who are deemed unable to understand and validly express their consent. In the latter cases, however, as we shall see in Sect. 3.10, various doubts arise as to the ethical admissibility of euthanasia.

By excluding the criminal relevance of suicide, not considering it necessary to punish the suicidal person even in cases where this was materially possible (as in the case of attempt), the legal system has limited criminal relevance exclusively to external conduct capable of encroaching on the personal sphere of the individual (whether through moral or material sharing). It is precisely from such external influences that the State is called upon to protect the right to life of every individual, especially those in a vulnerable or fragile condition.

The fragile or vulnerable subject is not necessarily mentally ill, mentally deficient, a minor or one whose consent is flawed, but on the contrary, it is undeniable that there are vulnerable and fragile subjects even outside these categories, whose right to

[86] Constitutional Court (2019) Judgment No. 242 of 22 November 2019, Constitutional Court of the Italian Republic, pt. 2, (*trans. by the author*). Available at: https://www.cortecostituzionale.it/documenti/download/doc/recent_judgments/S242_2019_en.pdf.

[87] Constitutional Court (2019) Judgment No. 242 of 22 November 2019, Constitutional Court of the Italian Republic, pt. 2, facts section. (*trans. by the author*). Available at: https://www.cortecostituzionale.it/documenti/download/doc/recent_judgments/S242_2019_en.pdf.

life in the absence of protection even with respect to the expression of their consent, could remain unprotected as well as subject to possible abuse.

In addition to the grounds of inadmissibility on which the Constitutional Court's ruling is based, it is also possible to point out further profiles that may prove useful for the purposes of the analysis in this work.

First of all, the presence of a provision protecting the most vulnerable individuals can be considered necessary for the fulfilment of obligations of an international nature by virtue of the sub-constitutional rank attributed to international treaties in the hierarchy of sources.[88]

According to this argument, the first source of international law to be considered violated in the event of repeal of the rule punishing the murder of consenting persons would be the ECHR. Specifically, Article 2, in stating that "The right to life of every person is protected by law",[89] establishes a positive obligation for each individual state 'not only to refrain from intentionally and unlawfully depriving life, but also to take appropriate measures to safeguard the life of persons subject to its jurisdiction. Generally speaking, this positive obligation has two aspects: (a) the duty to prepare a legal framework; and (b) the obligation to take preventive operational measures'.[90] The partial exclusion of the protection provided by the rules punishing the murder of the person giving consent to it could represent a breach by the State of its positive obligation to provide a legal framework capable of ensuring the protection of the value of life.

Although the case law of the European Court of Human Rights has interpreted Art. 2 ECHR (in conjunction with Art. 8 ECHR) as guaranteeing the right of "each individual to decide by what means and at what point his or her life will end",[91] at the same time it has consistently ruled out the possibility of the existence of a right to obtain from the State or third parties assistance in dying or death itself being interpreted as deriving from Arts. 2, 3 and 8 ECHR.[92]

---

[88] The ratification laws of international treaties—already since the twin judgments of the Cort. Cost. nos. 348 and 349 of 2007—acquire the value of an 'interposed' norm also following the amendment of Art. 6 of the E.U.T. made by the Treaty of Lisbon.

[89] Council of Europe (1950) Convention for the Protection of Human Rights and Fundamental Freedoms (European Convention on Human Rights), Rome, 4 November 1950, Art. 2. Available at: https://www.echr.coe.int/documents/convention_ita.pdf.

[90] European Court of Human Rights (2021) Guide on Article 2 of the European Convention on Human Rights—Right to life. Updated 31 August 2021. Available at: https://www.echr.coe.int/Documents/Guide_Art_2_ENG.pdf.

[91] On all see European Court of Human Rights (2002) Pretty v. the United Kingdom, App. No. 2346/02, Judgment of 29 April 2002. Available at: https://hudoc.echr.coe.int/eng?i=001-60,448.

[92] In a similar vein to *Pretty vs United Kingdom* see European Court of Human Rights (ECtHR) (2011) *Haas v. Switzerland*, Application no. 31322/07, Judgment of 20 January 2011. Available at: https://hudoc.echr.coe.int/eng?i=001-102940; European Court of Human Rights (ECtHR) (2012) *Koch v. Germany*, Application no. 497/09, Judgment of 19 July 2012. Available at: https://hudoc.echr.coe.int/eng?i=001-112282; European Court of Human Rights (ECtHR) (2014) *Gross v. Switzerland*, Application no. 67810/10, Judgment of 14 May 2013 (struck out 2014). Available at: https://hudoc.echr.coe.int/eng?i=001-119703.

In this sense, the exclusion of a regulation punishing homicide of the consenting person, in addition to the potential violation of Art. 2 ECHR, would also risk undermining the right to life as a fundamental human right also affirmed and recognised by Art. 3 of the Universal Declaration of Human Rights,[93] Art. 2 of the Universal Declaration on Bioethics and Human Rights[94] and Art. 10 of the Convention on the Rights of Persons with Disabilities.[95]

3.7 Euthanasia in Southern Mediterranean Countries: The Case of Spain and France

On 18 March 2021, the Spanish Chamber of Deputies definitively approved Bill No. 122/20, later published as Law No. 3/2021 on 24 March,[96] which dictates the general regulation of euthanasia, defining it as a real right to request and obtain the help necessary to die.

Spain, like Italy and Franca, is characterised by a strong Catholic influence. Compared to the Benelux European countries, the debate in the southern Mediterranean is more recent and, as far as Spain is concerned, even predates the well-known Ramón Sampedro Cameán case.[97]

[93] United Nations (1948) Universal Declaration of Human Rights. Adopted by the United Nations General Assembly on 10 December 1948. Available at: https://www.un.org/en/about-us/universal-declaration-of-human-rights.

[94] UNESCO (2005) Universal Declaration on Bioethics and Human Rights. Adopted on 19 October 2005 by the General Conference of UNESCO. Available at: https://unesdoc.unesco.org/ark:/48223/pf0000146180.

[95] United Nations (2006) Convention on the Rights of Persons with Disabilities (CRPD). Adopted by General Assembly resolution 61/106 of 13 December 2006. Available at: https://www.un.org/development/desa/disabilities/convention-on-the-rights-of-persons-with-disabilities.html.

[96] *Ley Orgánica 3/2021, de 24 de marzo, de regulación de la eutanasia.* Spain (2021) Boletín Oficial del Estado [Law on euthanasia] (BOE-A-2021-4628). Available at: https://www.boe.es/eli/es/lo/2021/03/24/3/.

[97] The well-known fisherman, who became a universal symbol thanks to the film Mare dentro, embarked on a long and difficult legal journey in 1993 to obtain recognition of his right to die, after he had been tetraplegic for twenty-nine years due to a serious accident caused by diving into the sea. Faced with the authorities' refusal to grant him a legal path to end his life, Ramón Sampedro organised his own suicide with the help of eleven friends. Each of them carried out actions that, according to Article 143 of the Spanish Penal Code of 1995, did not constitute a crime, as they were not acts 'necessary' to carry out the suicide, as required by the rule for the integration of the crime of cooperation in suicide. After Sampedro's death on 12 January 1998, the Public Prosecutor's Office investigated Ramona Maneiro, but the case was dismissed for lack of evidence. Only after the statute of limitations had expired, during an interview with Telecinco, did the woman confess to having placed the glass with cyanide next to the bed and to having filmed the last moments of Sampedro's life.

On the other hand, the case with an impact comparable to Fabiano Antoniani's was that of María José Carrasco[98] in 2019, following which, also thanks to the weight of public opinion, several bills were brought forward that later merged into *Ley organica* 3/2021.

The Spanish Penal Code of 1928, which came into force in 1929 after Primo de Rivera's coup d'état, introduced important innovations compared to the 1848 legislation on assisted suicide. Article 517 distinguished between 'simple' inducement or assistance (punishable by 4–8 years' imprisonment) and 'executive' inducement, i.e. determining suicide (punishable by 6–15 years). The latter sanction was particularly severe considering that voluntary manslaughter carried a penalty of 8–20 years. However, the second paragraph of Article 517 allowed the judge, assessing circumstances and reasons, to reduce the penalty or even, according to Article 518, to convert it from prison to imprisonment. The Spanish Penal Code of 1944 did not introduce significant changes to the previous discipline. Article 409 punished those who assisted or induced suicide with '*prisión mayor*' and, in cases where the assistance went as far as the execution of the act, with '*reclusión menor*'. This text also lacked a specific provision for the murder of consenting persons, which continued to be assimilated to voluntary manslaughter, following the approach already adopted by the previous penal code.

The doctrinal elaboration had difficulty accepting the possibility of excluding the punishability of a doctor who had caused death even if this had occurred through the administration of narcotics or drugs to soothe pain. Such behaviour was in fact considered contrary to the general principles of medical ethics as well as to the Catholic precepts of the unavailability of life (Cuello Calón 1955).

The patient's condition of absolute suffering and the request for release from it could only be considered as mitigating factors for liability, but the law in force did not provide for any mitigating factor connected with the defendant's status as a doctor. Contrary to the legislation in force at that time, part of the doctrine maintained that the doctor's conduct could not be equated with ordinary homicide by virtue of the special relationship between doctor and patient, which also led to an obvious psychological involvement.

On the other hand, Spain has long been open to passive euthanasia—by virtue of national law 41/2002[99] as well as those specifically enacted by some of the

---

[98] María José Carrasco was a 61-year-old Spanish woman who had suffered from multiple sclerosis for more than 30 years. The disease, degenerative and incurable, had reached a very advanced stage: Carrasco was completely dependent, bedridden, unable to move or take care of herself, and lived in constant pain. In spite of everything, she maintained full mental lucidity, and had long expressed her determination to end her suffering by requesting euthanasia. With no legal access to euthanasia in Spain, in April 2019 María José's husband, Ángel Hernández, decided to help her die at their home in Madrid, recording the entire process on video with his wife's consent. In the footage, Hernández repeatedly asks María José if she is sure of her decision and if she wishes to end her life, and following repeated firm affirmative answers, he administers a lethal substance to her, under sedation, self-reporting to the police.

[99] *Ley 41/2002, de 14 de noviembre, básica reguladora de la autonomía del paciente y de derechos y obligaciones en materia de información y documentación clínica.* Spain (2002)

seventeen Autonomous Communities—which equates the phenomenologically active conduct of interrupting medical treatment with an omissive conduct for which, if the request to interrupt or not to start medical treatment comes from the patient, no criminal liability can be ascribed to the doctor or health personnel.

Gimbernat Ordeig (1987) argued that in cases where the patient is close to death and in the grip of unbearable suffering, the euthanasia practice is not only permitted by virtue of a state of necessity of the subject to defend the individual's dignity and his ideological freedom, but even that keeping him alive forcibly could be considered a real violation of his rights if not inhuman treatment.

Spanish legislation too, going beyond the traditionalist conception of the unavailability of human life, has disassociated the assessment of the lawfulness of euthanasia from the evaluation of the type of conduct carried out by the third party but has linked it directly to the patient's fulfilment of certain requirements.

The new Spanish law is characterised by its openness towards active euthanasia practices by qualifying it as a true individual right. Article 1[100] states that the aim of the law is to regulate the right of each person who meets the required conditions to request and receive help in dying.

The existence of a genuine individual right to die is one of the most debated issues in doctrine. The reconstruction of the ECtHR has always excluded that the protection of Article 2 in conjunction with Article 8 of the Convention could be interpreted as guaranteeing the right to die on the part of the patient. In contrast, the Spanish legislation establishes a real right, under certain conditions, to obtain help in dying. The use of the expression *help in dying* overcomes the dichotomy between euthanasia and assistance to suicide in that it focuses on the result, the objective, namely death, with the intention of rendering the right effective regardless of the type of conduct capable of ensuring the protection invoked.

Despite this, doctrine has always been divided. According to some reconstructions, even recognising the right to die by means of a request to interrupt life-support treatment, which in most cases involves the intervention of medical personnel, means implicitly

---

Boletín Oficial del Estado (BOE-A-2002-22188). [Law 41/2002, of 14 November, Basic Law Regulating Patient Autonomy and Rights and Obligations in Matters of Clinical Information and Documentation]. Available at: https://www.boe.es/buscar/act.php?id=BOE-A-2002-22188; as amended by Spain (2010) *Ley Orgánica 2/2010, de salud sexual y reproductiva y de la interrupción voluntaria del embarazo.* Boletín Oficial del Estado (BOE-A-2010-3514). [Organic Law 2/2010 on Sexual and Reproductive Health and Voluntary Termination of Pregnancy] Available at: https://www.boe.es/buscar/doc.php?id=BOE-A-. Spain (2011) *Ley 33/2011, General de Salud Pública.* [Law 33/2011, General Public Health Law] Boletín Oficial del Estado (BOE-A-2011-15623). Available at: https://www.boe.es/buscar/doc.php?id=BOE-A-2011-15623.

[100] Ley Organica: Art. 1: "*El objeto de esta Ley es regular el derecho que corresponde a toda persona que cumpla las condiciones exigidas a solicitar y recibir la ayuda necesaria para morir*" [The purpose of this Law is to regulate the right of any person who meets the required conditions to request and receive the necessary assistance to die] art. 4 "*Se reconoce el derecho de toda persona que cumpla los requisitos previstos en esta Ley a solicitar y recibir la prestación de ayuda para morir*" [Every person who meets the requirements set out in this Law is recognised to have the right to request and receive the provision of assistance in dying] (*trans. by the author*).

recognising the right to die (Donini 2019). According to a certain point of view, in terms of disvalue, interrupting the operation of a respirator by injecting an anaesthetic while waiting for the onset of death or an immediately lethal dose would only become relevant in terms of the time between the administration of the drug and death.

If such a right were allowed, among other things, it would be endowed with maximum constitutional coverage as an expression of the right to self-determination and the protection of human dignity as a fundamental right.

The requirements of Art. 5 of the Spanish euthanasia law are as follows: (a) to have Spanish citizenship or legal residence in Spain, or a certificate of registry registration (*empadronamiento*) attesting to a permanence in Spanish territory of more than twelve months; to be of age and to be capable and aware at the time of the request; (b) to have available in writing the information available on their medical process, on the different alternatives and possibilities of intervention, including that of access to integral palliative care included in the common health services and the benefits provided by the legislation on assistance for non-self-sufficiency (c) having formulated two requests, voluntarily and in writing (or by another means enabling them to be documented), which are not the result of any external pressure, maintaining an interval of at least fifteen calendar days between each request; if the doctor in charge considers that the loss of the patient's capacity to provide informed consent is imminent, he/she may accept a shorter interval, deemed appropriate on the basis of the clinical circumstances, of which he/she must leave a record in the medical record (d) suffer from a serious and incurable illness or severe, chronic and disabling suffering, within the terms established by this law, certified by the doctor in charge; (e) give informed consent before receiving aid in dying. This consent shall be incorporated into the patient's medical record.

A particularly important element concerns the equivalence in terms of the right to request and obtain assistance in dying recognised in the definitions in Article 3 between physical suffering and psychic suffering. Well, the reference to psychic suffering, the afflictive value of which certainly cannot be disregarded, would probably merit greater procedural caution. This will be discussed at length in paragraph (3.10).

A final element that should be emphasised is the Spanish legislature's failure to provide that a patient who claims the right to be helped to die must be kept alive or require life-support treatment. This conclusion moves even further away from the requirements identified by Italian jurisprudence by moving towards a greater enhancement of the right to self-determination in order to protect one's dignity, while maintaining a procedural control that guarantees the permanence of the State's duty to protect the most vulnerable citizens.

In France, the discipline of euthanasia has undergone a complex development, marked by a progressive opening towards the right to die with dignity, while maintaining a clear distinction between active euthanasia and other end-of-life practices. On 27 May 2025, for the first time in history, the lower house of Parliament approved a bill on assisted dying, which will have to be passed in the Senate to become law.[101]

[101] See https://www.assemblee-nationale.fr/dyn/17/textes/l17b1100_proposition-loi?.

It is notable that the bill, as approved, does not provide for the patient to be in a condition requiring life-support treatment. Furthermore, it equates the condition of physical suffering with that of mental suffering. In addition, the legislation under consideration by the Senate does not differentiate between assisted suicide and euthanasia, acknowledging that in cases where the patient is unable or unwilling to self-administer the procedure, the physician is responsible for performing the act.

The most significant turning point in French regulatory evolution came with Law No 2005-370 of 22 April 2005, known as the *Loi Leonetti*, which introduced the right for patients to refuse medical treatment, including the use of therapeutic obstinacy, recognising the possibility of proceeding with deep and continuous sedation under certain conditions. This was followed by Law No 2016-87 of 2 February 2016 (*Loi Claeys-Leonetti*), which strengthened the protection of informed consent and formally established the right to deep and continuous sedation until death, in the event that the patient is in the terminal phase and is subject to suffering refractory to any treatment. In terms of case law, the French Court of Cassation and the *Conseil d'État* have played a central role in defining the limits of the legitimacy of end-of-life practices. Of particular importance was the Lambert case[102] defined by a ruling of the *Conseil d'État*[103] that recognised the possibility of interrupting life-support treatment for a patient in a permanent vegetative state, in application of the patient's previously expressed will and the medical assessment of his condition. The case also gave rise to a ruling by the European Court of Human Rights[104] that confirmed the compatibility of French legislation with Article 2 ECHR.

French doctrine, while expressing diversified positions, has largely recognised the importance of consent as the basis of the legitimacy of end-of-life practices, valuing the principle of patient autonomy and dignity. However, there has been no lack of criticism of the persistent ban on active euthanasia, judged by some authors as an incoherent denial of personal freedom, especially in situations of extreme and irreversible suffering. This is the context for the current debate on the proposed law

---

[102] Vincent Lambert was a French psychiatric nurse who became minimally conscious following a car accident in 2008. He was unable to communicate or perform significant voluntary acts and was artificially fed and hydrated via a gastric tube, although he did not need a respirator. In 2013, the doctor in charge of Vincent's care considered this to be a case of futile treatment and proposed the interruption of artificial nutrition, in accordance with the French law of 2005 (Loi Leonetti), which allows for the suspension of treatment in cases of unreasonable obstinacy. However, Lambert's parents, practising Catholics, strongly opposed this and started a long court battle to prevent the suspension of treatment. On the contrary, Lambert's wife and part of his siblings argued that Vincent would not want to continue living in that state. After a long legal battle, the case ended with the suspension of life-support treatment and Vincent's death only in 2019.

[103] *Conseil d'État* (2014) *Assemblée*, Decision No. 375081 of 24 June 2014 (Mme Lambert and others). Recueil Lebon. Available at: [Legifrance—CE 24 juin 2014, No 375081] https://www.legifrance.gouv.fr/ceta/id/CETATEXT000029141099/.

[104] European Court of Human Rights (2015) *Lambert and Others v. France*, Grand Chamber, Application no. 46043/14, Judgment of 5 June 2015. Available at: https://hudoc.echr.coe.int/eng?i=001-155352.

allowing controlled forms of active euthanasia or medically assisted suicide, in the wake of what has happened in other European legal systems. The bill currently under consideration in Parliament is in line with the opinion of the *Conseil Consultatif National d'Èthique* (CCNE), which for the first time opened up this possibility, recognising that the current law no longer fully responded to the plurality of social and moral demands expressed by contemporary French society.

3.8 The Judgment of 26 February 2020 by the German Federal Constitutional *Court* (*Bundesverfassungsgericht*)

We have so far observed through which arguments and by which steps the legalisation of euthanasia has been achieved in some Benelux countries as well as in the most important Catholic-based countries of the southern Mediterranean.

To conclude this brief comparative excursus, it is interesting to deal, albeit briefly, with the German case, which is quite distinct from the previous ones.

German law has also been influenced by case law. In particular, the Federal Constitutional Court (*Bundesverfassungsgericht*)[105] in its judgment No. 26 February 2020 affirmed a genuine right to die based on the protection of human dignity and the right to free development of the personality.

Prior to 2015, when Section 217 was introduced into the German Criminal Code with the aim of punishing professionalised assisting and abetting of suicide, there was no provision in Germany punishing those who helped others in dying. Following the reform, anyone who assisted others in dying through a recurrent activity, excluding relatives or close persons, was punished with imprisonment of up to three years. The introduction of this particular legislation obviously restricted the possibility of even medical personnel participating in the activity of aiding in dying unless they risked criminal prosecution. For this reason, people who wanted to die in a dignified way, under the supervision of qualified staff, and in a way that corresponded with their view of human dignity, often had to travel to Switzerland. This constraint forced individuals to take unusual routes to take leave of life termed *institutional mercilessness* (Hufen 2018, p. 1524). Following several appeals raising the question of the unconstitutionality of Art. 217, the German Federal Constitutional Court pronounced a historic ruling that introduced the individual right to die into German law for the first time (Göken and Zwießler 2022, pp. 661–671).

The argument put forward by the legislature, which was refuted by the constitutional body's ruling, was based on the assumption that suicide requests come in all cases from sick people without hope and that therefore the decision to ask to die can never really be autonomous (Gaede 2016). The introduction of suicide assistance within the national

[105] Federal Constitutional Court (Germany) (2020) Judgment of 26 February 2020—Right to a self-determined death, Case No. 2 BvR 2347/15. Available at: https://www.bundesverfassungsgericht.de/e/rs20200226_2bvr234715en.html.

health service risked that assisted suicide would be understood as a recurrent practice dangerously affecting people's free will and decisions (Roxin 2016).

The German court, on the other hand, admitted that the general right to the free development of one's personality includes the decision on how to end one's life and this is directly incorporated into the concept of the protection of human dignity. This entails the right to seek help from third parties and, to the extent that this help is offered, to avail oneself of it. According to the German court it is therefore not necessary to make the possibility of requesting help in dying subject to further requirements or material elements but "The right to a self-determined death as an expression of personal freedom is not limited to externally defined situations. The right of disposal over one's own life [. . .] is in particular not limited to serious or incurable illnesses or certain phases of life and illness" (Sachs 2020, p. 580) and, therefore, "does not require any explanation or justification".[106]

The German court broadens the interpretation of the right to self-determination to include the right to dispose of one's own life, identifying as a requirement only that the individual is capable of making free and conscious decisions. The conception of the dignity and meaningfulness of one's own existence is therefore the prerogative of the individual free from any assessment of motives. The Court, hoping for a legislative regulation of the matter, stated that the requirements for access to a self-determined death are not material but refer exclusively to the assessment of the seriousness and permanence of the suicidal will.

The right to develop one's personality autonomously entails not only the possibility of growth and expansion but also the possibility of stopping this process. Suicide, lacking material requirements, risks at the same time becoming ordinary and turning the right to life into a right on life.[107]

In this perspective, too, the slippery slope argument impressively returns. The normalisation of suicide as a way of taking leave of life could risk making the very weakest and most vulnerable people perceive that the identification of material requirements would aim to protect, a sort of social imperative or inducement to die.[108] According to some critics of the judgment, it did not take into account some significant data that would demonstrate a social tendency to habituate suicide as an ordinary mode of leave from existence taken from Switzerland where the number of suicides has doubled in the last 5 years or from the Dutch case where it has tripled in the last 10 years (Berghäuser et al. 2020, pp. 207–211).

The Court's decision was, of course, subjected to a number of criticisms, one of the main ones being that 90% of successful suicides in Germany were due to psychological disorders, casting doubt on the real self-determination of those who resorted to them (Spittler 2020, pp. 97–99).

---

[106] Federal Constitutional Court (Germany) (2020) Judgment of 26 February 2020—Right to a self-determined death, Case No. 2 BvR 2347/15, para 210. (*trans. by the author*) Available at: https://www.bundesverfassungsgericht.de/e/rs20200226_2bvr234715en.html.

[107] One could say that this consists with Promethean pride in refusing to owe anything, even oneself, to others, or in owing everything, even oneself, to oneself (Anders, 2003).

[108] This conclusion would be supported by the Dutch experience.

The common element in all the pronouncements and all the legislation seems to be the existence of the informed consent of the person and of a firm will to take leave of life to guarantee the existence of which the Court also identified the request for assistance to professional associations. The Court's choice seems to be that of deciding *in dubium pro vita* (Göken and Zwießler 2022) while providing for the prohibition of any form of commercialisation of suicide based on the prohibition of profiting from the death of others, but without taking into account that assisted suicide is evolving from "last resort in preventing a terrible death" to "a way out of a terrible life" (Berghäuser et al. 2020, p. 210).

The Court's reasoning[109] marks a clear break with the jurisprudence of the European countries analysed, and while it is in line with the supranational jurisprudence of the ECtHR, which recognises a wide margin of appreciation for the member States, it would probably merit harmonisation activities by the German legislature in order to counteract the tendency to take the slippery slope that seems to emerge from the analysis of older European experiences.

3.9 The European Court of Human Rights (ECtHR) and the Right to Assisted Dying

In order to fully analyse the path of argumentation that has supported some EU member states in making euthanasia and assisted suicide legal and others in maintaining the prohibition on the practice, it may be useful to refer to some of the most relevant case law precedents of the European Court of Human Rights also in order to verify whether conclusions can be drawn from the Court's pronouncements regarding the existence of a right to die with dignity.

Most of the plaintiffs turned to the European Court of Human Rights raising a claim for protection of their right to a dignified death and refusal of degrading treatment as complementary to their right to life affirmed by Article 2 ECHR.[110]

The plaintiffs argued that the right to life includes the right to interrupt the suffering resulting from an illness by means of a medically assisted euthanasia procedure, or at least that the mere prohibition of medical treatment to assist in dying conflicted with the right to life.

The best-known case in the jurisprudence of the European Court of Human Rights is certainly *Pretty v. United Kingdom.*[111]

---

[109] For an in-depth discussion see (Colaianni, 2020).

[110] Art. 2. Council of Europe (1950) Convention for the Protection of Human Rights and Fundamental Freedoms (European Convention on Human Rights), Rome, 4 November 1950. Available at: https://www.echr.coe.int/documents/convention_eng.pdf.

[111] European Court of Human Rights (2002) *Pretty v. United Kingdom*, Application No. 2346/02, Judgment of 29 April 2002. Available at: https://hudoc.echr.coe.int/eng?i=001-60448.

Diane Pretty was a woman suffering from amyotrophic lateral sclerosis (ALS) in its terminal phase; a disease for which no cure is available and which increasingly weakens the patient's muscles until they become immobile and cause death, often by suffocation. Despite the serious consequences on the body, the patient does not lose his or her capacity to make decisions.

Mrs Pretty had asked the British government to grant her husband criminal immunity if he helped her to die. The authorities refused.

In the appeal to the Court it was argued that Articles 2, 3, 8, 9 and 14 of the ECHR[112] had been violated in that respect for one's individual freedom also included the right to decide how and when to die, and that preventing this choice amounted to restricting human dignity. In the applicant's view, the prohibition on assisted suicide imposed unnecessary and cruel suffering, forcing her to undergo unbearable physical deterioration with no way out or possibility of improvement. Furthermore, she considered that the law, by preventing her from accessing suicide assistance, which would theoretically be possible for those physically capable of taking their own life, discriminated against persons with severe disabilities such as hers.

The Court dismissed the appeal, stating that there is no right to assisted suicide protected by the Convention.

While recognising that the decision on one's own death falls within the scope of the right to respect for private life, the Court found it legitimate for the State to prohibit suicide assistance as an expression of its duty to preserve life and protect the vulnerable.

It also made it clear that the right to life cannot be interpreted as a right to die, that the suffering caused by illness is not equated with inhuman treatment imputable to the state, and that there is no discrimination between persons capable or unable to commit suicide independently. Similarly, freedom of conscience does not include the right to act contrary to criminal law.

In conclusion, the Court held that the State's refusal to authorise assisted suicide did not constitute a violation of the Convention.

A little less than 10 years later, the Court affirmed again in *Haas v. Switzerland*[113] that end-of-life choices are in any case covered by Article 8 of the ECHR but that even in the case of *Ernst Haas* this did not entail a duty on the part of the State to actively provide the means for suicide outside the prescribed procedures.

Switzerland, in fact, already allowed assisted suicide following a medical prescription in 2011 with the legitimate aim of protecting people from hasty decisions or abuse, particularly with the use of dangerous substances.

---

[112] Article 2: right to life (also understood as the right to decide when and how to die) Article 3: prohibition of inhuman or degrading treatment; Article 8: right to respect for private and family life (including the right to self-determination); Article 9: freedom of thought and conscience; Article 14: prohibition of discrimination (with respect to persons capable of committing suicide on their own).

[113] European Court of Human Rights (2011) *Haas v. Switzerland*, Application No. 31322/07, Judgment of 20 January 2011. Available at: https://hudoc.echr.coe.int/eng?i=001-102,940.

Haas, however, despite having requested sodium pentobarbital from his doctors who refused the prescription, turned to the cantonal and federal authorities after twice attempting to commit suicide in order to obtain the drug without a prescription, but all applications were denied as they did not meet the requirements of the criminal law.

According to the plaintiff, the State's refusal violated his right to respect for private life, including the freedom to decide how and when to die. The Court recognised that the right to self-determination at the end of life falls under Article 8 of the Convention, but stated that this right does not impose a positive obligation on states to provide or facilitate access to lethal substances. Switzerland, according to the Court, acted lawfully by imposing control rules (such as prescription), with the aim of protecting vulnerable people and preventing abuse. There was therefore no violation of the Convention: the State, while admitting assisted suicide, retains a wide margin of appreciation in regulating the modalities, in particular to ensure that the decision is free, conscious and not the result of treatable or temporary suffering.

A different case law was reached by the Court following the case *Gross v. Switzerland.*[114] In the Gross case, the applicant was an elderly woman who wished to end her own life, although she was not suffering from a clinically diagnosed illness. Her motivation was the fear of facing an ageing process that she found humiliating and degrading. Although she had been deemed fit and able by a psychiatrist, no doctor wanted to prescribe the lethal drug she requested. After several refusals, the direct request to the state was also rejected. Gross appealed to the European Court of Human Rights, complaining that the Swiss authorities had violated her right to privacy by preventing her from deciding how and when she should die.

In May 2013, the Chamber of the Court ruled by a majority that there had been a violation of Article 8, noting that the Swiss law on assistance to suicide was not sufficiently clear. However, the case was referred to the Grand Chamber at the request of the Swiss government.

In the meantime, Ms. Gross had procured the drug and taken her own life in November 2011, before the case was finally heard, without informing either her own lawyer or the Court. When the government learned of her death, it raised a preliminary objection for abuse of the individual right to appeal. The Grand Chamber, in its judgment of 30 September 2014, upheld this exception, noting that Gross had intentionally concealed his death in order to avoid the interruption of the proceedings. Accordingly, it declared the appeal inadmissible on the ground of abuse of rights (Article 35 §§ 3(a) and 4 ECHR). The 2013 Chamber judgment, as it was not yet final, lost all legal value but remained useful for argumentative purposes in any case.

In *Lambert and Others v. France* (Grand Chamber judgment, 5 June 2015), the applicants were the parents, sister and half-brother of Vincent Lambert, a man

---

[114] European Court of Human Rights (2014) Gross v. Switzerland, Application No. 67810/10, Judgment of 14 May 2013. Available at: https://hudoc.echr.coe.int/eng?i=001-119,703.

quadriplegic and in an irreversible vegetative state following a serious car accident in 2008. They challenged the decision of the *French Conseil d'État*, which on 24 June 2014 had ruled that the treating doctor's decision to suspend Lambert's artificial nutrition and hydration, on the basis of a medical report drawn up by three specialists, was lawful, causing his death. According to the plaintiff family members, that decision violated Article 2 of the European Convention on Human Rights, i.e. the right to life.

The ECHR, however, ruled that the implementation of that decision would not constitute a violation of Article 2. Indeed, it recognised that, in the field of end-of-life, there is no unambiguous European consensus on the interruption of life-sustaining treatment, and that states must therefore be granted a wide margin of appreciation. In particular, it held that the French law of 22 April 2005—as interpreted by the *Conseil d'État*—provided a sufficiently clear and precise legal framework to regulate medical decisions in complex situations such as that of lambert. The Court emphasised that the proceedings at national level had been meticulous and thorough, involving several levels of jurisdiction, medical experts and ethical authorities. Furthermore, the Court reiterated that it was primarily up to the national authorities to ascertain the patient's wishes and the compatibility of the decision with domestic and conventional law.

An important element in the Lambert case is the conflict between the members of Lambert's family: on the one hand his wife, in favour of stopping treatment; on the other hand his parents, opposed for religious reasons (they were observant Catholics) and convinced that this choice constituted a violation of the right to life. Although the case formally concerned the suspension of life-sustaining treatment and not directly palliative sedation or the administration of euthanasia, the Lambert judgment also gained relevance in the debate on the interpretation of the right to death under the Convention. The Court found, in each case, that the decision-making process had been fair, transparent and respectful of fundamental rights, thus rejecting the family's appeal. The Court identified three basic requirements to determine whether Article 2 of the Convention was respected: First, the Court must ascertain whether a functional legal framework exists; second, it must take into account the will of the individual together with the opinion of medical professionals; third, it will assess whether this legal framework allows recourse to the courts in case of doubts as to whether the interests of the patient are respected. In the present case, it was assessed that the French legal system ensured compliance with the above criteria and that the decision of the Council of State therefore complied with Article 2 of the Convention.

More recently, two other pronouncements can be considered useful in order to reconstruct the interpretative structure of European end-of-life jurisprudence, the *Mortier v. Belgium* case of 2022 and the *Daniel Karsai v. Hungary* case of 2024.

The first case concerns the euthanasia of a woman suffering from chronic mental suffering, which was carried out without the children—the applicant and his sister—being informed. The mother had expressly requested that they not be involved, despite the fact that doctors had advised her several times to do so. The applicant alleged that the Belgian State had failed to adequately guarantee the mother's life, since—according to the applicant—all the procedural guarantees provided for by the euthanasia law had not been respected, and that there had been no proper investigation after the death.

The Court made it clear that the case did not concern the right to euthanasia per se, but the compatibility of the procedure followed with the ECHR. It therefore concluded that there had been no violation of Article 2 ECHR due to incompatibility with Belgian law: the legislation was sufficiently clear and respectful of the protection of life, and the act itself had been carried out in compliance with the established rules.

However, the Court recognised a violation of Article 2 from a procedural point of view, as the post-euthanasia monitoring system did not guarantee sufficient independence (in particular, the Federal Evaluation Commission had not been considered impartial) and the criminal investigation had lasted beyond the prescribed time. The Court also found that there was no violation of Article 8 as the doctors had acted in compliance with the patient's wishes, confidentiality rules and ethical guidelines.

In the second case, Daniel Karsai, suffering from advanced amyotrophic lateral sclerosis (ALS), claimed the right to decide when and how to die, before the disease degenerated irreversibly. Since he could not commit suicide by virtue of his disease, anyone who helped him would risk criminal prosecution. Karsai complained of a violation of his right to privacy and discrimination against terminally ill patients kept alive by life-support treatment who can refuse life-saving treatment.

However, the Court ruled that there had been no violation of the invoked articles. It pointed out that, despite a growing trend towards the legalisation of medically assisted suicide, most Council of Europe states still prohibit it, and that the issue raises serious social and ethical implications, including risks of error and abuse. It therefore granted Hungary a wide margin of appreciation, finding that the state had not exceeded the bounds of discretion in banning suicide assistance.

The Court also emphasised the ongoing social and regulatory changes in Europe, and reiterated the importance of access to high-quality palliative care, including palliative sedation and effective pain management, which, according to the experts, was available in Hungary and capable of ensuring a dignified death. Finally, it considered that the difference between refusing life-sustaining treatment and asking to be helped to die was justified, since only the first option is recognised as necessary as an international medical and ethical consensus affirmed among others in the Oviedo Convention.[115]

In the cases of which we have just outlined the salient features, it is possible to find some similarities in the arguments. First is the attempt to argue that the right to terminate one's life can be derived from a broad interpretation of Article 2 of the

[115] Council of Europe (1997) Convention for the Protection of Human Rights and Dignity of the Human Being with regard to the Application of Biology and Medicine: Convention on Human Rights and Biomedicine, Oviedo, 4 April 1997. Available at: https://rm.coe.int/168007cf98.

ECHR which enshrines the right to life. The appellants argued that the State's obligation to protect the absolute value of life applied to attacks by third parties, but not to those resulting from an individual's own free choice. In the context of the right of human beings to be free from inhuman or degrading treatment, as enshrined in Article 3 of the European Convention on Human Rights (ECHR), the applicants attempted to derive an obligation to stop an individual's suffering in any event, even by reason of an illness, from the positive obligation to avoid such treatment (e.g. torture).

In both cases, the Court concluded that attempts to broadly interpret the aforementioned obligations could not extend to encompass the right to state intervention to protect life or avoid degrading treatment by ending one's life.

Finally, virtually all of the applicants argued that the prohibition of medically assisted death also included a violation of Article 8, which establishes the right to protection of private and family life, interpreted to mean that conduct that has no impact other than on the person requesting and implementing it should be permitted on the basis of the autonomy and right to self-determination conferred by that article. There would be nothing more intimate and private than an individual's choice as to how to take leave of life.

On the contrary, the Court has shown that in addition to the literal predictions of certain possible interactions of states with private life, e.g. for the purpose of protecting public safety, public health and economic welfare, legislative interventions by member states with the purpose of placing limits on private autonomy find meaning precisely within the duty under Article 2 ECHR.

Indeed, the obligation to protect human life requires states to endeavour to protect the weakest and most vulnerable individuals, always with wide margins of appreciation as to the modalities also in virtue of the moral inclinations of their citizens. Indeed, considering that the desire to die materialises in situations of suffering, illness, solitude and therefore extreme weakness and vulnerability, the protection mechanisms adopted by the Member States find their justification precisely in these reasons.

In essence, the Court distinguishes between the patient's right to refuse any medical treatment or life-support in the context of the right to self-determination, even if this leads to death, and the patient's right to obtain from the State assistance in dying. In fact, while the former can be interpreted as a real obligation of the Member States towards their citizens, in the latter, the margin of appreciation of each State is greater, since the right to life is considered to prevail over the right to self-determination and private life, which is why the overturning of the hierarchical scale of values may find reasons in specific situations whose occurrence may be assessed exclusively by the member States.[116]

[116] For further discussion see Cohen & Hortensius (2018).

3.10 Are We on a Slippery Slope? The Koffie Case in the Dutch Supreme Court

As we have seen in the preceding paragraphs, in most cases legislative innovations are followed by the occurrence of concrete cases settled by case law. There are several jurisprudential cases as a result of which the legal system of European states has evolved. Emblematic are the Lambert (Casonato 2015) and Cappato cases (Razzano 2019; Poggi 2020) in France and Italy, which sparked debate a few years ago and perhaps led to the promulgation of the first euthanasia laws.

At the same time, while the general legitimacy of euthanasia and assistance to suicide is being debated in the rest of Europe, the Dutch Supreme Court, the first country in the world to have made it legal with a law promulgated in 2002, has excluded—with the well-known 'Koffie' judgement[117]—the punishability of a doctor who had practised euthanasia on a patient suffering from Alzheimer's disease, and therefore deemed not to be of sound mind, after having sedated her without her knowledge and without taking into account her actual will, since she had made a written declaration years earlier in which she had asked for euthanasia in the event of her future incapacity.

It is necessary to premise, in order to outline more clearly why it may be useful to deal specifically with this case, that the problematic elements of the application of the Dutch euthanasia law in execution of an earlier written request—provided for in section 2 of the Dutch euthanasia law[118] (Wtl)—arise mainly when the patient on whom euthanasia is practised is suffering from a mental disease and especially when there is a conflict between the advance request for euthanasia and the actual will.

It should be noted that the imprecise locution mental disease—which deliberately does not distinguish between psychiatric, neurodegenerative and psychic illnesses—will be used to indicate all those pathological states that directly or indirectly affect the individual's capacity to make decisions without resulting in a consequent and relevant functional or bodily limitation.

In order to be able to delve deeper into the question of the relationship between an advance request for euthanasia in the case of mental disease and the contrast between this and the applicant's current wishes, it is worth analysing in detail the case resolved by the Supreme Court of the Netherlands in judgment No. 19/04910

---

[117] Hoge Raad (2020) *Judgment of 21 April 2020, No. 19/04910 CW*. ECLI NL HR 2020:712. Supreme Court of the Netherlands. Available at: https://uitspraken.rechtspraak.nl/inziendocument?id=ECLI:NL:HR:2020:712.

[118] *Wet toetsing levensbeëindiging op verzoek en hulp bij zelfdoding* [Termination of life on request and assisted suicide law] Art. 2, c. 2: "If the patient aged sixteen or over is no longer capable of expressing his or her wishes, but before reaching that state has been deemed capable of a reasonable assessment of his or her interests in this regard and has submitted a written statement containing a request for termination of life, which has been completed, the physician may comply with this request. The duties of care set out in the first paragraph shall apply mutatis mutandis" (*trans. by the author*).

of 21 April 2020. The case arose out of an appeal by Attorney General *Jos Silvis* against a ruling by the District Court of The Hague, which found a geriatric doctor not guilty of euthanasia in the case of a patient suffering from Alzheimer's disease, as the patient had made a written declaration in which she had requested euthanasia in advance in the event that she had reached such a state of health that she had lost her capacity to understand and to be admitted to a nursing home.

Specifically, immediately after being diagnosed with Alzheimer's disease, the patient drew up an advance euthanasia declaration[119] (AED), requesting euthanasia when she felt her quality of life was too low. After being forced into a nursing home, her living conditions fluctuated between brief periods of well-being, primarily in the mornings and during visits from her relatives and husband, and periods of profound distress characterised by insomnia and outbursts of anger towards the nursing home staff.[120]

In any case, when asked if he wanted to be euthanised, he replied, 'Not yet; it's not that bad' (Miller et al. 2019, p. 3). On the day of the euthanasia—and this is the most controversial element of the case, from which the name 'Koffie' (coffee) derives—the doctor, in order to avoid the patient's resistance during the execution of the euthanasia, first administered a sedative in her coffee, without her knowledge, and then injected her with the lethal drug with the help of her relatives who prevented her from moving and getting out of bed.

Despite this, the doctor who performed the euthanasia was found not guilty by both The Hague Tribunal and the Supreme Court. Unlike the Dutch *Euthanasia Review Committee* (RTE) and the Attorney General's Office, they considered that the requirements for diligence set out in Dutch euthanasia legislation had been met. Compliance with these requirements means that the doctor cannot be punished.[121]

As we have seen, the Dutch End of Life and Assisted Suicide Act (Wtl) provides, in fact, for the exclusion of the punishability of the doctor who has performed euthanasia if the latter has complied with the criteria of diligence laid down in Article 2(1).[122] At the same time, subsection 2 provides that the doctor may also take into consideration and execute a written request for euthanasia

[119] The patient's statement was as follows: "I would like to use the legal right to be given voluntary euthanasia, when I think the time is right. I do not want to be placed in a nursing home for elderly people with dementia. I want to say goodbye to my loved ones in a timely and dignified manner. My mother in her time had been in a nursing home for 12 years before she died, so I have close experience of it. I know what I am talking about. I definitely do not want to experience this, it has traumatised me severely and really saddened the whole family. Trusting, that when the quality of my life is so low, that at my request euthanasia will be performed" (Asscher and van de Vathorst, 2020, pp. 71–75).

[120] For a timely account of every detail of the case, see Miller et al. (2019, pp. 84–89).

[121] The requirements for diligence that were not met according to the RTE related to the voluntariness and sufficient weighting of the request and the necessary implementation through compliance with the principles of medical activity (Miller et al. 2019, p. 4).

[122] Art.1 *Wet toetsing levensbeëindiging op verzoek en hulp bij zelfdoding* [Act on Termination of Life on Demand and Suicide Assistance] Netherlands (2020) Available at: https://wetten.overheid.nl/BWBR0012410/2020-03-19.

received from a patient over the age of sixteen who is currently incapacitated if, at the time of the request, he or she is considered to be capable of understanding and aware of his or her request, provided that the requirements of subsection 1 apply *mutatis mutandis.*

Well, one of the most problematic issues is the possibility, which seems to have been recognised by the Dutch Supreme Court, of performing euthanasia even against the currently manifested will and despite the unconsciousness of the patient, who is considered to be no longer capable of understanding. In analysing the various pronouncements made so far, as well as the various arguments put forward by the doctrine, one element is common to all: the need for the person requesting help to die to express an informed, free, conscious, current and explicit request.

Our intention is not to limit ourselves to analysing the Dutch case, but rather to use it as a starting point to explore some relevant ethical and philosophical questions.

In order to pronounce the doctor's non-punishability, the Dutch Supreme Court focuses its attention on the recurrence—*mutatis mutandis*—of the same requirements of diligence as provided for in paragraph 1 of Art. 2 Wtl, without it mattering whether the causes of the patient's present incapacity include mental disease. Obviously, the Court clarifies, in order to be able to execute a previous written request for euthanasia, it is appropriate to exclude any doubt as to the patient's present capacity; the fact that the latter is able to express himself verbally does not prevent the doctor from carrying out an assessment as to his capacity in any event.

According to the Court, the doctor must ascertain that the patient's current situation corresponds to what is envisaged in the written request for euthanasia and that the stated conditions are actually fulfilled. To do so, it is necessary to analyse the content of the request considering not only the literal text, but also the patient's intentions and all the circumstances of the case. Substantial ambiguities may hinder the execution of the request, but not every slightest contradiction is relevant. The written declaration must explicitly provide for euthanasia in the case of advanced dementia that prevents the expression of one's future wishes. If the patient wishes euthanasia even in the absence of unbearable physical suffering, he or she must make it clear that he or she considers the suffering resulting from the dementia itself intolerable. It is therefore essential that the doctor carefully assesses the current clinical situation and compares it with what is indicated in the advance request.[123]

The relationship between the will previously manifested by the patient in the written declaration and the will manifested when euthanasia was performed is one of the most problematic elements of the ruling.

[123] Hoge Raad (2020) Judgment of 21 April 2020, No. 19/04910 CW. ECLI NL HR 2020:712. para. 4.5.2. Supreme Court of the Netherlands. Available at: https://uitspraken.rechtspraak.nl/inziendocument?id=ECLI:NL:HR:2020:712.

On this point, the Dutch Minister of Health, in a memorandum addressed to the President of the House of Representatives of the Parliament, had already raised the question of the cases in which the will of a patient who has expressed his or her written request for euthanasia in advance and who has meanwhile become incapacitated, may or may not be considered to be current when the conditions indicated in the written request are fulfilled and, above all, in cases in which the patient's behaviour or outward expressions are no longer in line with what is written in the declaration. Indeed, it is not insignificant if the patient, having become incapacitated, expresses himself in a sense contrary to the execution of euthanasia, since there is no certainty, the memorandum states, that the patient, even if the conditions indicated in the declaration were to be fulfilled, would still be in favour of ending his own life.

Well, the problem seems to have been resolved by the Court in the sense of excluding the relevance of the current will expressed by the patient who has become incapacitated. At the time of verifying the conditions set out in the written request, it would appear that the patient loses the right to modify their request, and consequently the right to their own life. According to the Court, since the patient no longer has the capacity to consent, the responsibility and the power to assess the existence of the requirements of diligence laid down in Article 2 of the Wtl and of the possible good reasons for not granting the written request for euthanasia will be attributed exclusively to the doctor. Based on the Court's reasoning, words spoken by an incapacitated person cannot be considered relevant in either requesting euthanasia or revoking a previous request.

The 'Koffie' judgment in essence—by excluding the punishability of the doctor who had administered a sedative to the patient in the coffee shop in order to be able to perform euthanasia without any 'hindrance' on the part of the patient himself—tends to affirm that, even when the patient's right to life, dignity and health is at stake, it is not necessary, if one considers the patient incapable of coherently assessing his or her own interests, to investigate his or her actual will, but one can act in the patient's unconsciousness even against his or her will.

The Dutch Supreme Court's ruling, as well as the euthanasia law itself, present several critical issues.

The application, *mutatis mutandis*, of the requirements of Art. 2 par. 1 of the Wtl, stipulates that euthanasia may only be administered in the case of mental disease if the patient is suffering unbearable and present suffering with no future hope of obtaining any clinical improvement. The existence of such unbearable suffering, the ruling states, is difficult to determine precisely with this type of illness and therefore, this assessment—to be made on a case-by-case basis—must be the sole responsibility of the doctor. It is the doctor who must assess whether the patient, who is no longer capable of understanding, is actually suffering unbearably.

To do so, the Court suggests, it may take into account any further pathologies or physical suffering, or, in the absence thereof, it must take into consideration the existence of other conditions (the ruling refers e.g. to sadness, withdrawal from food, refusal to drink, etc.) which must correspond to those set out in the written request for euthanasia and which must be such as to lead to the belief that the patient is suffering intolerably. The Court adds that the mere correspondence between the elements indicated in the written request and the actual ones is not a sufficient condition for intolerable suffering to be considered to exist but that this may be considered by the doctor as a useful clue.

The Supreme Court's pronouncement seems to admit that the assessment of intolerable suffering afflicting the patient can be derived from the analysis of the clauses included in the written statement, from conversations with close relatives, from the current observation of the patient and of the patient's life circumstances, in essence, can be deduced from circumstantial elements.[124] In the present case, evidence of unbearable suffering was considered from observation of the patient such as: signs of agitation, restlessness, stress, fear, sadness, anger and panic for most of the day.

The manner in which the euthanasia was carried out and the doubts as to whether the patient was actually suffering unbearably at the time it was administered highlight several weaknesses of the Wtl as well as of the very idea of euthanasia being performed on mentally ill patients.

Without dwelling on the lack of further requirements of diligence under the Wtl—such as, for example, informing the patient of his condition and of the various alternatives to euthanasia or arriving with the patient at the conviction that there was no alternative but to terminate life—it is sufficient for our purposes to point out that the Court's provision that the requirements of due care must be applied in so far as the factual situation permits, does no more than provide, in essence, that in cases where the patient is incapable of understanding certain requirements may be disregarded (van Delden 2004, pp. 447–451), in effect diminishing the protection for some patients compared to others.

The question has also been raised as to whether the requirement of unbearable suffering must be permanent or whether it is sufficient that at some times of the day the patient suffers unbearably and at others not. To this question the regional euthanasia review commissions (RTE), set up to verify *ex post* the regularity of euthanasia procedures, have responded by stating that it is not necessary for the patient to suffer intolerably every moment of the day, but just enough to consider the suffering unbearable. On this point, too, it is probably necessary for the assessment of the patient's condition to take place on the basis of different assumptions; the life of every human being is in fact marked by more or less positive periods, periods of depression and suffering, sometimes even intolerable, but to establish when the weight of suffering is such as to justify the interruption of life would require a more in-depth assessment (Miller et al. 2019, pp. 84–89) or at any rate the identification of more stringent, if not objective, requirements.

[124] Hoge Raad (2020) Judgment of 21 April 2020, No. 19/04910 CW. ECLI NL HR 2020:712. Supreme Court of the Netherlands, para. 4.6.3. Available at: https://uitspraken.rechtspraak.nl/inziendocument?id=ECLI:NL:HR:2020:712. In the present case, evidence of intolerable suffering was considered sufficient to establish intolerable suffering from observation of the patient such as: signs of agitation, restlessness, stress, fear, sadness, anger and panic for most of the day.

The insights offered by the analysis of some of the justificatory elements of the Dutch Supreme Court's ruling allow for some ethical and philosophical reflections on the execution of euthanasia for persons with mental disease, that all the legislation analysed seems to admit.

One of the critical points of the discipline that provides for the possibility of euthanasia for patients suffering from mental disease is the establishment of the requirement of intolerable suffering.

In the balancing of the fundamental values and rights underlying the recognition of the possibility of access to euthanasia or assistance to suicide, the protection of the right to self-determination and human dignity takes on an essential role, as opposed to the state's duty to protect the lives of its citizens, especially those in a weak or fragile state (such as the sick or disabled).

The rationale of the rules on euthanasia rests on the recognition of the existence of certain special situations in which the patient's objective conditions are such as to give greater weight to the need to protect the dignity of the human being and his right to self-determination than to the general duty to protect the lives of citizens. This inversion of values, which is based on a feeling of solidaristic compassion towards the sick person, requires certain requirements in order to be effective (van Delden 2004, p. 449).

Unless one were to adhere to an absolutely subjectivist view such as that held by the German Federal Constitutional Court, one of the particular conditions that permits the inversion of the hierarchical scale of the principles of the legal system is precisely the patient's unbearable suffering. Well, speaking of suffering and intolerability in the context of mental disease certainly predisposes one to certain evaluations that go beyond the realm of objectivity, requiring instead that the doctor's own evaluation be linked to the particular case. It cannot be denied that suffering is directly linked to the individual's perception of it and that in itself it is not an objective element; neither is intolerability of suffering, which subjectifies any evaluation even more.

Added to the patient's subjective perception is the doctor's subjective perception of the suffering of others. In fact, when it comes to mental disease, which are not evidently connected to further physical illnesses or obvious functional limitations,[125] the ascertainment of suffering and its intolerability requires even more rigour and places the evaluator in a condition of greater uncertainty, especially in the case of an advance request for euthanasia based on a forecast of future unbearable suffering.[126] And this is precisely one of the further controversial elements of the ethical admissibility of advance euthanasia declarations.

In cases of advance request for euthanasia, one is faced with a situation in which the individual foresees one or more specific conditions—considered to be

[125] Reference is made to the case in which the certainty of intolerable suffering can be derived from the obvious functional limitations associated with the illness, such as the inability to perform any movement or particularly severe limitations.

[126] It is not easy to predict the experience of mental decline or its future effects on one's quality of life.

a harbinger of unbearable suffering—upon the occurrence of which he requests euthanasia to be performed. The individual, therefore, does not know but anticipates his own suffering without ever having experienced that particular condition. An anticipated request for euthanasia expressed at a time when one is unable to imagine or empathise with the patient's condition has limited validity. Indeed, the absence of awareness may fuel prejudice towards illness and disability by making one imagine unbearable conditions of suffering instead of a more balanced idea that also includes moments of joy and pleasure (Miller et al. 2019, p. 86).[127] It is undoubtedly not easy to predict the experience of cognitive decline and its future effects on the quality of life (Miller et al. 2019, p. 86) as anticipating the emotional burden is also complicated because people often underestimate their ability to adapt to their state of health after developing an illness or disability (Menzel et al. 2002, p. 2150).

Moreover, the time elapsing between the moment of the advance declaration of euthanasia and its execution runs the risk of bringing out the so-called *then-self versus now-self problem* (Menzel and Chandler-Cramer 2014, p. 23).[128] That is, the idea that the individual at the time of the AED and the individual at the time of the illness are different subjectivities that develop simultaneously as the illness progresses. The idea is that in such cases there is doubt as to whether the advance request for euthanasia made by one subject is actually being performed with respect to a substantially different subject. On the other hand, taking a Lockian definition, it can be said that the individual against whom euthanasia is performed is not a complete individual, by which is meant a thinking, intelligent being capable of reasoning and reflection who perceives himself as the same thinking entity in different times and spaces (Locke 1824, [1690]) in which self-determination is a decisive element (Korsgaard 2009, p. 25). Moreover, an individual's personality due to mental illness can vary and also allow him to experience moments of absolute lucidity in which his 'old-self' can emerge (Menzel and Steinbock 2013).

The same problematic issue relates to the ascertainability of the suffering at the time it occurs. In fact, the doctor is required to verify that the unbearable suffering is present at the moment when euthanasia is carried out and that therefore, the condition set out in the advance declaration has occurred.

The doctor's recourse to presumptions, clues and evaluations are clearly fallible insofar as they refer to highly subjective conditions and, above all, are often drawn directly from verbal confrontation with the patient, whose condition of capacity or incapacity cannot but affect the evaluations themselves.

---

[127] See also (Menzel and Steinbock 2013, p. 490; Asch 2005, p. s32).

[128] "One concern about the use of advance directives is distinctively philosophical: the possibility that, in certain cases in which a patient undergoes massive psychological change, the individual who exists after such change is literally a (numerically) distinct individual from the person who completed the directive. If this is true, there is good reason to question the authority of the directive in question, since it is supposed to apply to the individual who completed it, not to someone else. This may be called 'the someone else problem'' (De Grazia 1999, p. 374) See also (Walsh 2020, p. 54).

Both suffering and the intolerability of it—even more subjective—require that their existence be communicated or transferred directly by the patient experiencing them. This need for communication, however, finds a limit precisely in the subjective condition of the person who communicates it, at that given moment affected by an illness that could alter his or her capacity to understand.

Added to this is the fact that an early request for euthanasia is subject to less scrutiny as to whether the requirements are met than an actual request for euthanasia, which makes the subsequent assessment even more uncertain.

The problem inherent in the application of an advance request for euthanasia in the case of a patient suffering from mental disease is obvious, and all the passages just discussed can be extended in their application to cases where the mental disease occurs simultaneously with a physical one. It is true that presumptions may have greater weight in such cases, but they are still presumptions. The high degree of subjectivity and unconsciousness that characterises all the steps in the procedure runs the risk of rendering the execution of euthanasia illegitimate precisely because of the failure to comply with the requirements laid down by the law itself and shared by doctrine and jurisprudence, even that of the German Federal Constitutional Court.

The limitation, which is probably insuperable, is the expectation that the requirements will be met at the present time.

Even the requirement that requests for euthanasia must be voluntary and well considered by the patient can present serious difficulties in cases where the request was made several years ago and the patient is no longer capable of understanding. How can the doctor who has to assess the existence of the requirements be sure that the advance request for euthanasia going back several years, perhaps at a time when the patient was not in his care, was written without any external conditioning? (van Delden 2004, p. 448).

Furthermore, with regard to the individual's possibility of establishing *a-priori*, and therefore without any phenomenal experience capable of giving him certainty, the conditions that in his opinion would produce unbearable suffering in the future, two questions arise: on the one hand, as already mentioned, it is problematic to admit that a prognostic judgement on possible future unbearable suffering can be considered a sufficient condition for determining the reversal of values—outlined above—necessary for the execution of a euthanasia practice. On the other hand, the temporal context in which the subject's future will is manifested is relevant. Indeed, the moment at which the request for euthanasia is drawn up does not seem to have any relevance (in Belgium the validity of the advance request has been extended indefinitely) in any of the sources analysed so far. It could be said, however, that this moment should be taken into account in view of the evolution of the human psyche and soul in the course of life. Indeed, the same individual, in going through the different stages of life, tends to change his or her conceptions, on dignity, life, death and illness, to such an extent that he or she can also change his or her judgement and will with regard to the execution of euthanasia or the conditions under which it can be requested (van Delden 2004, p. 448).

As anticipated in paragraph (3.4) some of the indications formulated in the "Koffie" judgement have been incorporated into the Euthanasia Code 2022 which has specifically implemented the requirements of due care for cases in which this is performed on a patient in an advanced stage of dementia on the basis of an advance request for euthanasia. In any event, even applying further precautions, it is not considered possible to overcome the problems highlighted above implemented by an additional element.

Finally, the provision that the patient no longer has the right to withdraw his or her request for euthanasia openly contradicts the European Convention on the Rights of Persons with Disabilities (CRPD).[129]

It is stated in Article 12 of the CRPD that persons with disabilities enjoy the same legal capacity as other persons in all aspects of life; consequently, States are obliged to provide the necessary measures to make this equality effective.[130]

As stated by Rozemond (2021, p. 3) on the other hand, the right of the mentally ill patient to express his or her wishes and to decide when and whether to end his or her life, was absolutely violated by the conduct of the defendant doctor in the 'Koffie' judgment, who did not even inform the patient that he or she had decided to perform euthanasia. The most serious thing, according to Rozemond, is that the doctor's conduct was approved by the Supreme Court, which did not consider it necessary to consult with the patient or to inform him about the execution of euthanasia, and this precisely because the patient was incapacitated. Again according to Rozemond, a differentiation of human rights based on the condition of illness or disability seems absolutely unjustifiable since the CRPD did not specifically state new rights of the sick or disabled but simply sanctioned the need for fundamental human rights, already in force, to be ensured also and above all for the weakest and most disadvantaged.

The application of the principles enshrined in Article 12 of the CRPD therefore determines that the incapacity of a person with a disability cannot be a justification for not informing the patient about decisions taken and/or for sedating him/her without his/her consent in order to perform a euthanasia practice (Arstein-Kerslake and Flynn 2016) or in performing it against his/her will.

Moreover, if the patient's incapacity were to result in the expression of his present will becoming irrelevant, the moment of ascertaining incapacity would acquire a decisive value. Not only is the ascertainment of incapacity particularly difficult, especially in the case of certain pathologies, but when the effect of that ascertainment is the loss of the right to ask to continue living, it becomes even more

[129] United Nations (2007) Convention on the Rights of Persons with Disabilities (CRPD). Available at: https://www.un.org/development/desa/disabilities/convention-on-the-rights-of-persons-with-disabilities/convention-on-the-rights-of-persons-with-disabilities-2.html.

[130] CPDR, Art. 12: "States Parties reaffirm that persons with disabilities have the right to recognition everywhere as persons before the law. States Parties shall recognize that persons with disabilities enjoy legal capacity on an equal basis with others in all aspects of life. States Parties shall take appropriate measures to provide access by persons with disabilities to the support they may require in exercising their legal capacity".

problematic. In determining the person's capacity to make a decision, especially in view of the broad temporal scope of reference. Establishing when the patient crosses the threshold of incapacity can mean the difference between life and death.

Lastly, taking into consideration that the doctor who performs euthanasia and assesses the patient's present capacity is not always the same one who assessed the patient's capacity at the time the written request for euthanasia was drawn up, and in any case, the unnecessary correspondence between the advance request and the present will, (Kim et al. 2020) it is possible to argue that the termination of a patient's life in a condition of frailty and weakness such as that of the mentally ill patient is subject to excessive discretion and lacks the necessary caution that the overturning of a right as important as the right to life would instead require. Evidently, accepting the idea that the patient who has become legally incapacitated no longer has the right to express his or her will would tend to exclude the problem of actuality through a legal fiction that considers external manifestations of the patient's will irrelevant, but in reality, as we have already seen, this interpretation has several weak points.

The retrospective nature of advance euthanasia requests in allowing a doctor to act on the basis of his or her personal judgement on such a controversial issue probably requires a more thorough evaluation and a procedure marked by greater formality, (van Delden 2004, p. 451) which gives legal relevance to the patient's current wishes and wellbeing, at least when this conflicts with the previous advance euthanasia request (Dresser 1995, 2017).

The aim in fact—also by virtue of the principles affirmed within the CRPD—is that legal systems should provide a series of extra safeguards for individuals who by their very nature are in a condition of extreme weakness and fragility, especially in those conditions in which doubts may arise as to whether the necessary conditions for access to euthanasia exist.

If self-determination and the protection of the dignity of the human being are the elements on the basis of which the right to request and obtain assistance in dying, through informed consent, is affirmed, one wonders whether the possible fallacy of consent can only undermine the justification underlying the request for assistance in dying.

One wonders what element of procedural justification is so solid and what absolute certainty can determine that despite the patient's claim that he or she does not want to die, it can be admitted that euthanasia is being carried out against his or her will, violating his or her right to life.

In cases where the effectiveness, autonomy, and actuality of consent is at risk, it is probably necessary to acquire a higher degree of certainty, especially when such an injury occurs against the actual will of the patient who is considered to be incapacitated.

The advance request for euthanasia, especially in the case of mental disease, is drawn up on the basis of a future idea of unbearable suffering characterised by a high degree of unconsciousness. The patient's perception of suffering and its intolerability is also highly subjective, as is the perception and assessment by the doctor who must establish whether the patient is suffering unbearably and from what moment onwards he is no longer capable of understanding and therefore from what moment onwards the expressed will no longer has any value. The margin of error seems to be too high, and although the recognisability, in certain situations, of a right to help in dying now seems out of the question, the evolution of the disciplines that will regulate its implementation cannot but require the application of high standards of certainty and guarantee of protection of the rights of the human being.

It is true that euthanasia aims to protect individuals who are often afflicted by terminal and/or incurable illnesses. These illnesses are a source of atrocious suffering, and the individuals are in such difficult conditions that they find themselves in a state of infirmity (or psychic deficiency), or a psychological state that is difficult to assess. For this reason, there are objective difficulties in ascertaining the authenticity of their consent. However, the rule of law cannot completely abdicate its main task of protecting the lives of citizens. In any case, particular attention must be paid to the forms of consent, which must necessarily pass through specific procedures that guarantee respect for the duty to protect the weak and vulnerable, as identified above.

Dworkin argued that the interest of an able-bodied person in securing a death consistent with their personal values should take priority over their future care interests (Dworkin 1993). Conversely, some argue that establishing the relationship between the weight of an early request for euthanasia and the patient's current welfare and interests is a challenging task that cannot be entrusted to the individual judgement of a physician (van Delden 2004, p. 451).

Just as the criminal justice system would rather avoid punishing one innocent person than punish all the guilty, so a euthanasia law that respects fundamental human rights should aim to ensure that no one who is not entitled to it is deprived of life, especially against their will, in order to protect the right to life of all human beings.

Otherwise, one would run the risk of violating the fundamental rights of the weakest and most fragile individuals, which the laws allowing euthanasia and the European Convention on the Rights of Persons with Disabilities aim to protect more than any other. This matter concerns matters of life and death, and the termination of life is irreversible, which is why it would be better to ensure a higher level of certainty and maintain a more restrictive interpretation of the rules (Miller et al. 2019, p. 12).

3.11 Is There a Right to a Dignified Death?

Among the various ethically and politically divisive issues that have emerged in the course of the analysis carried out within this chapter, the recognition of a right to a dignified death is certainly the one that, due to its possible social and legal implications, is most relevant in today's debate.

Very often, changes in legal structures influence social ones, and many other times, instances from the evolution of social bodies determine legal ones. In this case, it is technological and scientific progress, allowing human beings to survive in situations unimaginable just a few decades ago, that has raised new questions, including whether or not there is a right to a dignified death.

From the analysis of European case law as well as from the main positions of the doctrine two opposing approaches emerge within which the different conceptions adopted by the member states are placed (Simoncini 2022, p. 347). One defined as *dignitarian* in which both the homicide of the consenting person and assistance to suicide are punished and close to which one can place the French or Italian approach, and a second defined as *libertarian* in which euthanasia is considered an individual right and in which assistance to suicide and homicide of the consenting person are not considered crimes. This is the approach taken by the Benelux countries and Spain. Between these two positions lies the German approach, which recognises the broad autonomy of the individual in end-of-life decisions but states that there are reasons for limiting aid to suicide (including the risks of commercialisation and profit).

At the same time, the European Court of Human Rights does not seem to want to take a clear position on the possibility of deciding on one's own life but, on the contrary, seems to pursue an approach centred on attempting to protect the *marge d'appréciation* of the individual member states, recognising in some way that although closely linked to fundamental human rights, the question of the end of life has an implicit connection with the prevailing morality of the peoples to whom the rules should be applied. For this reason the margin of appreciation that is usually recessive before fundamental human rights in this case seems to retain its centrality (Shany 2005). This is probably because the need to strike a balance between the different constitutional values at stake can be achieved more effectively at the national rather than supranational level.

The ECtHR findings seem to call for a necessary balancing act between the right to decide when and how to end one's life provided one has the possibility of directing one's will and acting accordingly (based on Art. 8 ECHR) and the right to life (Art. 2 ECHR) from which a right to die cannot be derived.

However, some of the pronouncements and legislative sources analysed (such as the Spanish *Ley organica* or the ruling of the German Federal Constitutional Court) have admitted the existence, under certain conditions, of a right to die or to receive help in dying. The evolution of national case law is probably moving in the direction of an increasing recognition of help in dying understood as a right to a dignified life.

This conclusion, in fact, could also find a further argument. While prolonging the human being's life chances is certainly a sensible goal to pursue, it may be appropriate to ask to what extent and under what conditions it is good for this to happen. Indeed, living is one thing, surviving is another.

Similarly, Giovanni Fornero (2019) argues that the right to die should be considered an extension of the right to life, not its negation: the right to die can be understood as an internal articulation of the right to live. Such reflections have prompted a greater focus on distributive justice in end-of-life care, raising the issue of equitable access to euthanasia and palliative care based on criteria of equity and not just affordability (Engelhardt 1996). In short, the contemporary debate on the end of life moves between respect for individual self-determination and the moral and social implications of assisted dying choices, seeking a balance between individual freedom, medical duty and public interest.

This distinction may require a re-conceptualisation of the very idea of life. What is life? When can one say one is alive? Is it necessary to recognise a qualitative as well as quantitative lowest common denominator to existence? To date, there is no unambiguous and universally accepted definition of 'life'. Rather, life is described in scientific terms through a series of properties and functions that distinguish living beings from inanimate matter. According to classical biology, a living organism is characterised by its cellular organisation, metabolism, growth, reproduction, response to stimuli, homeostasis and evolutionary capacity (Koshland 2002). A minimalist approach, widely used in astrobiology, instead identifies life as an autonomous chemical system capable of Darwinian evolution (Deamer and Fleischaker 1994). Theoretical biology and complex systems theory propose an organisational definition: a living being is an autopoietic system, i.e. capable of self-organisation and regeneration through its own internal processes (Maturana and Varela 1980).

The concept of human life, however, may presuppose additional dimensions beyond the purely biological, subjectivity or self-awareness, relational capacity, potential autonomy, possible moral and legal recognition. Can dignity be included among these? Can it be said that life is only really life when it is dignified? When is the dignity of the person respected? And who is responsible for this judgement? Can the dignity of an existence be assessed by someone other than the very subject whose life is being discussed?

Attempting to answer these questions would likely constitute an act of excessive presumption. However, if the affirmation of dignity as an essential human right is unquestionable and an inherent element of life, and if the biological meaning of life itself becomes a motive for violating human dignity in some cases, then perhaps this dichotomy represents a way to hypothesise a right to assisted dying, as a meeting point between libertarian and dignitarian approaches.

The life of which Art. 2 ECHR speaks is intrinsically connected to the dignity of the human being, if biological life and therefore the biological conditions of life are such as to exclude dignity from life, it is precisely in order to protect life and its dignity that the element detrimental to dignity, biological life, must be excluded. Death can in some way represent the modus to protect not only the autonomy of the human being but also life understood in a sense that conforms to the essential characteristics affirmed by the ECHR.

If this reasoning is valid, the question remains as to who is deputed to assess the dignity of a given existence, whether this assessment can be left to individual autonomy or whether objective criteria can be identified to define an existence as undignified.

From this point of view, it is indisputable to affirm that the assessment of the dignity of one's existence can only be delegated to individual freedom and autonomy, since no one, be it an individual or an institution, could ever arrogate to himself the right to define an existence as undignified against the perception and will of the individual himself.

Secondly, to remain consistent with what has been said above, the lack of dignity must be based on reasons related to biological life and thus to biological living conditions. It cannot and must not be accepted that a conception of life without dignity is based on social, relational, economic elements or on which the States can directly or indirectly influence. It could not, for example, be accepted that a homeless person—forced to live on the streets, without food, in degrading living conditions—should be granted assistance to die because they consider their own life undignified; not so much because one cannot understand the judgement of one's own life, but because one cannot accept that the States should participate in eliminating the outcomes of a condition that they have determined.

According to this reading, the existence of a right to die can only be recognised in the case of the existence of certain biological conditions (in essence, illness), the verification of which is independent of the States and institutions.

The State's duty of protection towards its citizens, according to a Hobbesian securitarian perspective, both from other individuals and from its own choices, implies the burden of verifying that the request for help to die is truly free, autonomous, current and stable and is not due to additional or contingent factors other than the biological conditions of life and that the same are permanent and irreversible. In that case, in fact, the dignity of life could be protected by means of another pathway for which the State itself would have to take responsibility. If this were the case, instead of recognising and protecting its citizens' right to life, the state would be abdicating its own role.

While recognising the existence of a right to die under certain conditions, not only the question of autonomy but also that of the actuality of consent remains central. When it is a question of definitively ending one's existence, what the Italian Constitutional Court has affirmed regarding the need to guarantee *usque ad vitae supremum exitum* the effectiveness of a possible reconsideration seems highly sensible.

At the same time, to avoid raising questions about discrimination between individuals who can administer the lethal drug themselves and those who cannot (usually because they are completely immobile), it would be necessary to invest in technologies that would allow the autonomous administration of the drug to be activated through *eye-tracking* alone. This would address concerns that the latter group may be disadvantaged by not having access to euthanasia, or that they may not be guaranteed the possibility of having second thoughts until the last moment (enjoying less protection). Such technological developments are certainly feasible and would help to overcome one of the most widely debated issues in doctrine besides conscientious objection.

Finally, we should briefly mention one last issue that has been widely debated, concerning conscientious objection. Despite extensive academic speculation on this issue, it has not been deemed necessary to examine it in depth, as it is clear that even if conscientious objection were considered a true right to be balanced against other rights, it would be overridden in areas relating to the right to life and health, such as abortion, assisted reproduction and euthanasia. This is why, when it comes to rights, it is the state that must provide safeguards to guarantee them. If one concludes that euthanasia is a true and proper right under certain conditions and must be administered as part of an institutionalised medical procedure, conscientious objection can be ruled out and administration can be a duty of medical personnel.

In all cases in which it is admitted that conscientious objection can be opposed to a right on the basis of the fact that it is believed that the healthcare facility will find within its ranks personnel capable of guaranteeing that right, it is theoretically admitting the legitimacy of a generalised refusal and therefore admitting, in complete contrast to the right of the individual, that all personnel can oppose the practice, rendering the very existence of that right ineffective. Those who wish to access public health employment positions must therefore accept that their duties and obligations include guaranteeing the human rights that directly depend on them, like euthanasia or abortion.

In conclusion, although the stipulation that assistance in dying can be granted solely upon the provision of access to palliative care and pain therapy is a matter of substantial plebiscite, in order to ensure that death is not perceived as a mere means of evading pain and suffering, even if such an outcome is not deemed dignified, it is asserted that the aforementioned stipulation can only be enshrined in legislation if it is proposed within a specified time frame. This is done in order to avoid the prolongation of suffering and pain that is often associated with the inefficient functioning of state healthcare systems. On the basis of this latter assumption, emergency situations come to the fore with respect to the end-of-life issue, whose response by States must be immediate and in which time plays a key factor.

These situations, empirically demonstrated during the last Covid-19 pandemic, will be discussed in the last Sect. 3.12

3.12 Euthanasia and Triage

As we have seen, the debate presents a broad spectrum of issues and questions whose resolution does not merely touch upon legal, medical and/or social aspects, but above all aspects related to the intimate moral convictions of those who approach it.[131]

The issues discussed, deserving of ever wider consideration, have probably acquired greater relevance in the wake of the global *Coronavirus* emergency.[132]

---

[131] *Comitato Nazionale di Bioetica, Riflessioni Bioetiche sul Suicidio Medicalmente Assistito* [National Bioethics Committee, (Italy) Bioethical Reflections on Medically Assisted Suicide, Opinion No. 135 of 18 July 2019. The CNB within the document drafted following the Constitutional Court Ruling no. 207/2018 carried out an interesting work aimed at providing indications for the identification of an *ethically sustainable* approach in regulating the cases of medically assisted suicide.

[132] Coronaviruses are 'a large family of viruses known to cause illnesses ranging from the common cold to more serious diseases such as Middle East Respiratory Syndrome (MERS) and Severe Acute Respiratory Syndrome (SARS)'. Specifically, the current infection was caused by 'a novel Coronavirus (nCoV) which is a new strain of coronavirus that has not previously been identified in humans', http://www.salute.gov.it/portale/nuovocoronavirus/dettaglioFaqNuovoCoronavirus.jsp?lingua=italiano&id=228.

With each passing week and the growing fear of an uncontrolled spread of the virus, the conviction grew that the question of how to regulate the practices of suicide assistance and euthanasia was far more urgent than was previously thought.

This conviction began with 13 doctors from the Papa Giovanni XXIII Hospital in Bergamo in a letter published in the New England Journal of Medicine—Catalyst Innovations in Care Delivery, on 21 March 2020, in which they depicted the dramatic scenario following the Coronavirus outbreak: "Our own hospital is highly contaminated, and we are far beyond the tipping point: 300 beds out of 900 are occupied by Covid-19 patients. Fully 70% of ICU beds in our hospital are reserved for critically ill Covid-19 patients with a reasonable chance to survive. The situation here is dismal as we operate well below our normal standard of care. Wait times for an intensive care bed are hours long. Older patients are not being resuscitated and die alone without appropriate palliative care, while the family is notified over the phone, often by a well-intentioned, exhausted, and emotionally depleted physician with no prior contact" (Nacoti et al. 2020).

The complaint of the doctors of the Papa Giovanni XXIII Hospital, who were forced to reserve their hospital beds for patients with a reasonable chance of survival, seems to confirm what the Italian Society of Anaesthesia Analgesia Resuscitation and Intensive Care (SIAARTI) had hypothesised only a few days earlier (6 March 2020) in a document entitled 'Clinical Ethics Recommendations for admission to and withdrawal from intensive care in exceptional conditions of imbalance between need and available resources'.[133]

The need to publish guidelines through which to establish criteria for access to intensive care and to enable physicians to adopt common principles in assessing the 'increased life expectancy' of patients, with a view to the efficient allocation of healthcare resources, shows that the occurrence of such a serious scenario is indeed considered plausible. The possible application of principles that have arisen in the sphere of 'disaster medicine' highlights, for the reasons we shall see below, the need for careful reflection on the different ways in which to regulate the cases of suicide assistance and euthanasia.

We have already seen the distinction between cases where death is directly brought about by the administration of a lethal drug, and those of medicalised suicide assistance, where instead the lethal drug is made available to the patient, who takes it on his own initiative. From the analysis carried out in the preceding paragraphs, the prevailing orientation emerges that assisting and abetting conduct is not punishable if certain requirements are met. Among these, it is often required that the doctor does everything within his power to offer the patient alternative routes to death.

This conclusion adheres to the fundamental principles of medical ethics that enshrine the doctor's duty to endeavour to alleviate the suffering of the sick person, even if the latter refuses medical treatment, by offering him or her pain treatment and therapy.

[133] The recommendations drawn up to manage the admission to intensive treatment, as specified by SIAARTI can only be applied 'after all possible efforts have been made by those involved to increase the availability of deliverable resources', https://www.sicp.it/wp-content/uploads/2020/03/CS-SIAARTI_Racc-di-etica-clinica_09-mar-20.pdf.

Access to palliative care and pain therapy,[134] therefore, should be guaranteed as part of the essential levels of care by the national health services, in order to ensure respect for the dignity and autonomy of the human person, the need for health, equity of access to care, the quality of care and its appropriateness with regard to specific needs.

While on the one hand, the ethical and legal admissibility of death-supporting conduct seems to be gaining ground in European legal systems, as well as in supranational jurisprudence, at the same time the parallel need to guarantee access to pain therapy and palliative care in all cases in which it is necessary to alleviate and/or control the pain suffered by the patient, either because of the ineffectiveness of treatments to counteract the evolution of the disease or because of the refusal of such treatments, is affirmed.

On the other hand, the actual availability of palliative treatments and pain therapies is a fundamental element precisely for the purpose of acquiring full and free consent. Death, in fact, must not be chosen as the only plausible solution to pain and suffering, but must be chosen as adhering to one's own conception of dignity.

The issue of the relationship between euthanasia, assistance to suicide and the need to provide palliative care and pain therapy takes on singular connotations when observed in the light of the spread of the Coronavirus epidemic and CoViD-19.[135] The premise of the following reflections is the recognition of the right to health as a fundamental right of the individual[136] as well as the need for the State, even in a situation such as that of a global pandemic characterised by an imbalance between necessary and available healthcare resources, to intervene to the maximum of its possibilities to ensure that every sick person has access to the highest possible level of care.[137]

---

[134] Palliative care and pain therapy, mean respectively the set of therapeutic, diagnostic and assistance interventions, addressed both to the sick person and to his or her family unit, aimed at the active and total care of patients whose basic illness, characterised by an unstoppable evolution and an inauspicious prognosis no longer responds to specific treatments, as well as the set of diagnostic and therapeutic interventions aimed at identifying and applying suitable and appropriate pharmacological, surgical, instrumental, psychological and rehabilitative therapies, variously integrated with each other, to chronic morbid forms, in order to develop suitable diagnostic and therapeutic paths for the suppression and control of pain'.

[135] The disease caused by the new coronavirus is called 'COVID-19' (where 'CO' stands for corona, 'VI' for virus, 'D' for disease and '19' indicates the year in which it occurred). This was announced by WHO Director-General Tedros Adhanom Ghebreyesus, http://www.salute.gov.it/portale/nuovocoronavirus/dettaglioFaqNuovoCoronavirus.jsp?lingua=italiano&id=228. A press briefing during a break in the Extraordinary Forum on the virus on 11 February 2020 consultation 5/04/2020.

[136] Art 14, c.2: "the enjoyment of the highest attainable standard of healthis one of the fundamental rights of every human being". UNESCO (2005) Universal Declaration on Bioethics and Human Rights. Adopted on 19 October 2005 by the General Conference of UNESCO. Available at: https://unesdoc.unesco.org/ark:/48,223/pf0000146180.

[137] UNESCO International Bioethics Committee (IBC) & World Commission on the Ethics of Scientific Knowledge and Technology (COMEST) (2020) Statement on COVID-19: Ethical Considerations from a Global Perspective. Available at: https://unesdoc.unesco.org/ark:/48223/pf0000373115.

However, the scenario from which we will take our cue—the one denounced by the doctors of the Pope John XIII Hospital—has occurred in several European countries as well as in the rest of the world, and there have been many cases in which hospitals have actually found themselves in the position of not being able to treat all patients and having to choose who to treat, refusing admission to intensive care even for serious cases with a lower chance of survival.[138]

National health systems risked collapse and the need to assess patients' chances of survival and not being able to hospitalise those with the least chance of recovery—who by definition would probably be those in the worst health conditions and therefore destined to suffer the worst—had its negative effects on thousands of individuals.

The questions raised by the ineffective response of health systems to the coronavirus emergency are various. Among these, of particular importance is the question of what should be done in the event that an unspecified number of suffering people, thousands if compared to the worldwide emergency, in a precarious and/or perhaps tragic condition, wishing to be treated, cannot be granted the fundamental right to health and consequent access to care.

In the emergency situation that mankind has gone through—and in which the EU Member States could find themselves again, whether for reasons related to new pandemics or the ongoing geopolitical crisis—the tragic circumstance has occurred whereby States have been unable to treat their sick. Well, in cases where health conditions are particularly serious, marked by enormous suffering and the disease, with a very high degree of certainty, can lead to death, there would be no choice but to attempt to ensure the administration of palliative care and pain therapy.

Indeed, in the situation where a patient with a serious health condition cannot be hospitalised due to insufficient health resources, the minimum burden on States would be the containment of the patient's suffering and physical pain.

However, as emerged in Italy from the letter published by the Bergamasque doctors, the implementation of the law on palliative care and pain therapy at a European level is characterised by lights and shadows, with strong inhomogeneities at a national, regional and local level and with situations in which doctors and the organisation, in the hospital and on the territory, are not yet sufficiently prepared to recognise and address these needs in time and to offer an early, integrated and complex intervention.

If one considers that the system of palliative care and pain therapy at the European level is scarcely efficient and that in emergency situations this efficiency could decrease drastically, it is then appropriate to assume the collapse of European national healthcare systems.

---

[138] Symptoms of Covid-19 include, in the most severe cases, pneumonia and severe acute respiratory syndrome (SARS) such that the patient may die, https://www.cdc.gov/coronavirus/2019-ncov/symptoms-testing/symptoms.html.

The States at this point would neither be able to attempt to cure the sick nor to try to accompany them *'in'* dying, due to the absence of hospital beds and specialised medical personnel.

An alternative would be to passively accept that these people are condemned to suffer a slow, painful and agonising death, for themselves and their relatives.

In this case, the neo-liberal policies of the last decades, guilty of cuts in public spending, the consequent impoverishment of health systems and the absence of adequate *preparedness*,[139] would highlight the *indirect* responsibility of States in their inability to ensure their citizens the protection of the main human rights. In fact, it is undeniable that political choices of macro-distribution of resources have decisive effects on micro-distribution and on the consequent capacity of healthcare facilities to provide an adequate level of care.[140]

At this point, the question arises as to whether in such an exceptional condition the principle affirmed by the European Court of Human Rights in Judgment No. 2346/02[141] and endorsed by the Italian Constitutional Court in Judgment No. 242/2019, according to which from Article 2 Const.—not differently from Article 2 ECHR—descends the State's duty to protect the life of every individual: not that—diametrically opposed—of recognising to the individual the possibility of obtaining from the State or from third parties an aid to die. Or, whether, in a logic of balancing the fundamental rights of the individual, the acclaimed inability of States to recognise effectively the right to health and the consequent right to life, imposes, on the other hand, at least to recognise fully the right to self-determination and the right to die with dignity.

The question on which most European Courts seem to focus is whether the very application of Articles 1, 2 and 3 ECHR, at least in the emergency situations hypothesised, can give rise to a real right to a good death or at least to the best

---

[139] Comitato Nazionale per la Bioetica (2020) Covid-19: la decisione clinica in condizioni di carenza di risorse e il criterio del "triage in emergenza pandemica" [National Bioethics Committee (2020) Covid-19: Clinical decision-making under conditions of scarce resources and the criterion of "triage in a pandemic emergency"] (Opinion No. 136/2020). Available at: https://bioetica.governo.it/media/4248/p136_2020_-covid-19-la-decisione-clinica-in-condizioni-di-carenza-di-risorse-e-il-criterio-del-triage-in-emergenza-pandemica.pdf. CNB highlights the lack of planning of action strategies in the public health sphere in view of exceptional conditions despite the fact that a *'National Plan for Preparedness and Response to an Influenza Pandemic'* had been prepared after the avian flu in 2003 and abandoned in 2006, and above all, despite the alert on the risk of global pandemics launched by the Global Preparedness Monitoring Board (GPMB) and entitled *A World at Risk, Annual Report on Global Preparedness for Health Emergencies* with the report published in September 2019, https://apps.who.int/gpmb/assets/annual_report/GPMB_annualreport_2019.pdf.

[140] UNESCO International Bioethics Committee (IBC) & World Commission on the Ethics of Scientific Knowledge and Technology (COMEST) (2020) Statement on COVID-19: Ethical Considerations from a Global Perspective, p. 2. Available at: https://unesdoc.unesco.org/ark:/48,223/pf0000373115.

[141] European Court of Human Rights (2002) *Pretty v. United Kingdom*, Application No. 2346/02, Judgment of 29 April 2002. Available at: https://hudoc.echr.coe.int/eng?i=001-60,448.

possible death. The right to expect the State to help alleviate the suffering that the State itself is unable to mitigate, owing to its own culpability.

Moreover, in such a serious context, even the solution put forward by those who admit recourse to direct active euthanasia practices[142] would probably be insufficient. In fact, even those who believe that listening to and accepting a request for medically assisted suicide, under the conditions envisaged, should be clearly distinguished from incitement to suicide, and should be accepted on account of the ethical principles of self-determination and the physician's duty to be charitable[143] and that the balancing of values in favour of assisting medically assisted suicide is ethically and legally legitimate because the person has the right to preserve his or her dignity even and especially in the final stages of life[144] requires, however in order to legitimise the decision to medically assist suicide and for the values protected by the legal system to be balanced, that certain conditions be met simultaneously. The plausible, and probably necessary, precautions devised for the execution of medical assistance to suicide would, however, probably be unworkable in the course of a general health emergency. Indeed, in the event of a collapse of the health care system, it is to be expected that certain stipulated requirements will not be met.

A useful food for thought might come from reading the recommendations published on 10 February 2020 by the French High Authority for Health[145] (Has), which, in the context of the reform of the law *'on the end of life'*, allow the family doctor to directly prescribe a drug[146] for deep and continuous sedation and to be able to obtain it, for the completion of medical procedures, directly from the pharmacy. In France,

---

[142] It should be emphasised that most countries that allow euthanasia practices stipulate that the final act of dying is performed by the patient himself, drinking a medicine or, in cases of immobility, operating a plunger with his mouth that injects the lethal solution. This eventuality constitutes a case of medically assisted suicide, for which the help of the doctor, who arranges everything necessary so that the act can be performed, is essential.

[143] *Comitato Nazionale per la Bioetica (2020) Covid-19: la decisione clinica in condizioni di carenza di risorse e il criterio del "triage in emergenza pandemica"* [Covid-19: Clinical decision-making under conditions of scarce resources and the criterion of "triage in a pandemic emergency"] (Opinion No. 136/ 2020). Available at: https://bioetica.governo.it/media/4248/p136_2020_-covid-19-la-decisione-clinica-in-condizioni-di-carenza-di-risorse-e-il-criterio-del-triage-in-emergenza-pandemica.pdf.

[144] *Comitato Nazionale per la Bioetica (2020) Covid-19: la decisione clinica in condizioni di carenza di risorse e il criterio del "triage in emergenza pandemica"* [Covid-19: Clinical decision-making under conditions of scarce resources and the criterion of "triage in a pandemic emergency"] (Opinion No. 136/ 2020). Available at: https://bioetica.governo.it/media/4248/p136_2020_-covid-19-la-decisione-clinica-in-condizioni-di-carenza-di-risorse-e-il-criterio-del-triage-in-emergenza-pandemica.pdf.

[145] *Haute Autorité de Santé* (2018) *Comment mettre en œuvre une sédation profonde et continue maintenue jusqu'au décès* [How to implement deep and continuous sedation maintained until death]. Available at: https://www.has-sante.fr/jcms/c_2832000/fr/comment-mettre-en-oeuvre-une-sedation-profonde-et-continue-maintenue-jusqu-au-deces.

[146] The drug in question is *Midazolam*, a drug of the benzodiazepine class with ultra-short action used in anaesthesia today.

as we have seen, already since 2016 the so-called *Claeyes-leonetti* law,[147] allows the doctor to practise deep and continuous sedation directly at the patient's home if certain conditions are met, but until the reform a few weeks ago, the doctor did not have direct access to the drug, always having to go through a hospital pharmacy.

The French case could, at this point, provide useful food for thought on the answers to the questions posed at the beginning of this chapter.

It is true that this refers to exceptional situations, but also in the light of the *EU Preparedness Union Strategy to prevent and react to emerging threats and crises*[148] it may be necessary to assume regulatory interventions in this direction. In cases where it is not possible to hospitalise the patient and where no other life-sustaining treatment is possible, general practitioners (Cimbalo 2003) would play an essential role, carrying out the assessment of the requirements for carrying out euthanasia practices directly at the patient's home.

In the event of incapacity and the collapse of national health services, it might be essential to provide for the possibility of procuring the necessary medicines directly from pharmacies and to be able to supply them not only to doctors, but also directly to sick people or their families, rather than providing for support criteria between member States.

The solutions that can be envisaged are different, and they will certainly have to take into account the balancing of the various interests at stake, but regardless of their identification, it is certainly of fundamental importance to carry out a serious reflection on the issue capable of stirring consciences.

Exceptional situations clearly differ from ordinary ones, and the precautions taken in different cases can only be taken at different levels. What is certain is the necessary weighing of all the aspects involved so as to avoid superficial and insufficiently thorough conclusions.

Choices in these cases, regulatory or otherwise, can make the difference between life and death, determine who lives and who dies, and above all deprive or guarantee the dignity of the human being until the last possible moment.

In conclusion, both themes addressed in this book involve decisions that lead to irreversible consequences: the coming into being of a new life and the deliberate cessation of an existing one. These are not merely private choices but decisions that

---

[147] *Cleays-Leonetti* law, made euthanasia practices legal accompanied by deep and continuous sedation. *Loi n° 2016–87 du 2 février 2016 créant de nouveaux droits en faveur des malades et des personnes en fin de vie* [Law No. 2016–87 of 2 February 2016 creating new rights for patients and persons at the end of life], known as the Claeys-Leonetti Law. Available at: https://www.legifrance.gouv.fr/affichTexte.do?cidTexte=JORFTEXT000031970253&categorieLien=id.

[148] Regulation (EU) 2022/2371 on 25 March 2025, was issued, requiring the Commission to develop a Union plan for prevention, preparedness and response to crisis situations. The key objectives and actions of the strategy include the need to protect the essential functions of European society, including the development of a minimum standard of preparedness for crucial services such as hospitals, schools, transport and telecommunications; as well as the strengthening of coordination and cooperation in crisis response: by establishing or improving the integration of existing crisis management structures and the development of emergency protocols for responding to critical situations.

are situated at the ontological thresholds of human existence, where ethical complexity is intensified by the finality of the act. Actions with profound ethical and legal implications, touching on fundamental human rights such as the right to life, the right to health, human dignity, personal autonomy, and protection from exploitation and commodification. Precisely because of their definitive and non-reversible nature, such practices demand a normative framework grounded in caution, responsibility, and ethical foresight.

For these reasons, Hans Jonas's concept of the heuristics of fear (Jonas 1984) provides a compelling ethical framework can provide useful food for thought. Indeed, Jonas argues that in the age of technological power—particularly biomedical and biopolitical interventions—classical ethics prove insufficient. Our actions have far-reaching effects, both temporally and spatially, including on future generations and vulnerable populations. Traditional utilitarian calculations or rights-based liberalism may fail to capture the weight of these consequences. According to Jonas, in the face of technological power capable of reshaping human life and death, ethical deliberation must be guided not by optimism but by a responsible anticipation of the worst possible outcomes. Fear, in this context, is not a paralyzing emotion but a rational and moral tool aimed at preventing irreversible harm and safeguarding the conditions for human dignity and social coexistence. The heuristic of fear thus becomes a principle of ethical anticipation, a call to responsibility for what might be destroyed—life, dignity, nature—without the possibility of restoration. This approach demands that wherever human agency intersects with life's most fragile and irreversible moments, the burden of proof lies with those who wish to permit, rather than prohibit. As such, Jonas's ethical framework is especially relevant in guiding bioethical decisions where the margins for error are morally unacceptable and where the societal stakes—both symbolic and material—are exceedingly high.[149]

Ultimately, the ethical treatment of surrogacy and euthanasia cannot be reduced to questions of consent or autonomy alone. Rather, a broader and more cautious ethical paradigm is required—one that acknowledges the limits of our foresight, the asymmetry of power in many of these practices and the irreversible nature of choices concerning the thresholds of life and death. This approach does not oppose progress or the exercise of individual freedom; rather, it emphasises that when legislation concerns fundamental thresholds of life and death, our primary responsibility is to ensure that what we permit respects the irreversible nature and profound ethical significance of such decisions.

References

Adamo U (2020) La Corte costituzionale apre (ma non troppo) al suicidio medicalmente assistito mediante una inedita doppia pronuncia. BioLaw J 1:27–64

[149] A similar concept is supported by Stephen Gardiner (2011) on climate changes who argues for ethical restraint in contexts marked by uncertainty and potential for profound harm, framing it as a duty of intergenerational justice.

Alfonzo A (2016) La sperimentazione clinica "con" il minore: il necessario bilanciamento tra diritti individuali e interessi collettivi. BioLaw J 3:253–277

Amato S (2016) Forum: eutanasia e minori: il primo caso Belga. BioLaw J 3:15–16

Anders G (2003) L'uomo è antiquato I. Considerazioni sull'anima nell'epoca della seconda rivoluzione industriale. Bollati Boringhieri, Torino, p 58

Aquinas T (1920) Summa Theologiae, Part II–II, Question 64 (trans: Fathers of the English Dominican Province, (revised edn). Burns, Oates & Washbourne, London

Aristotle (2009) Nicomachean ethics. In: Ross D (trans), Brown L (ed). Oxford University Press, Oxford

Arstein-Kerslake A, Flynn E (2016) The general comment on article 12 of the convention on the rights of persons with disabilities: a roadmap for equality before the law. Int J Human Rights 20:4

Asch A (2005) Recognizing death while affirming life: can end-of-life reform uphold a disabled person's interest in continued life? Hastings Cent Rep 35(6 Suppl):s31–s36. https://doi.org/10.2307/3528402

Asscher ECA, van de Vathorst S (2020) First prosecution of a Dutch doctor since the Euthanasia Act of 2002: what does the verdict mean? J Med Ethics 46(2):71–75. https://doi.org/10.1136/medethics-2019-10587

Augustine (1957) City of god, volume I: books 1–3. In: McCracken GE (trans). Loeb Classical Library 411. Harvard University Press, Cambridge, MA

Augustine (2014) Confessions, volume I: books 1–8. In: Hammond CJ-B (trans). Loeb Classical Library 26. Harvard University Press, Cambridge, MA

Aurelius M (1902) Meditations. In: Long G (trans). J. M. Dent & Sons, London

Berghäuser G, Boer TA, Borasio GD, Hohendorf G, Rixen S, Spittler JF (2020) Brauchen wir eine Neuordnung der Sterbehilfe in Deutschland? Medizinrecht 38(3):207–211. https://doi.org/10.1007/s00350-020-5484-4

Bignami M (2018) Il caso Cappato alla Corte costituzionale: un'ordinanza ad incostituzionalità differita. Questione Giustizia

Camus A (2000) Il mito di Sisifo. In: Sartelli F, Bompiani M (trans). Originally published as: Camus A (1942) Le Mythe de Sisyphe. Gallimard, Paris

Canestrari S (2019) Una sentenza 'inevitabilmente infelice': la 'riforma' dell'art. 580 c.p. da parte della Corte costituzionale. Rivista Italiana di Diritto e Procedura Penale 62(4):2159–2179

Canestrari S (2021) Ferite dell'anima e corpi prigionieri: suicidio e aiuto al suicidio nella prospettiva di un diritto liberale e solidale. In: Seminario Giuridico della Università di Bologna, no. 308. Bononia University Press, Bologna. https://doi.org/10.30682/sg308

Carnevale P (1997) Il referendum abrogativo e i limiti alla sua ammissibilità nella giurisprudenza costituzionale. CEDAM, Padova

Casavola FP (2013) Bioetica. Una rivoluzione postmoderna. Salerno Editrice, Roma

Casonato C (2015) Un diritto difficile. Il caso Lambert fra necessità e rischi. BioLawJournal 9:489–501

Casonato C (2016) Introduzione: il primo caso di eutanasia minorile in Belgio. BioLaw J 3:5–7

Catalano S (2020) La sentenza 242 del 2019: una pronuncia additiva molto particolare senza 'rime obbligate'. Osservatorio AIC 2:15–25

Catechism of the Catholic Church (1997) Libreria Editrice Vaticana/United States Conference of Catholic Bishops, 2nd edn. Washington DC

Cavanaugh TA (2006) Double-effect reasoning: doing good and avoiding evil. Clarendon Press, Oxford

Cicero (1927a) Tusculan disputations, volume I. In: King JE (trans). Loeb Classical Library 141. Harvard University Press, Cambridge, MA

Cicero (1927b) Tusculan disputations. In: King JE (trans). Loeb Classical Library 222. Harvard University Press, Cambridge, MA

Cimbalo G (1989) I rapporti finanziari tra Stato e Confessioni religiose nei Paesi Bassi. Giuffrè, Milano

Cimbalo G (2003) Euthanasia, palliative care and the right to a dignified life in the recent legislation of Denmark, Holland and Belgium. Il Foro Italiano 126(2):9

Cohen M, Hortensius J (2018) A human rights approach to end of life? Recent developments at the European court of human rights. Revista Do Instituto Brasileiro de Direitos Humanos (COEHN) 17(18):193–210

Colaianni N (2020) L'aiuto al suicidio tra Corte costituzionale 242/2019 e BundesVerfassungsGericht 26 febbraio 2020. Stato, Chiese E Pluralismo Confessionale

Cuello Cal6n E (1955) El problema penal de la eutanasia. In: Tres temas penales. Barcelona, pp 119–173

Cupelli C (2018) Il caso Cappato, l'incostituzionalità differita e la dignità nell'autodeterminazione alla morte. Diritto Penale Contemporaneo 2(19):533–546

Cupelli C (2019) Il cammino parlamentare di riforma dell'aiuto al suicidio: spunti e prospettive dal caso Cappato fra Corte costituzionale e ritrosia legislativa. Diritto Penale Contemporaneo 11(1):1–12

Cupelli C (2020) Il caso Cappato e i nuovi confini di liceità dell'agevolazione al suicidio. Dalla 'doppia pronuncia' della Corte costituzionale alla sentenza di assoluzione della Corte di Assise di Milano. Cassazione Penale 60(4):1428–1450

Cuttini M, Casotto V, de Vonderweid U, et al (2009) Neonatal end-of-life decisions and bioethical perspectives. Early Human Dev 85(10 Suppl):S21–S25

D'Agostino F (2018) Bioetica. Questioni di confine. Studium, Roma

D'Alessandro G, Di Giovine O (eds) (2020) La Corte costituzionale e il fine vita. Un confronto interdisciplinare sul caso Cappato-Antoniani. Giappichelli, Torino

D'Aloia A (1998) Diritto di morire? La problematica dimensione costituzionale della "fine della vita". Politica del Diritto 4:601–636

De Grazia D (1999) Advance directives, dementia, and 'the someone else problem'. Bioethics 13(5):373–391

Deamer DW, Fleischaker GR (1994) Origins of life: the central concepts. Jones and Bartlett Publishers, Boston

Dierickx S, Deliens L, Cohen J, Chambaere K (2015) Comparison of the expression and granting of requests for euthanasia in Belgium in 2007 versus 2013. JAMA Int Med 175(10):1703–1706

Diogenes Laërtius (2008) Vite dei filosofi. In: Indelli G (trans). BUR, Milano

Donini M (2016) La necessità di diritti infelici. Il diritto di morire come limite all'intervento penale. Rivista Italiana Di Medicina Legale E Del Diritto in Campo Sanitario 38(2):555–581

Donini M (2019) Il caso Fabo/Cappato fra diritto di non curarsi, diritto a trattamenti terminali e diritto di morire. L'opzione "non penalistica" della Corte costituzionale di fronte a una trilogia inevitabile. In: Marini FS, Cupelli C (eds) Il caso Cappato. Riflessioni a margine dell'ordinanza della Corte costituzionale, n. 207 del 2018. Editoriale Scientifica, Napoli, § 5

Donini M (2020) Libera nos a malo. I diritti di disporre della propria vita per la neutralizzazione del male. Sistema Penale (web edition)

Dresser R (1995) Dworkin on dementia: elegant theory, questionable policy. Hast Cent Rep 25(6):32–38

Dresser R (2017) On legalizing physician-assisted death for dementia. Hast Cent Rep 47(4):5–6

Dworkin R (1993) Life's dominion: an argument about abortion, euthanasia, and individual freedom. Vintage Books, New York

Engelhardt HT Jr (1996) The foundations of bioethics, 2nd edn. Oxford University Press, New York

Epictetus (1925) Discourses, volume I. In: Oldfather WA (trans). Loeb Classical Library 131. Harvard University Press, Cambridge, MA

Epicurus (1974) Epistola a Meneceo. In: Cambiano G (ed). Opere. UTET, Torino, pp 196–204

Epicurus (1983b) Vatican saying IX. In: Long AA, Sedley DN (eds) The hellenistic philosophers, vol. 1: translations of the principal sources with philosophical commentary. Cambridge University Press, Cambridge, p 215

Eusebi L (2018) Un diritto costituzionale a morire «rapidamente»? Sul necessario approccio costituzionalmente orientato a Corte cost. (ord.) n. 207/2018. DisCrimen 19 December 2018
Fiandaca G (2020) Fino a che punto è condivisibile la soluzione costituzionale del caso Cappato? DisCrimen 3 Feb 2020
Flores d'Arcais P (2010) Albert Camus. Filosofo del futuro. Codice Edizioni, Torino
Foot P (2001) Morality, action, and outcome. In: Woodward PA (ed) The doctrine of double effect: philosophers debate a controversial moral principle. University of Notre Dame Press, Notre Dame, pp 67–82
Fornasari G, Picotti L, Vinciguerra S (eds) (2019) Autodeterminazione e aiuto al suicidio. Padova University Press, Padova
Fornero G (2020) Indisponibilità e disponibilità della vita: una difesa filosofico-giuridica del suicidio assistito e dell'eutanasia. UTET, Milano
Fornero M (2019) Il diritto di andarsene. Einaudi, Torino
Francis (2022) Catechesis on St. Joseph: 11. St. Joseph, Patron of the good death. General Audience, Vatican City
Francis N (2016) Neonatal deaths under Dutch Groningen protocol very rare despite misinformation contagion. J Assisted Dying 1(1):7–19
Gaede K (2016) The criminalization of facilitating suicide as a recurring pursuit—§ 217 StGB. Juristische Schulung 53(7):385
Gardiner SM (2011) A perfect moral storm: the ethical tragedy of climate change, environmental ethics and science policy series. Oxford Academic
Gensabella Furnari M (2008) Vulnerabilità and Cura, Bioetica ed esperienza del limite edn. Rubbettino, Soveria Mannelli
Gimbernat Ordeig E (1987) Eutanasia y Derecho Penal. Revista de la Facultad de Derecho de la Universidad de Granada 12:107–112
Göken H, Zwießler F (2022) Assisted suicide in Germany: the landmark ruling of the German Federal Constitutional Court of February 26, 2020. German Law J 23(4):661–671
Griffiths J, Bood A, Weyers H (1988) Euthanasia and law in the Netherlands. Amsterdam University Press, Amsterdam
Gusmai A (2019) Il diritto all'autodeterminazione: una libertà "perimetrata" dal sapere scientifico? Dirittifondamentali.it 1:5
Hegel GWF (1977) Phenomenology of spirit (trans: Miller AV). Oxford University Press, Oxford. Originally published as: Hegel GWF (1807) Phänomenologie des Geistes. Joseph Anton Goebhardt, Bamberg and Würzburg
Hegel GWF (1999) Lineamenti di filosofia del diritto. Diritto naturale e scienza dello Stato in compendio, con le Aggiunte di Eduard Gans. Laterza, Roma–Bari
Hegel GWF (2003) Elements of the philosophy of right (trans: Nesbit HB). Cambridge University Press, Cambridge
Herremans J, Genicot G (2016) Minors in the Belgian law on Euthanasia: a welcomed extension of patient's autonomy. BioLaw J 3:9–14
Hufen F (2018) Self-determined dying—the rejected fundamental right. Neue Juristische Wochenschrift 1524
Hume D (1985) Essays, moral, political, and literary. In: Miller EF (ed) Liberty Fund, Indianapolis
Hutchinson DS (1994) Introduction. In: Inwood B, Gerson LP (eds) The Epicurus reader: selected writings and testimonia. Hackett Publishing Company, Indianapolis, p vi
Illich I (1975) Medical Nemesis: the expropriation of health. Calder & Boyars, London
Jonas H (1984) The imperative of responsibility: in search of an ethics for the technological age. University of Chicago Press, Chicago
Kant I (1984) Lezioni di etica (trans: Capra F, Bari L). Originally published as: Kant I (1924) Eine Vorlesung Kants über Ethik: im Auftrag der Kantgesellschaft. Reuther & Reichard, Berlin
Kant I (1998) Groundwork of the metaphysics of morals (trans: Gregor MJ). Cambridge University Press, Cambridge

Kant I (2003) Sull'etica del suicidio: dalle Riflessioni e Lezioni di Immanuel Kant con i Preparativi di un infelice alla morte volontaria di un anonimo del Settecento. In: Aportone A (ed). I biancospini 5. Le Lettere: Firenze, p 138

Kim SYH, Mangino D, Nicolini M (2020) Is this person with dementia (currently) competent to request euthanasia? A complicated and underexplored question. J Med Ethics 46:459–460. https://doi.org/10.1136/medethics-2019-105860

Korsgaard C (2009) Self-constitution: agency, identity, and integrity. Oxford University Press, Oxford

Koshland DE (2002) The seven pillars of life. Science 295(5563):2215–2216

Kübler-Ross E (1975) Death: the final stage of growth. Simon & Schuster, New York

Lerner BH, Caplan AL (2015) Euthanasia in Belgium and the Netherlands: on a slippery slope? JAMA Intern Med 175(10):1640–1641

Lewis P (2007) The empirical slippery slope from voluntary to non-voluntary euthanasia. J Law Med Ethics 35(1):197–210

Locke J (1824) An essay concerning human understanding. In: The works of John Locke, vol 1. Thomas Tegg, London

Maltoni M, Pittureri C, Scarpi E, Piccinini L, Martini F, Turci P, et al (2009) Palliative sedation therapy does not hasten death: results from a prospective multicenter study. Ann Oncol 20:1163–1169

Manna A (2019) Does a right to die exist? Reflections between the Italian and German Constitutional Courts. Criminalia 2019:203–220

Marini FS, Cupelli C (eds) (2019) Il caso Cappato. Riflessioni a margine dell'ordinanza della Corte costituzionale n. 207 del 2018. Editoriale Scientifica, Napoli

Materstvedt LJ, Clark D, Ellsershaw J, Førde R, Gravgaard AM, Müller-Busch HC, Porta i Sales J, Rapin CH (2003) Euthanasia and physician-assisted suicide: a view from an EAPC Ethics Task Force. Palliat Med 17:97–101

Maturana HR, Varela FJ (1980) Autopoiesis and cognition: the realization of the living. D. Reidel, Dordrecht

Menzel P, Dolan P, Richardson J, Olsen JA (2002) The role of adaptation to disability and disease in health state assessment: a preliminary normative analysis. Soc Sci Med 55(12):2149–2158

Menzel PT, Steinbock B (2013) Advance directives, dementia, and physician-assisted death. J Law Med Ethics 41(3):484–500

Merrill KR (1999) Hume on suicide. Hist Phil Quart 16(4):395–412

Miller DG, Dresser R, Kim SYH (2019) Advance euthanasia directives: a controversial case and its ethical implications. J Med Ethics 45(2):84–89. https://doi.org/10.1136/medethics-2017-104644

Nacoti M, Ciocca A, Giupponi A, et al (2020) At the epicenter of the Covid-19 pandemic and humanitarian crises in Italy: changing perspectives on preparation and mitigation. NEJM Catalyst Innov Care Deliv 1(2)

Nietzsche F (1966) Beyond good and evil: prelude to a philosophy of the future (trans: Kaufmann W). Vintage Books, New York. Originally published as: Nietzsche F (1886) Jenseits von Gut und Böse. C. G. Naumann, Leipzig

Orsi L, Giannini A, Vergano M, Gristina GR (2015) Le cure di fine vita in Italia: il problema e la sua possibile soluzione nella prospettiva dei clinici. BioLaw J 4(2):227–234

Padovani T (2019) Dovere di vivere e aiuto al suicidio: un sintagma. In: Istigazione e aiuto al suicidio e valori costituzionali: un orizzonte da delineare, proceedings of the seminar held at the Senate of the Republic, 15 March 2019. BioDiritto

Palazzani L (2020) Il suicidio assistito medicalizzato: riflessioni filosofico-giuridiche sulla sentenza n. 242/2019 della Corte costituzionale. BioLaw J (2):287–301

Paul II J (1995) Evangelium Vitae: encyclical letter on the value and inviolability of human life. Catholic Truth Society, London

Pellizzone I (2020) Aiuto al suicidio e sindacato di costituzionalità: pars destruens e pars construens delle pronunce della Corte Costituzionale come chiave di lettura della tecnica decisoria e della ratio decidendi del caso Cappato. Forum di Quaderni Costituzionali 2/2020

Pessina A (2007) Eutanasia. Della dignità del morire nell'epoca della tecnologia. Cantagalli, Siena

Pizzetti FG (2019) L'ordinanza n. 207/2018 della Corte costituzionale, pronunciata nel corso del "Caso Cappato", e il diritto del paziente che rifiuta le cure salvavita a evitare un'agonia lenta e non dignitosa. BioLaw J 2019(2):151–170. https://doi.org/10.15168/2284-4503-416

Plato (1926) Laws. In: Bury RG (trans). Loeb Classical Library 192. Harvard University Press, Cambridge, MA

Plato (1990) Phaedo. In: Fowler HN (trans). Loeb Classical Library 36. Harvard University Press, Cambridge, MA

Plato (2016) The Republic. In: Reeve CDC (trans) 2nd edn. Hackett Publishing Company, Indianapolis

Poggi (2020) Il caso Cappato: la Corte costituzionale nelle strettoie tra uccidere e lasciar morire. BioLaw J 1/2020

Rachels J (1975) Active and passive euthanasia. N Engl J Med 292(2):78–80

Razzano G (2019) La Corte costituzionale sul caso Cappato: può un'ordinanza chiedere al Parlamento di legalizzare il suicidio assistito? Dirittifondamentali.it 1/2019

Ricci Ascoli A (2002) L'opera creativa della giurisprudenza olandese in tema di eutanasia attiva e suicidio assistito: commento alla sentenza del tribunale circoscrizionale di Haarlem, sez. collegiale, 30 ottobre 2000. In: Fiandaca G (ed) Sistema penale in transizione e ruolo del diritto giurisprudenziale, Il diritto penale XXI secolo 1. Edizioni Scientifiche Italiane, Padua, pp 119–129

Risicato L (2020) La Consulta e il suicidio assistito: l'autodeterminazione "timida" fuga lo spettro delle chine scivolose. Legislazione penale, web edn, 1–12

Rodotà S (2012) La vita e le regole. Tra diritto e non diritto, 2nd expanded edn. Feltrinelli, Milano

Ross WD (1930) The right and the good. Clarendon Press, Oxford

Roxin C (2016) Assisted suicide intended as a recurring pursuit as a criminal offence and the proposal of an alternative. Neue Zeitschrift Für Strafrecht 185:189–197

Rozemond K (2021) Euthanasie bij mensen met dementie volgens het supported decision-making regime van artikel 12 van het Verdrag inzake de Rechten van Personen met een Handicap [Euthanasia in persons with dementia according to the decision-making regime supported by Article 12 of the Convention on the Rights of Persons with Disabilities]. Handicap and Recht 6:3

Sachs M (2020) Constitutional rights: right to a self-determined. Juristische Schulung 580:580

Sartre JP (2003) Being and nothingness: an essay on phenomenological ontology. In: Barnes HE (trans). Routledge, London

Schopenhauer A (1969) The world as will and representation. In: Payne EFJ (trans). Dover Publications, New York

Schopenhauer A (1974) Parerga and paralipomena. In: Payne EFJ (trans). Clarendon Press, Oxford

Seneca LA (1920) Epistles. In: Gummere RM (trans). Loeb Classical Library 75. Harvard University Press, Cambridge, MA

Seneca LA (1928) Moral Essays, Volume I: De Providentia. De Constantia. De Ira. De Clementia. In: Basore JW (trans). Loeb Classical Library 214. Harvard University Press, Cambridge, MA

Sessa A, (2018) Le giustificazioni procedurali nella teoria del reato: profili dogmatici e di politica criminale. Edizioni Scientifiche Italiane, Naples. ISBN 978-88-495-3632-4

Shany Y (2005) Toward a general margin of appreciation doctrine in international law? Eur J Int Law 16(5):907–940

Siegel AM, Sisti DA, Caplan AL (2014) Pediatric euthanasia in Belgium: disturbing developments. JAMA Int Med 311(19):1963–1964

Simoncini A (2022) Towards the elaboration of a right to a dignified death in the European experience. Some food for thought. In: Cerruti T (ed) L'elaborazione di un diritto a una morte dignitosa nell'esperienza europea. Editoriale Scientifica. Naples, pp 347–371
Snijdewind MC, van Tol DG, Onwuteaka-Philipsen BD, Willems DL (2015) A study of the first year of the end-of-life clinic for physician-assisted dying in the Netherlands. JAMA Int Med 175(10):1633–1640
Spittler JF (2020) Assisted suicide in Germany – a neurological-psychiatric point of view. Neue Juristische Online Zeitschrift 20(19):97–99
Steinbock B, Norcross A (eds) (1994) Killing and letting die. Fordham University Press, New York
Tamburini C (2020) Per non morire di inerzia: piste di riflessione per una legge italiana su alcuni aspetti del fine vita. BioLaw J 2020(3):261–270. https://doi.org/10.15168/2284-4503-705
Tedesco M (2017) Dutch protocols for deliberately ending the life of newborns: a defence. J Bioethical Inquiry 14(2):251–259
The Holy Bible (1989) New revised standard version. In: Division of Christian education of the national council of the churches of christ in the United States of America. New York
Tigrino A (2021) La riflessione penalistica spagnola in materia di fine vita: dalle elaborazioni d'epoca franchista alla Ley Orgánica de regulación de la eutanasia del 18 marzo 2021. La legislazione penale 2021(2):1–20
Tripodina C (2018) Quale morte per gli "immersi in una notte senza fine"? Sulla legittimità costituzionale dell'aiuto al suicidio e sul "diritto a morire per mano di altri. BioLaw J 3:147
Trombetti Budriesi AL (2013) Un gallo ad Asclepio: morte, morti e società tra antichità e prima età moderna. Bologna
van Delden JJ (2004) The unfeasibility of requests for euthanasia in advance directives. J Med Ethics 30(5):447–451
van der Berg JH (1969) Medische Macht en Medische Ethiek. Callenbach, Nijkerk
Verhagen E, Sauer PJ (2005) The Groningen protocol—euthanasia in severely ill newborns. N Engl J Med 352:959–962
Veronesi P (2019) L'ordinanza n. 207/2018 sul c.d. 'Caso Cappato': cosa c'è, cosa non c'è (né poteva esserci) e a cosa potrebbe preludere. Forum di Quaderni Costituzionali 2019(6):1–10
Vinciguerra S (2020) L'aiuto al suicidio dopo il giudizio di costituzionalità. Una risposta e qualche domanda. Il Foro Italiano 145(3):843–850
Vinciguerra S, Ricci Ascoli A (1997) Il diritto giurisprudenziale olandese in tema di eutanasia attiva e suicidio assistito. In: Fiandaca G (ed) Sistema penale in transizione e ruolo del diritto giurisprudenziale. CEDAM, Padova
Wach B (2020) Dutch protocol from Groningen (the so-called Groningen Protocol). The problem of deliberate causing of death in newborns ("neonatal euthanasia"). Analiza I Egzystencja 49:53–87
Walker RM (2001) Physician-assisted suicide: the legal slippery slope. Cancer Control 8(1):25–31
Walsh E (2020) Cognitive transformation, dementia, and the moral weight of advance directives. Am J Bioeth 20(8):54–64
Zagrebelsk V (2020) Aiuto al suicidio. autonomia, libertà e dignità nel giudizio della Corte europea dei diritti umani, della Corte costituzionale italiana e di quella tedesca. Legislazione penale

Chapter 4
The Ethical Triage Dilemma

In the domain of healthcare management and resource allocation, the subject of triage is characterised by its sensitivity and complexity. In addressing issues concerning the micro-allocation of healthcare resources, it is imperative to elucidate the parameters and scope of research activities from their inception.

The issue of healthcare resource allocation has been a subject of interest to scholars of economic policy, medicine, bioethics, philosophy and law for many years. This is due to the fact that it involves a series of choices that must take into account different areas and aspects. The contemporary debate, which has endured since that time, commences with the earliest cases in the field of allocation from the 1940s[1] and 1960s.[2]

In the context of health resource allocation, it is imperative to delineate the distinct macro, meso and micro levels of decision-making. Each level is associated with a distinct scale of intervention, and each is characterised by specific actors, constraints, and ethical tensions.

Decisions pertaining to the overall structure, funding and priorities of the healthcare system are made at the macro level by national or regional authorities. This encompasses the conceptualisation of public health insurance schemes, the delineation of essential benefits packages, pharmaceutical pricing, and the formulation of population-wide health strategies. Ethical issues at this level are frequently associated with distributive justice, intergenerational equity, and the balance between individual rights and collective welfare.

The meso level is concerned with institutional or organisational decisions, such as those made by hospitals, health agencies, or clinical networks. In this

[1] Where expert committee allocated—without public input—then-novel penicillin to American soldiers before civilians, using expected efficacy and speed of return to duty as criteria (McGough et al. 2005).

[2] During the 1960s, committees in Seattle allocated scarce dialysis machines using prognosis, current health, social worth, and dependants as criteria (McGough et al. 2005).

A. Ferrara, *Bioethical Reflections on the Border between Life and Death*, European Union and its Neighbours in a Globalized World 32,
https://doi.org/10.1007/978-3-032-09985-3_4

context, the allocation of resources is characterised by the establishment of budgets across various departments, the formulation of eligibility criteria for specific interventions, and the management of waiting lists. The ethical challenges intrinsic to this level pertain to the principles of transparency, consistency, and the equitable treatment of diverse patient demographics within a unified healthcare system.

Finally, the micro level refers to decisions made at the bedside by clinicians and care teams. Decisions pertaining to individual treatment plans, the process of informed consent, the withholding or withdrawal of therapies, and the prioritisation of one patient over another in routine clinical practice are all included. Within the domain of medical ethics, prevailing concerns are typically centred on the relationship between patient and physician, the importance of respect for autonomy, and the management of uncertainty in clinical decision-making.

Despite their analytical distinctiveness, these levels are interdependent. The formulation of macro-level policies gives rise to the shaping of meso-level constraints, which in turn condition micro-level decisions. It is therefore essential that a coherent ethical framework encompasses all three dimensions, thereby ensuring that justice, efficiency, and care are promoted consistently across the system.

In this chapter, however, it should be demonstrated that to avoid violating fundamental human rights, the decision-making process regarding the criteria for the allocation process, including the micro-allocation level, must be determined at the meso or macro level, starting from the analysis of the closest level of healthcare resource allocation to the patient (i.e., micro-allocation) in an emergency situation.

We will therefore refer more specifically to cases in which demand for healthcare resources exceeds supply. While some scholars consider scarcity to be endemic to healthcare systems, we will focus on allocation decisions in emergency situations similar to those that occurred during the SARS-CoV-2 pandemic. After analysing specific cases regarding the different approaches adopted in some European states, the USA and Brazil, we will attempt to verify which ethical approach seems to be more justifiable. Subsequently, we will carry out a further philosophical analysis of some of the criteria in order to offer useful considerations that can inform the current debate and help to avoid the violation of fundamental human rights, even in emergency situations, as much as possible. This is particularly important in light of the Common EU Protocol on Crisis Preparedness.

To clarify the boundaries of our research, it is important to note that, given the broad scope of the debate on healthcare resources, we will distinguish ordinary healthcare scarcity from emergency scarcity by three factors compared to ordinary conditions: firstly, the quantitative exacerbation of scarcity conditions; secondly, the inestimable value of time in both the selection of the criterion and the utilisation of the resource; and thirdly, the fatal outcome for patients who are not allocated healthcare resources. This outcome would not have been fatal in ordinary triage, but would have enabled the patient to survive.

4.1 General Principles of the Medical Ethics. Criteria for Resource Allocation

As outlined in preceding chapters, technological progress in the medical field has engendered novel possibilities that have resulted in benefits for patients that would have been arduous to achieve in the past. It has been asserted that an increase in life expectancy, population growth, rising costs and a shortage of medical and nursing staff are indicative of the possible limitations of medicine. However, alternative perspectives posit that the manner in which financial resources are distributed exerts a significant influence on the perception of their sufficiency (Light 1997).

The allocation of resources has always been and continues to be one of the most significant ethical challenges of our time. The domain of medical ethics is the study of the moral and ethical implications of healthcare practices, encompassing the stages of life from birth to death. This subject inherently gives rise to profound philosophical interrogations concerning fundamental questions about human nature. The concept of resource allocation in economics is defined as the rationalisation of resources and their utilisation in accordance with a specific logic. The concept of rationalisation, understood as the optimisation of resources and the equitable management of constraints, is economically imperative, legally and ethically justifiable, yet manifestly incomplete, despite its pervasive implementation. An enhancement in efficiency is observed, yet this is counterbalanced by the presence of practical limitations.

The principles underpinning micro-allocative choices in healthcare resources are fundamentally aligned with the fundamental principles of medical ethics established by Beauchamp and Childress (2001).

Autonomy refers to the capacity of individuals to make informed, uncoerced decisions about matters affecting their own bodies and lives. In medical ethics, respect for autonomy means that patients must be treated as agents capable of rational self-determination. This entails not only obtaining informed consent but also ensuring that patients are given adequate information, time, and freedom to make decisions consistent with their values and beliefs. The principle of beneficence obliges healthcare professionals to act in ways that promote the well-being of their patients. It goes beyond avoiding harm (as in non-maleficence) and requires active contribution to the health and welfare of individuals. This includes the duty to diagnose accurately, treat effectively, relieve suffering, and offer comfort. Beneficence also involves a balancing act: not every possible benefit can be pursued at any cost, and clinicians must weigh expected outcomes against potential burdens or side effects. Closely related to beneficence, the principle of non-maleficence is captured by the ancient maxim *primum non nocere*. It represents a fundamental commitment to refrain from actions that might cause unnecessary injury, suffering, or risk. In clinical practice, this translates into careful risk–benefit assessments, the avoidance of futile or disproportionate interventions, and sensitivity to iatrogenic harm. Unlike beneficence, which invites positive action, non-maleficence imposes a constraint: if an action carries significant risk of harm without sufficient potential benefit, it should be avoided.

Justice, in the context of medical ethics, is concerned with fairness in the distribution of healthcare resources, responsibilities, and burdens. It requires that patients in similar circumstances be treated alike, and that access to care is not arbitrarily determined by irrelevant factors such as race, gender, socioeconomic status, or geography. At the micro level, justice demands impartiality in clinical judgment; at the macro level, it calls for structural mechanisms to ensure that healthcare systems are equitable and inclusive.

It is important to note that these four principles should not be regarded as rigid rules; rather, they are moral considerations that must be balanced in light of context. Conflicts between these principles are a common occurrence, as illustrated by the scenario in which the pursuit of beneficence for one patient results in the limitation of justice for others. In such cases, ethical reasoning involves a process of evaluation in which principles are considered alongside the consequences of their application. This process is informed by both professional standards and societal values.

The ethical debate on resource allocation is chiefly concerned with the conflict between the individual and the community, as well as the tension between divergent conceptions of justice in resource allocation.

Various distributive models can be articulated within the principle of justice, such as utilitarianism (which aims to maximise overall benefit), egalitarianism (which ensures equal access), prioritarianism (which gives preference to those who are worst off) and sufficientarianism (which guarantees a minimum threshold of care). We will focus on these models later.

The establishment of priorities can facilitate the implementation of targeted rationing, with the urgency of treatment being determined by the diagnostic and therapeutic levels. The fundamental objective of the process must be to ensure equitable allocation. The fundamental principles underpinning this concept are those of rationalisation, rationing and priority.

In everyday clinical settings, triage functions as a routine tool for managing access to healthcare services when demand exceeds available capacity in a given moment, but not under conditions of extreme scarcity. Ordinary triage operates within the boundaries of normal institutional functioning and is guided by a more stable set of ethical and clinical assumptions.

The underlying ethical framework of ordinary triage reflects a balance between deontological obligations toward individual patients and consequentialist considerations related to clinical efficiency and procedural fairness. Most health systems adopt a need-based model of justice (Rawls 1971; Daniels 2008), which prioritises patients according to the severity of their condition, the urgency of intervention, and the likelihood of therapeutic benefit. This approach is grounded in the principle that healthcare should respond first to those in greatest need, provided that some benefit is reasonably foreseeable. This approach is predicated on the principle that healthcare should be primarily focused on addressing the needs of those who are most in need, provided that a reasonable degree of benefit can be reasonably foreseen. The following operational criteria are of paramount importance: In the context of healthcare provision, three principles govern the prioritisation of patients according to their medical urgency. Firstly, patients facing the highest and most immediate risk of deterioration or death are prioritised. Secondly, those most likely to benefit from intervention are generally favoured within a given urgency category. Thirdly, waiting time and procedural fairness are considered. In cases where urgency and prognosis are equivalent, the principle of "first come, first served" is often applied to ensure transparency and avoid arbitrariness (Persad et al. 2009).

These principles reflect a prioritarian ethic, which gives moral weight to the needs of the worst-off, while also recognising the limits of resource availability. Ordinary triage does not aim to maximise total benefit across the population, but rather to allocate care based on a combination of clinical justice and institutional feasibility. In practice, this means that care is denied or delayed only when justified by relative clinical prioritisation.

Moreover, ordinary triage is embedded in a relational model of medicine, in which the physician maintains an ethical commitment to each individual patient, even when navigating institutional constraints. This distinguishes it sharply from emergency triage, where the clinician may be explicitly tasked with distributive decisions at the population level, often contrary to the usual fiduciary role (Berlinger et al. 2020). Thus, ordinary triage is not ethically neutral: it institutionalises a particular conception of fairness—one that seeks to reconcile clinical effectiveness, moral equality, and procedural transparency, without abandoning the primacy of patient-centred care. The duty of care and its ramifications are the primary focus of clinical ethics.

4.2 Medical Ethics in Times of Crisis: The Allocation of Health Resources in Emergency Contexts

In contexts of large-scale emergencies—such as pandemics, natural disasters, or humanitarian crises—the principles of medical ethics are subjected to intense pressure and often require reconfiguration. When healthcare systems are overwhelmed and resources become critically scarce, the ethical landscape shifts from patient-centred care to public health ethics, where the focus moves to population-level outcomes and collective survival (Thompson et al. 2006; Emanuel et al. 2020).

Emergency triage often is characterised by a utilitarian rationale: decisions are made with the explicit aim of maximising the number of lives saved, or in some cases, maximising life-years or quality-adjusted life expectancy (White and Lo 2020). The underlying assumption is that when not everyone can be treated, priority must be given to those with the greatest probability of survival with treatment, and the lowest expected use of scarce resources, such as ventilators or intensive care beds.

This shift entails profound ethical consequences. While ordinary triage relies on principles of urgency and individual benefit, crisis triage introduces exclusion criteria, ranking systems (such as the SOFA score or Clinical Frailty Scale), and triage committees, all designed to standardise decisions and reduce moral distress among frontline professionals (Christian et al. 2014). In this model, autonomy may be limited, informed consent becomes conditional, and the physician's fiduciary duty may be subordinated to public interest.

The criteria commonly employed in emergency triage include: Short-term survival probability (based on clinical scores and comorbidities); Long-term prognosis or life expectancy (used as a tiebreaker or secondary criterion); Instrumental value (giving priority to healthcare workers or individuals crucial to the response effort); Age thresholds, though highly contested, are sometimes invoked to maximise life-years or avoid therapeutic futility (Persad et al. 2009).

These criteria raise significant ethical challenges. The risk of discrimination, particularly against older adults, persons with disabilities, or those with chronic illnesses, is widely recognised. As a response, many triage protocols include explicit anti-discrimination clauses and require public accountability and procedural transparency (Berlinger et al. 2020).

Ultimately, crisis ethics requires a recalibration of core principles: justice becomes distributive, beneficence becomes collective, autonomy becomes constrained, and non-maleficence is reinterpreted in terms of avoidable harm to society rather than to the individual alone. This does not imply the suspension of medical ethics, but rather its transformation under exceptional constraints.

It is precisely these issues that will be discussed later on. The objective—starting from the most recent case of the coronavirus emergency—is to analyse the criteria adopted in some of the countries that have been most affected by the shortage of medical resources and then discuss them in an attempt to identify, if any, the criteria that seem most ethically acceptable. The present study will hypothesise that the real ethical dilemma does not lie in the kind of criteria that are used. Rather, the study will propose some solutions that may help to avoid violations of fundamental human rights and discrimination.

4.3 Triage and COVID-19: The Emergency Response in the United States, Brazil and Italy

The COVID-19 pandemic can be considered the most disastrous health emergency since the so-called Spanish pandemic of 1918; especially when compared to the scientific progress of the twenty-first century. The pandemic, declared by the World Health Organisation on 11 March 2020,[3] has shown the deep connection

[3] World Health Organization. (2020). WHO Director-General's opening remarks at the media briefing on COVID-19–11 March 2020. Available at: https://www.who.int/director-general/speeches/detail/who-director-general-s-opening-remarks-at-the-media-briefing-on-covid-19–11-march-2020.

between the economic systems of all the world's states, highlighting how the interdependence between them is an aspect to be taken into deep consideration when making health policy choices.

At the same time, it was possible to verify how the strategies adopted by different countries to counter the evolution of the pandemic did not really make a difference in the containment of contagions, especially following the so-called *first wave* (March–May 2020).

The protection of some basic human rights has been put at serious risk. The excessive demand for access to intensive and sub-intensive care treatment compared to the potential of hospitals and the impossibility of providing all patients with the necessary care has probably represented a serious threat to the effective right to health, and in some cases to life, of a large part of the population.

The suffering of intensive care wards and the difficulties in managing admissions and related healthcare resources has forced, in the absence of legislative intervention on the point, the doctors and healthcare workers themselves to identify certain criteria through which to establish how to allocate the available healthcare resources.

In this scenario, in fact, the insufficiency of healthcare resources put a strain on national systems, which often had to adopt triage protocols on their own initiative in order to justify the choice of who to treat and who not to.

The fundamental problem in this scenario was in fact, who to treat first, and on the basis of what criteria, given that this choice could have made the difference between the life and death of the patient by affecting the fundamental rights of the population.

It is undeniable that choices of this pervasiveness require a substratum of justification based not only on scientific but also on ethical principles, which should have matched each other as perfectly as possible.

Committees all over the world have endeavoured to identify inviolable principles to be applied to triage in the event of a disproportion between necessary and available healthcare resources, but despite this, the criteria adopted have been the most disparate.

The application of such different approaches has given rise to a heated ethical and philosophical debate on what criteria should be applied in allocating scarce healthcare resources.

The debate was fervent, and still, the triage dilemma does not seem to have been resolved.

In this section, we will be briefly analyse the protocols adopted in some of the countries most affected by the pandemic—specifically Brazil, the USA and Italy—to later verify whether the utilitarian approach prevalently applied, can actually find an ethical justification. Subsequently, a further philosophical analysis of some of the criteria will be carried out in order to offer some useful considerations that can feed the current debate in the direction of avoiding as much as possible, even in emergency situations, the violation of fundamental human rights.

Brazil, with 26.27% of global deaths (data from 15 April 2021), is the country most affected by the consequences of the pandemic. The ratio between the number of inhabitants and the infrastructures available to the Brazilian health system has contributed to a less effective response to the pandemic emergency, and at the same time very quickly led to a disproportion between the health resources available and those needed to deal with the pandemic. The problem of insufficient health resources led to the intervention of the Brazilian Society of Bioethics[4] in order to produce a document through which to provide useful guidelines, in the fight against COVID-19, for an ethical allocation that respects fundamental human rights.

The aforementioned recommendations, starting from the assumption that it is necessary, in the allocation of healthcare resources, to refer to a Unified Healthcare System through which to guarantee that intensive care places, both in public and private clinics, are allocated without violating the rights of the most fragile and socially disadvantaged people, identify certain parameters to be respected precisely in the case of insufficient resources.

The basis for any decision in the field of resource allocation is the protection of the dignity of the human being without any form of discrimination of socially fragile and vulnerable persons, groups of persons or communities being abstractly accepted.

Again according to the SBB if the flower is human dignity, the stem at its base is the right to life,[5] health, privacy and equality, rights without which, human dignity itself could not be protected.

After highlighting the need to eliminate the conditions by virtue of which society is effectively faced with the choice of whom to care for, the Brazilian Society reaffirms—on the basis of its role identified by the Universal Declaration on Bioethics and Human Rights[6]—the objective, even in extreme cases such as pandemics, of being able to provide adequate care to anyone in need in order to ensure "the right of every person to enjoy the highest possible level of physical and mental health"[7].

---

[4] Brazilian Society of Bioethics (SBB), Recommendation n.1/2020. Available at: http://www.sbbioetica.org.br/.

[5] Brazilian Society of Bioethics (SBB), Recommendation n.1/2020, 1. Available at: http://www.sbbioetica.org.br/.

[6] UNESCO. (2005). Universal Declaration on Bioethics and Human Rights. Paris: United Nations Educational, Scientific and Cultural Organization. Available at: https://unesdoc.unesco.org/ark:/48223/pf0000146180.

[7] United Nations. (1966). International Covenant on Economic, Social and Cultural Rights, 16 December 1966, UNTS Vol. 993, p. 3. Article 12. Available at: https://www.ohchr.org/en/instruments-mechanisms/instruments/international-covenant-economic-social-and-cultural-rights.

One of the cardinal principles of triage—which must be based exclusively on scientific evidence—is the need to take into account, when allocating healthcare resources, not only Sars-CoV-2 patients, but the entire patient population.

Moreover, criteria adopted by medical personnel to assess the patients to whom they should administer available healthcare should take into account certain risks inherent to triage. These certainly include social vulnerability, biological vulnerability, discrimination or stigmatisation of frail individuals and lack of respect for cultural or sexual diversity.

In addition to the SBB, the main medical associations also had to produce their own guidelines in order to provide healthcare professionals involved in the allocation of resources, which were insufficient, with a uniform reference. In a document prepared by AMIB, ABRAMEDE, SBGG, ANCP[8] the operating methods for scientifically as well as ethically validated triage were identified. Before outlining the clinical-operational modalities of triage, the four associations that signed the document outlined the ethical objectives on which to base the protocol. The choice of whom to treat should therefore be based on the need to save as many lives as possible and save as many years of life as possible.[9] Mention is also made of the criterion according to which it would be necessary to try to give each individual the same opportunity to go through the different stages of life, in fact valuing the patient's age.

The analysis of the protocol makes it possible to verify that the criteria underlying triage consist mainly of clinical criteria. The first parameter taken into consideration in order to save the greatest number of lives, and therefore, not to

[8] AMIB, ABRAMEDE, SBGG, ANCP (2020). Recomendações da AMIB (*Associação de Medicina Intensiva Brasileira*), ABRAMEDE (*Associação Brasileira de Medicina de Emergência*), SBGG (*Sociedade Brasileira de Geriatria e Gerontologia*) e ANCP (*Academia Nacional de Cuidados Paliativos*) de alocação de recursos em esgotamento durante a pandemia por COVID-19. [Recommendations from AMIB (Brazilian Intensive Medicine Association), ABRAMEDE (Brazilian Association of Emergency Medicine), SBGG (Brazilian Society of Geriatrics and Gerontology), and ANCP (National Academy of Palliative Care) for resource allocation in situations of exhaustion during the COVID-19 pandemic] Available at: https://www.amib.org.br/fileadmin/user_upload/amib/2020/abril/24/VJS01_maio_-_Versa__o_2_-_Protocolo_AMIB_de_alocac__a__o_de_recursos_em_esgotamento_durante_a_pandemia_por_COVID.pdf.

[9] AMIB, ABRAMEDE, SBGG, ANCP (2020). Recomendações da AMIB (Associação de Medicina Intensiva Brasileira), ABRAMEDE (Associação Brasileira de Medicina de Emergência), SBGG (Sociedade Brasileira de Geriatria e Gerontologia) e ANCP (Academia Nacional de Cuidados Paliativos) de alocação de recursos em esgotamento durante a pandemia por COVID-19. [Recommendations from AMIB (Brazilian Intensive Medicine Association), ABRAMEDE (Brazilian Association of Emergency Medicine), SBGG (Brazilian Society of Geriatrics and Gerontology), and ANCP (National Academy of Palliative Care) for resource allocation in situations of exhaustion during the COVID-19 pandemic] 1. Available at: https://www.amib.org.br/fileadmin/user_upload/amib/2020/abril/24/VJS01_maio_-_Versa__o_2_-_Protocolo_AMIB_de_alocac__a__o_de_recursos_em_esgotamento_durante_a_pandemia_por_COVID.pdf.

'waste' available healthcare resources, consists of the SOFA score[10] (Vincent et al. 1996); a scientific protocol applicable to patients admitted (or in need of admission) to intensive care through which to predict the success rate of healthcare treatment. The second parameter, on the other hand, is based on the ECOG scale[11] (Oken et al. 1982), which instead determines the general health condition through an objective examination of the patient's condition. Lastly, the presence of co-morbidities with a life expectancy of one year or less is assessed.

For each step, the protocol provides for the assignment of a higher score to the patient in the worst clinical condition and the subsequent allocation of the health resource to the patient with the lowest score, i.e. in the best condition. Obviously, it should be emphasised that these criteria deviate purely from the classical criteria of clinical ethics, but apply a utilitarian approach—which will be discussed below—aimed at maximising the cost-benefit ratio for society, understood as the sum total of the individual interests of each member of society.

The United States of America is characterised by a 'peculiar' healthcare system, in which public health protection is limited (only in 2010 with the so-called *Obamacare* was the number of beneficiaries of public healthcare extended) and inequalities in access to healthcare services are just as serious as the social ones.

The debate on the issue of triage has been heated from the outset and there are still different schools of thought on the correct way to allocate insufficient healthcare resources.

In addition to the institutional bioethics commissions, the first body to express an opinion on the subject was the Ethics Commission of the American College of Surgeons[12] through some guidelines made available to its members.

The two fundamental objectives to be pursued in the allocation of insufficient healthcare resources were to save as many lives as possible and as many years of life as possible.[13] To assist and support doctors in triage, again according to the ACS, it was necessary to set up triage teams in hospitals that could ensure transparency and consistency in triage management and relieve the individual doctor of the emotional burden of choice.

---

[10] The SOFA (Sequential Organ Failure Assessment) score is a clinical tool used to assess the extent of a patient's organ function or rate of organ failure. Originally developed to describe the progression of organ dysfunction in intensive care units, it evaluates six organ systems (respiratory, cardiovascular, hepatic, coagulation, renal, and neurological), assigning each a score from 0 (normal function) to 4 (severe dysfunction), with the total score helping to estimate morbidity and mortality risk. See Vincent et al. (1996).

[11] The ECOG (Eastern Cooperative Oncology Group) Performance Status Scale is a widely used clinical tool that assesses a cancer patient's level of functioning in terms of their ability to care for themselves, carry out daily activities, and engage in physical activity. Scores range from 0 (fully active) to 5 (death), and are commonly used to evaluate prognosis, determine treatment eligibility, and guide clinical decision-making in oncology. See Oken et al. (1982).

[12] American College of Surgeons (ACS) 2020. Ethical Framework for the Allocation of Resources in the Event of Shortages, https://www.facs.org/covid-19/ethics.

[13] American College of Surgeons (ACS) 2020. Ethical Framework for the Allocation of Resources in the Event of Shortages, p. 1 https://www.facs.org/covid-19/ethics.

The objectives of triage should be pursued through the use of clinical protocols based on objective parameters such as SOFA (also seen in Brazil) or PELOD[14] (Leteurtre et al. 2006).

Further interesting food for thought, however, was provided by the ethics committee of the Society of Critical Care Medicine.[15]

The pivotal criterion—utilitarian in nature—suggested by the SCCM for the allocation of healthcare resources in the event of insufficient resources is summarised in the assumption 'greatest good for the greatest number'.[16] According to this principle, in order to achieve the greatest benefit for the greatest number of people, it is permissible for *the triage team*, in a contingency phase between necessary and available healthcare resources, to refuse even life-support to a patient in need; or in the case of 'critical capacity'[17] to suspend a life-support treatment if, after a maximum period of time, it proves ineffective, allowing a patient on the waiting list to receive the necessary treatment.

Priority should be given to patients most likely to benefit from treatment, based on clinical criteria freely predetermined by the facility, applied consistently and without being influenced in any way by considerations of race, gender, ethnicity, disability, sexual orientation, religious beliefs, citizenship and socio-economic status.

Even more detailed is the document promulgated by the Department of Critical Care Medicine (DCCM) of the University of Pittsburgh[18] in which a clear and specific set of ethically justifiable criteria were identified to identify the most correct way of performing triage.

---

[14] The PELOD (Pediatric Logistic Organ Dysfunction) score is a validated clinical tool used to quantify the severity of multiple organ dysfunction in critically ill children admitted to intensive care units. It assesses the function of several organ systems—including neurological, cardiovascular, respiratory, renal, and hematologic—assigning scores based on physiological and laboratory parameters. Higher scores are associated with increased mortality risk. See Leteurtre et al. (2006).

[15] Society of Critical Care Medicine (SCCM), 2020. Society of Critical Care Medicine Crisis Standard of Care Recommendations for Triaging Critical Resources During the COVID-19 Pandemic (SCCM), https://www.sccm.org/getattachment/179d65cb-9076-4cf2-a06a-3ae7c928e634/Triaging-Critical-Resources.

[16] Society of Critical Care Medicine (SCCM), 2020. Society of Critical Care Medicine Crisis Standard of Care Recommendations for Triaging Critical Resources During the COVID-19 Pandemic (SCCM), p. 1. Available at: https://www.sccm.org/getattachment/179d65cb-9076-4cf2-a06a-3ae7c928e634/Triaging-Critical-Resources.

[17] Society of Critical Care Medicine (SCCM), 2020. Society of Critical Care Medicine Crisis Standard of Care Recommendations for Triaging Critical Resources During the COVID-19 Pandemic (SCCM), p. 2. Available at: https://www.sccm.org/getattachment/179d65cb-9076-4cf2-a06a-3ae7c928e634/Triaging-Critical-Resources.

[18] (DCCM) Department of Critical Care Medicine (2020) Allocation of Scarce Critical Care Resources During a Public Health Emergency, University of Pittsburgh, published on 15 Apr 2020. Available at: https://www.ccm.pitt.edu/sites/default/files/2023-05/Allocation_of_Critical_Care_in_Public_Health_Emergency_June2021-FINAL.pdf.

According to Pittsburgh physicians, the primary objective of triage is to achieve the greatest possible benefit for the patient community as a whole; to do this, it is necessary to identify the patient to whom care should be administered, establishing the patient with the greatest number of life-saving years.[19]

The DCCM of the University of Pittsburgh also states that no choice should ever be motivated by whether or not a patient belongs to any category; on the contrary, it totally excludes, in the case of triage following emergencies characterised by absolute dynamism (such as pandemic emergencies), that categorisation can be used in order to allocate or not health resources. Such an allocation structure for scarce resources must never be able to identify a priori the categories to be excluded from the possibility of receiving the relevant care. There are many reasons for this; the prediction of categories to be excluded a-priori would deviate even further from ordinary medical criteria, creating real discrimination without at the same time maximising general public health and conveying the idea that certain categories of patients do not deserve to be treated[20] while at the same time fuelling the population's distrust and sense of injustice in the resource allocation system, which instead needs, especially during a health emergency, a strong consensus on the part of the population.

A convincing element—albeit with some corrections—consists in the justification of the assessment of short-term life expectancy as a criterion for resource allocation. Indeed, the DCCM scholars argue that using the criterion of the longest life expectancy in the long term, already used for example in the choice of lung transplant recipients (Egan et al. 2006), would lead to clear discrimination against patients with a reduced life expectancy due to a disability, other illnesses or otherwise conditions exacerbated by social inequalities. The principle that short-term life expectancy should be valued, irrespective of the outcome of the disease for which the healthcare resource is needed at that time, is based on the desire to avoid discrimination due to the age factor pure and simple and to ensure greater certainty in the clinical assessment made at triage. In fact, life expectancy is only valued in the event that, regardless of whether the current, acute phase of the illness has passed, it is less than five years.

The procedure, developed in detail by the Pittsburgh scholars, involves the assignment of a final score resulting from the summation of the values attributed on the basis of the greatest chance of benefiting from treatment and the patient's short-term life expectancy. Patients with a higher probability of survival through intensive care should be given priority over patients with a lower probability.

---

[19] (DCCM) Department of Critical Care Medicine (2020) Allocation of Scarce Critical Care Resources During a Public Health Emergency, University of Pittsburgh, published on 15 Apr 2020, p. 1. Available at: https://www.ccm.pitt.edu/sites/default/files/2023-05/Allocation_of_Critical_Care_in_Public_Health_Emergency_June2021-FINAL.pdf.

[20] (DCCM) Department of Critical Care Medicine (2020) Allocation of Scarce Critical Care Resources During a Public Health Emergency, University of Pittsburgh, published on 15 Apr 2020, p. 7. Available at: https://www.ccm.pitt.edu/sites/default/files/2023-05/Allocation_of_Critical_Care_in_Public_Health_Emergency_June2021-FINAL.pdf.

Patients who, in the short term, do not have a compromised prognosis are given priority over those with a high risk of death, even if the acute phase of the disease is overcome.[21]

Patients are therefore subjected to a triage based exclusively on clinical-prognostic criteria that tend to value the cost-benefit ratio associated with the use of the healthcare resource, through the application of the SOFA score (which assigns a higher score to patients in the worst condition) and the subsequent assessment of short-term life expectancy (with only patients with a life expectancy of less than 5 years and 1 year being given a score). For the resolution of the *ex aequo*, on the other hand, a number of options are proposed in order to correctly identify the prioritising elements, among which, belonging to the category of health professionals or being among the individuals who have not yet had the opportunity to go through the different stages of life.[22] According to the doctors of the University of Pittsburgh, who justify this statement by also referring to popular common feeling (Biddison et al. 2014), giving all individuals an equal chance to experience the different stages of life is a shareable ethical goal (Emanuel et al. 2020; Neuberger et al. 1998).

The protocols whose salient features have just been reported are only some of those produced in the USA. In fact, the absence of any directive promulgated by state or supra-state bodies has allowed each hospital or medical association to produce its own guidelines and recommendations for triage (Antommaria et al. 2020), generating what could be considered a real disparity between individuals residing in the same state or sometimes in the same city.

The Italian National Health System was among the first to be confronted with insufficient healthcare resources. As stated in the previous chapter as early as 21 March 2020, thirteen doctors from the Papa Giovanni XXIII Hospital in Bergamo wrote and published a letter in the 'New England Journal of Medicine—Catalyst Innovations in Care Delivery' (Nacoti et al. 2020), in which they denounced the insufficiency of available healthcare resources.

At the same time, the Italian Society of Anaesthesia Analgesia Resuscitation and Intensive Care, published a document entitled 'Recommendations of Clinical Ethics for the admission to and suspension of intensive care in exceptional conditions of imbalance between need and available resources' (2020), which identified criteria through which to choose who to treat and who not to. This document, by virtue of the continuation of the pandemic emergency, was

[21] (DCCM) Department of Critical Care Medicine (2020) Allocation of Scarce Critical Care Resources During a Public Health Emergency, University of Pittsburgh, published on 15 Apr 2020, p. 6. Available at: https://www.ccm.pitt.edu/sites/default/files/2023-05/Allocation_of_Critical_Care_in_Public_Health_Emergency_June2021-FINAL.pdf.

[22] (DCCM) Department of Critical Care Medicine (2020) Allocation of Scarce Critical Care Resources During a Public Health Emergency, University of Pittsburgh, published on 15 Apr 2020, p. 7. Available at: https://www.ccm.pitt.edu/sites/default/files/2023-05/Allocation_of_Critical_Care_in_Public_Health_Emergency_June2021-FINAL.pdf.

subsequently reworked[23] on behalf of the Italian National Institute of Health, on the basis of a shared reflection with jurists and with representatives of the Italian Society of Legal Medicine and Insurance. The Working Group's analysis started from the identification of the founding principles of bio-legal reasoning (principle of equality, social solidarity, dignity of the individual, self-determination) and then subsequently became explicit in a series of statements produced in order to outline the criteria that must guide triage in the case of a disproportion between available and necessary healthcare resources. The most relevant statements, for the present work, are those from 4 to 7 and more specifically: At each level of intensity of care, in the case of a saturation of care resources such that the indicated treatment cannot be guaranteed for all patients, it is necessary to resort to triage, rather than to a chronological criterion (order of arrival of patients) or a random criterion (draw). The purpose of intensive care triage is, in accordance with the above-mentioned principles, to guarantee life-support treatment to as many patients as possible who can benefit from it. Triage must be based on defined clinical-prognostic parameters that are as objective and agreed upon as possible. The assessment, aimed at stratifying the likelihood of overcoming the current critical condition with the support of intensive care, must proceed on the basis of the global assessment of each individual patient through the following parameters: (a) number and type of comorbidities; (b) past functional status and frailty; (c) severity of current clinical picture; (d) likely impact of intensive care, also taking into account the patient's age; (e) The patient's wishes regarding intensive care should be investigated as early as possible in the initial triage phase.

Age should be considered in the context of the overall assessment of the sick person and not on the basis of predefined cut-offs.[24]

The document in question, which is intended to offer healthcare professionals a tool for responding to the disproportion between available and necessary healthcare resources, stimulates various reflections when analysed in its entirety, especially with regard to the use of certain systems, such as Charlson's comorbidity index (1987) or the frailty scale (Rockwood et al. 2005), the use of which probably runs the risk of directly conflicting with the ethical and legal assumptions set out in the document itself.

[23] Italian Society of Anaesthesia, Analgesia, Resuscitation and Intensive Care (SIAARTI) & Italian Society of Legal and Insurance Medicine (SIMLA). (2021). Decisioni per le cure intensive in caso di sproporzione tra necessità assistenziali e risorse disponibili in corso di pandemia di COVID-19 [Decisions on intensive care in cases of disproportion between healthcare needs and available resources during the COVID-19 pandemic]. 13 January 2021. Available at: https://www.omceomi.it/docs/default-source/default-document-library/documento-cure-terapia-intensiva-a-covid.pdf?sfvrsn=0.

[24] Italian Society of Anaesthesia, Analgesia, Resuscitation and Intensive Care (SIAARTI) & Italian Society of Legal and Insurance Medicine (SIMLA). (2021). Decisioni per le cure intensive in caso di sproporzione tra necessità assistenziali e risorse disponibili in corso di pandemia di COVID-19 [Decisions on intensive care in cases of disproportion between healthcare needs and available resources during the COVID-19 pandemic]. 13 January 2021. Statement 4 to 7. Available at: https://www.omceomi.it/docs/default-source/default-document-library/documento-cure-terapia-intensiva-a-covid.pdf?sfvrsn=0.

In fact, despite the fact that the goal indicated is to save as many lives as possible, thus avoiding the waste of resources, the guidelines drawn up seem to directly emphasise certain elements that might deviate from purely *clinical-prognostic* criteria. Although within the promulgated recommendations reference is always made to an overall and discretionary consideration of the patient's condition, the prognostic assessment should be limited as much as possible, to avoid that assessments that are too discretionary or in any case uncertain may be included within the triage.

The document published by SIAARTI and SIMLA, however, sets out a number of guidelines to meet the criterion of the greatest number of lives saved and the greatest number of years of life saved, as fundamental corollaries of triage, also arguing that a utilitarian approach is certainly preferable.

In order to comprehend the criteria that were utilised in the administration of limited health resources, it is also possible to make reference to other studies that could assist in elucidating whether the fundamental question pertains to 'who should receive medical care first?' or 'how should we decide who should receive medical care first?'.

A study published in the Annals of Internal Medicine, compared 29 different triage policies provided by 29 different hospitals in the United States: "In terms of explicitly stated triage criteria, the 5 most commonly mentioned are benefit (25 policies [96.2%]), need (14 [53.8%]), age (13 [50.0%]), conservation of resources (10 [38.5%]), and lottery (9 [34.6%]). Only 6 (23.1%) policies utilize a first-come, first-served allocation framework. No policy utilized lottery or first-come, first-served as its sole or exclusive criterion. Ten (38.4%) policies give preference to health care workers: 5 (19.2%) on the basis of reciprocity (recognition of their voluntary acceptance of risk), 4 (15.4%) on the basis of narrow social utility, 1 (3.8%) on the basis of both reciprocity and narrow social utility, and 2 (7.7%) without articulating a specific reason. In specifying need and benefit, 21 (80.8%) policies use scoring systems, and the most commonly used scoring system is the Sequential Organ Failure Assessment (SOFA) score or the Modified SOFA (MSOFA) score, used in 20 (95.2% of policies that use scoring systems). Twelve (46.2% of all policies) utilize specific clinical diagnoses as allocation criteria—for example, excluding patients with cardiac arrest or severe burns. Although 13 (50.0%) policies utilize age criteria, only 2 (7.7%) specify age thresholds ("[...]"). Seventeen (65.4%) policies also specify criteria that should not be considered in allocation decisions. These include the ability to pay, insurance status, or socioeconomic status (13 [50.0% of all policies]); race (12 [46.2%]); broad social utility (social status or social worth) (11 [42.3%]); ethnicity (9 [34.6%]); and citizenship, gender, religion, or sexual orientation (8 [30.8% each]). Only 7 (26.9%) policies specify that decisions should not be based on disability, and 4 (15.4%) prohibit decisions based on age" (Antommaria et al. 2020).

As pointed out in the aforementioned study, each hospital in the United States followed different triage criteria and policies. At the same time, in the rest of the world, physicians had to deal with the absence of uniform criteria, independently deciding how to cope with the shortage of health resources. Another important study is the one published on *Bioethics*, showing that in Europe several professional associations published COVID-19 triage recommendations in an extremely short time (Ehni et al. 2021). In fact, even within the European borders, each country issued its own different guidelines and recommendations regarding the fundamental criteria to be applied in the presence of scarce resources. After analyzing the various ethical and practical approaches adopted in Italy, Austria, Switzerland, Germany and Belgium, Hans-Jörg Ehni, Urban Wiesing and Robert Ranisch affirmed: "Given the recommendations that have been presented here there is still a lot to be done on the ethics of triage" (Ehni et al. 2021, p. 134).

Another inspiring study conducted in UK, and which involved 763 people (both men and women) between 18 and 86 years, who were called to respond to a survey: "Presented with a set of hypothetical COVID-19 triage dilemmas, respondents prioritised patients who would have a higher chance of survival, longer duration of survival, shorter duration of treatment, lower age or lesser degree of frailty. Where there was a small difference between two patients, a larger proportion elected to toss a coin to decide which patient to treat. Respondents were more egalitarian in scenarios relating to patients with pre-existing disability. A majority were prepared to withdraw treatment from a patient in intensive care who had a lower chance of survival than another patient currently presenting with COVID-19. More participants were prepared to withhold than withdraw life-saving treatment in equivalent cases. Respondents also indicated a willingness to give higher priority to healthcare workers and to patients with young children" (Wilkinson 2020).

A similar finding was made in a study carried out in the United States by Buckwalter and Peterson. The result of the survey saw the majority supporting the idea that healthcare resources must be allocated primarily to patients with the greater chances of recovery, instead contradicting the principles that are based on the social utility of patients. In addition, a preference for the principle of an allocation based on utilitarian criteria emerged, although this would be to the detriment of the elderly (Buckwalter and Peterson 2020).

4.4 The Principle of Justice in Triage: Utilitarianism, Egalitarianism, Prioritarianism and Sufficientarianism

The analysis of the guidelines and criteria applied in three of the states most affected by the COVID-19 pandemic and the focus on the studies mentioned earlier allows some general legal-philosophical considerations to be made. The aim of these considerations is to verify—taking the criteria examined above as a starting point—whether there really are ethically sustainable criteria on the basis of which healthcare resources can be allocated in the event of a disproportion between those available and those needed.

The comparative study carried out highlights the emergence of an almost ubiquitous tendency to conceive of triage as based on a purely utilitarian approach that departs from the classical approach of clinical ethics inspired by the Hippocratic oath.

The adoption of a utilitarian approach, in fact, contrasts with the usual protection of the individual interest (Jöbges et al. 2020) with respect to the collective interest and with the physician's duty to act—according to his skills and judgement—in order to pursue the utility for the sick person and to avoid directing care towards the patient who would benefit most from it (Leven 1998). At the same time, it would conflict with the egalitarian principle founded on the pursuit of substantive equality for all human beings and the need to direct attention towards caring for those most in need (Raynaud 2003).

To be more specific could be usefull to analyse the foundamental ethical approaches to healthcare allocation, starting properly from the utilitarian one.

Utilitarianism remains one of the most influential normative frameworks in the ethical debate on the allocation of scarce healthcare resources. Its core principle—maximizing overall well-being or utility—has informed public health policies, cost-effectiveness analysis, and triage protocols in both routine and emergency medical settings. However, utilitarianism is not a monolithic theory; it encompasses multiple formulations, each offering a distinct account of what it means to produce “the greatest good.”

The most classical expression of utilitarianism, articulated by Jeremy Bentham and developed in contemporary bioethics by authors such as Peter Singer, aims to maximize the aggregate amount of utility across all individuals. In healthcare contexts, this approach justifies allocating resources to patients whose treatment will yield the highest total benefit, often measured in terms of life-years saved or quality-adjusted life years (QALYs). As a result, this model can permit the sacrifice of individuals who would benefit less, if doing so increases the overall gain (Singer 2011, p. 95). While intuitively powerful in maximizing outcomes, classical utilitarianism has been criticized for ignoring fairness and distributive justice.

A variant of this framework—average utilitarianism—shifts the focus from the total sum of benefits to their mean per capita distribution. This version seeks to enhance the average level of well-being within a population, rather than its total quantity. It may, for instance, avoid prioritizing a small number of highly beneficial treatments if they substantially lower the well-being of others or leave large groups underserved. Yet average utilitarianism, too, has limits, particularly when it comes to defending the interests of the worst-off, whose needs may be overlooked for the sake of maintaining a higher average (Broome 1991, p. 158).

Preference utilitarianism, meanwhile, defines utility not in terms of pleasure or health metrics, but as the satisfaction of individual preferences. In this framework, healthcare decisions should aim to fulfill the desires of patients, assuming these are informed and autonomous. While this model aligns closely with liberal values such as autonomy and consent, it raises difficult questions about the comparability and normative validity of preferences, particularly in settings where they are shaped by social inequalities or misinformation (Parfit 1984, pp. 493–494).

Finally, rule utilitarianism diverges from act-based versions by proposing that we should follow general rules or policies that, when applied consistently, maximize utility over time. In healthcare, this translates into support for standardized triage protocols, such as the use of SOFA scores or age-based prioritisation during pandemics, on the basis that such rules yield better long-term outcomes and institutional trust. However, rule utilitarianism can appear rigid or even unjust in specific cases where exceptions would yield better individual results (Hooker 2000, p. 74).

Despite their differences, all utilitarian approaches are united by the conviction that healthcare resources should be used to achieve the best overall outcomes, a view that continues to influence ethical and policy debates. Their divergence lies not in the goal, but in how benefits are conceptualized, measured, and distributed.

Egalitarianism, as an ethical approach to the allocation of healthcare resources, is grounded in the principle that all individuals have equal moral worth, and that justice requires equal access to health and healthcare opportunities. In its strictest form, egalitarianism demands that all patients receive the same treatment regardless of differences in need, prognosis, or social contribution. However, contemporary egalitarian theories typically endorse a more nuanced conception of equality, allowing for differential treatment when it serves to correct structural disadvantages or to ensure genuine equal opportunity.

One of the most influential formulations of egalitarian justice is found in John Rawls's theory of justice as fairness, which holds that social and economic inequalities are justifiable only if they benefit the least advantaged members of society (Rawls 1971, pp. 75–83). In healthcare, this Rawlsian approach supports allocating resources in ways that equalize access to meaningful health opportunities, for example by prioritizing the socially disadvantaged, the chronically ill, or those with limited life prospects due to systemic inequities. From this perspective, equality is not about identical treatment but about ensuring that everyone has a fair chance to attain a normal life span and health status (Daniels 2008, pp. 101–103).

Egalitarianism also informs critiques of allocation systems that rely solely on cost-effectiveness or outcome-maximisation. These systems risk perpetuating health disparities by systematically favoring individuals who are already better off—those with higher baseline health or greater access to care. Egalitarian ethics instead call for policies that recognize and rectify unjust background conditions, often through affirmative prioritisation of the disadvantaged. This view has influenced numerous public health initiatives, including efforts to reduce disparities in vaccination rates, access to organ transplants, and preventive care.

Nevertheless, egalitarian theories face several challenges. One central tension lies between equality and efficiency: treating all patients equally or prioritizing the disadvantaged may result in fewer lives saved or less overall benefit compared to strictly utilitarian models. Another difficulty concerns the metric of equality—whether it should refer to health outcomes, opportunities, life expectancy, or some broader conception of human flourishing. Despite these tensions, egalitarianism remains a foundational component of ethical discourse in health justice, particularly in contexts that involve vulnerable populations or structural health inequalities.

Prioritarianism offers a compelling alternative to both utilitarian and egalitarian approaches by asserting that the moral value of a benefit increases the worse off the person is who receives it. This principle does not demand equal treatment for all individuals—as egalitarianism might—nor does it aim to maximize total or average benefit, as in utilitarianism. Instead, it posits that improving the well-being of those in the worst conditions is ethically more urgent than producing similar or even greater gains for those who are better off. In the context of healthcare allocation, prioritarianism supports giving priority to patients who are severely ill, socially disadvantaged, or have had fewer life opportunities, even if others might experience greater health gains from treatment.

The intuitive moral appeal of prioritarianism lies in its sensitivity to both outcomes and fairness. It recognizes the importance of producing beneficial outcomes while refusing to treat all benefits as morally equal. For instance, saving five life-years for a young patient with a disability may be judged ethically more important than saving ten life-years for a healthy older person, because the former is in a more disadvantaged position. Philosophers such as Larry Temkin have argued that well-being improvements for the disadvantaged matter more, not just in terms of compassion, but as a matter of justice (Temkin 2003, pp. 18–21).

In practice, prioritarian reasoning has informed various healthcare policies, including pandemic triage frameworks that incorporate age, baseline health, and life-cycle considerations. These frameworks often combine prognostic scores (such as SOFA) with ethical modifiers designed to give extra weight to the worst-off, whether measured by life expectancy, comorbidities, or social conditions. Such approaches seek to balance efficiency with equity, avoiding both the strict egalitarian demand for equal treatment and the utilitarian risk of neglecting vulnerable individuals.

However, prioritarianism also faces challenges. A major difficulty is defining and operationalizing "worse off" in ethically justifiable ways. Should the metric be current health status, total expected life-years, socio-economic status, or cumulative disadvantage? Moreover, in certain cases, prioritizing the worst-off may lead to suboptimal use of scarce resources, especially when their chance of recovery is very low. Despite these concerns, prioritarianism remains a rich and flexible ethical framework that captures both the urgency of need and the moral significance of disadvantage.

Sufficientarianism presents a distinct ethical approach to healthcare allocation by shifting the moral focus from equality or maximisation to the idea of ensuring that everyone reaches a minimum threshold of well-being. According to sufficientarian theories, what matters most is not how benefits are distributed across the population, but whether each person receives "enough"—a sufficient level of goods, opportunities, or capabilities to live a decent life. Once this sufficiency threshold is met, further improvements in an individual's condition are considered less morally urgent. In healthcare, this translates into a commitment to guaranteeing access to essential treatments and basic health services, even at the cost of forgoing efficiency or further gains for those already above the threshold.

In ordinary contexts, prioritarianism and sufficientarianism provide valuable moral guidance by addressing long-term structural inequalities and by prioritizing those who are either worse off or below a threshold of basic well-being. However, emergency scenarios—such as pandemics, wars, or natural disasters—create acute scarcities, where every patient is in immediate and life-threatening need, and each available resource (e.g. a ventilator, ICU bed, or antiviral drug) represents the difference between life and death. Under such conditions, both theories face serious normative pressure.

In theory, prioritarianism would continue to favor those who are "worse off". But when all patients face the same lethal risk, the meaningfulness of "worse off" becomes ambiguous. Are all equally in need, or does some deeper form of disadvantage persist—e.g., a younger patient with a shorter life lived, or a person from a historically oppressed group?

Some interpretations of prioritarianism seek to preserve moral differentiation even in such cases, by weighing life-years lost or "life-cycle fairness" (i.e., younger patients may be seen as worse off because they have had fewer life opportunities). Others, however, argue that when death is imminent and equally likely without intervention, the claim of being "worse off" loses practical force, and decision-making may shift toward randomisation or clinical prognosis.

Sufficientarianism faces a distinct but parallel challenge. If "sufficiency" is interpreted as having access to life-saving treatment, then everyone below that threshold has an equally urgent and identical claim. This undermines the theory's ability to prioritize: no one can be considered "more insufficient" than another when each person will die without the resource.

Moreover, if the threshold is defined as "having a chance to survive," then all patients are, again, below the threshold, and sufficientarianism collapses into egalitarianism or default triage protocols. In such cases, the theory struggles to provide a discriminating principle for allocation.

An additional issue concerns what constitutes "sufficiency" in emergency medicine: Is it survival alone? Is it survival with minimal suffering? Or does it include long-term recovery prospects? These questions remain under-theorized in many sufficientarian accounts and create practical ambiguity in triage settings (Crisp 2003, pp. 751–753).

What these tensions reveal is that both prioritarianism and sufficientarianism are better suited to chronic scarcity and structural injustice than to acute, symmetrical crises. In emergencies where each life has equal urgent moral weight, ethical decision-making may need to incorporate hybrid principles—balancing fairness (e.g., lottery or "first come, first served"), clinical prognosis (likelihood of benefit), and societal considerations (e.g., key worker status or life-cycle stages).

In such contexts, the role of prioritarianism and sufficientarianism might shift from allocation criteria to institutional design principles, informing how systems prepare before crises (e.g., investing more in disadvantaged communities or early warning systems) rather than guiding bedside triage in the moment.

This approach is especially relevant in public health systems that aim to secure universal access to primary care, vaccinations, and life-saving treatments. It offers a moral justification for prioritizing patients who have not yet attained a basic level of health or functioning, regardless of how effective the treatment may be in terms of cost-efficiency or life-years saved. By focusing on sufficiency, rather than comparative advantage, sufficientarianism aligns with human dignity and minimum standards of justice, and it resonates strongly with rights-based and capability-based theories of justice (Crisp 2003, p. 757).

Yet sufficientarianism also faces important challenges. The first concerns the definition and measurement of the sufficiency threshold: what exactly counts as "enough"? Should it be based on survival, functional autonomy, the capacity to pursue personal goals, or access to a minimum healthcare basket? The second issue lies in its inflexibility once the threshold is met: sufficientarianism offers limited guidance in cases where multiple individuals are above the threshold and compete for further resources. In such contexts, it may fail to account for morally relevant differences in prognosis, outcome, or need.

Despite these limitations, sufficientarianism contributes an essential perspective to the ethics of health resource allocation. It draws attention to those below morally significant thresholds and emphasizes the duty to lift people out of states of deprivation, a consideration that remains crucial in both national and global health policy.

From what we have seen above utilitarianism, is founded on the objective of maximising the benefits for society as a whole by protecting the individual interests of the majority of members of society, attempting to improve the cost-benefit ratio and to deploy healthcare resources for those people who can benefit most from them. This particular type of health consequentialism implies that the goal of the public health system is to improve the health status of as many people as possible (Wynia 2005).

The criticisms made by some scholars (Gutman 2020; Barilan and Brusa 2016; Persad et al. 2009) towards the adoption of a utilitarian approach in triage are based on the assumption that any approach based on maximising the benefits for society would entail, as an indirect consequence, the discrimination of the weakest and most fragile subjects, whom the universally recognised solidaristic principles would tend to protect most strongly. Choosing the patient to whom to give the necessary medical care on the basis of an assessment of the probability of its success, rather than on the patient's life expectancy (after recovery) would mean that the elderly, the disabled, the frail or those with co-morbidities, would a-priori have a lesser chance of being treated. On the contrary, critics of an egalitarian approach to triage (Satomi 2020; Jöbges et al. 2020, p. 958), based on the need to treat primarily those in the worst condition or to apply the criterion of randomness, point out that such criteria would lead to the waste of resources and the worsening of general public health conditions, creating mistrust in the healthcare system and at the same time violating the fundamental rights of a larger section of society.

Indeed, in times of crisis, the population's trust in the healthcare system is a fundamental element that must be taken into consideration. It is only through the people's consent that the application of any criteria can become effective and efficient. It should be pointed out that utilitarian approaches can be very varied and pursue in their specificity very different objectives based on the interpretation of the concept of inviolability of certain fundamental human rights. In fact, the attempt to save as many lives as possible, rather than the greatest number of life years or even, the greatest number of 'quality' life years (QALYs), determines, from an ethical point of view, the sharing of absolutely opposing principles (Savulescu et al. 2020).

In any case, the desirable goal of saving as many lives as possible without violating patients' rights (Liddell et al. 2020), is particularly difficult to pursue. Even the very idea of triage in the case of insufficient healthcare resources presupposes the violation of certain fundamental rights of the patient who, despite having the right, as well as the possibility, to receive the care necessary to save his or her life, may be denied it on the basis of a certain triage policy. The choice (or non-choice) to apply one criterion rather than another cannot therefore prevent the violation of the right to health, the right to life, as well as the protection of the dignity of at least one human being, namely the patient to whom treatment will be denied.

Given that, therefore, no approach to triage seems to be able to prevent the violation of certain fundamental human rights, because the same definition of emergency of triage take with it the violation of fundamental rights.

Nevertheless, it is worth to examining whether there are grounds for considering one approach ethically preferable to the others.

Specifically, an attempt will be made to ascertain whether there are indeed motivations that tend to make one prefer the utilitarian approach adopted in almost all cases, and more specifically the two most frequently adopted criteria, the pursuit of the goal of saving as many lives as possible and as many years of life as possible.

4.5 Justifying Utilitarian Approaches: The Duty to Protect Future Generations

The intention to maximise, even though triage, the overall utility for the majority of the population can probably find justification in mankind's ancestral tendency. This tendency to "safeguard and promote the interests of the present and future generations"[25] seems to be able to justify, in an emergency situation, the adoption of criteria that favour the protection of plurality over individuality.

The ethical imperative to ensure the survival of the human species finds strong theoretical grounding in both classical and contemporary thought. In Leviathan, Thomas Hobbes identifies self-preservation as the most fundamental of natural

[25] Art 2., princ. g, UNESCO. (2005). Universal Declaration on Bioethics and Human Rights. Paris: United Nations Educational, Scientific and Cultural Organization. Available at: https://unesdoc.unesco.org/ark:/48223/pf0000146180.

laws, grounding the formation of social contracts and civil order on the rational imperative to avoid death. Although Hobbes formulates this principle in terms of individual survival, his logic can be extended to collective and intergenerational preservation. Hans Jonas expands this perspective in The Imperative of Responsibility, where he articulates a new categorical imperative for the technological age: to act so that the effects of our actions are compatible with the permanence of genuinely human life on Earth. While Jonas applies this imperative to the ethical challenges posed by modern technology, the same principle can be usefully extended to the ethics of emergency medicine and public health: in contexts where human life is at stake, preserving the conditions for future human existence must remain a guiding criterion. Building on this foundation, Brian Patrick Green argues that humanity's survival should be our first ethical priority, contending that the extinction of the human species would render all other moral considerations meaningless. Complementing this anthropocentric view, Paul W. Taylor's biocentric ethics maintains that every living being, including humanity, has a good of its own that ought to be respected and preserved. Contemporary scientific research supports this philosophical intuition: Schaller et al. have demonstrated the existence of evolved psychological systems dedicated to self-protection and disease avoidance—mechanisms that enhance individual and collective survival. Likewise, Capraro's work on human sociality highlights how intuitive moral heuristics, such as fairness and harm aversion, are evolutionarily shaped to promote cooperation and long-term group viability. Together, these philosophical and scientific perspectives converge on a shared ethical foundation: the survival of humankind is not merely a biological instinct, but a morally justified and rationally grounded imperative.

To justify the adoption of such criteria, it may be useful to consider the interests being protected and exaggerate the outcomes of one choice over another.

Therefore, in order to establish whether adopting a utilitarian criterion is ethically sustainable in a health emergency, a borderline situation could be hypothesised that is characterised by verisimilitude. In the event of a global pandemic, the consequences of which would far exceed those of COVID-19, putting the very survival of mankind at risk, the ethical sustainability of allocating healthcare resources towards those with the greatest chance of survival must be considered. The question must be posed: would it even be ethically sustainable to give priority in the delivery of care to those with the best chance of life itself remaining on earth? In the interest of the principles of non-discrimination and solidarity between individuals, would it be more appropriate to sacrifice humanity itself in the name of an individualistic ethic? While it is indeed possible to draw parallels between facing a pandemic and facing the extinction of the human race, it is equally possible to argue that the evolution of the effects of a pandemic caused by an unknown virus could, on a theoretical but plausible level, lead to an extreme situation such as the one hypothesised. It is reasonable to consider the hypothesis that the uncontrolled development of the pandemic could potentially undermine the survival of the human species at any given time. Consequently, it seems plausible that utilitarian criteria should be adopted in order to both ensure the prevention of current conditions of risk and to enhance the chances of survival of the species.

Furthermore, although it may be argued that avoiding the extinction of the human species is not necessarily an end connoted by moral value and that the concepts of society and species are abstractions of utilitarian ethics, it is possible to consider the self-preservation of the species as nothing more than the sum total of the interests and rights of each individual. Indeed, when utilitarianism is considered as acting in accordance with the interests of the greatest number of individuals, it is possible to argue that the preservation of the human race on Earth (as a species) consists in recognising and protecting each individual's right to life and existence. Conversely, the value of the right to life, which is inextricably linked to the right to health, is affirmed and recognised as fundamental by Art. 2 of the ECHR[26] (1950), Art. 3 of the UDHR[27] (1948) and Art. 2 UDBHR.[28] Furthermore, in the preamble of the Universal Declaration on Bioethics and Human Rights it is clearly stated that: "human beings are an integral part of the biosphere, with an important role in protecting one another and other forms of life". The aforementioned principle functions as a useful indicator of the universally recognised intrinsic value of the existence of every species and form of life on Earth. It thus follows that this principle legitimises a reasoning that, utilitarianistically, aims to prevent the risk of extinction of the human race itself as well as of every species present in the biosphere. In terms of fundamental rights, the interest in the continuation of the species, as well as being able to have a different and autonomous moral value (the same for which we attribute value to the survival of an animal species), can also be interpreted as an extrinsic expression of the right to life individually recognised for each human being.

One of the primary contentions advanced by critics of the utilitarian approach pertains to the notion that the selection of beneficiaries based on the probability of survival rather than the number of years of life saved inevitably gives rise to discriminatory practices against those who are most fragile and vulnerable (the elderly, disabled, and patients afflicted with comorbidities). The observations presented herein are predicated on the notion that the inherent value and dignity of a single human life is commensurate with that of multiple human lives,

---

[26] "Everyone's right to life shall be protected by law. No one shall be deprived of his life intentionally save in the execution of a sentence of a court following his conviction of a crime for which this penalty is provided by law". Council of Europe. (1950). European Convention for the Protection of Human Rights and Fundamental Freedoms. Rome, 4 November 1950. Available at: https://www.echr.coe.int/documents/convention_eng.pdf.

[27] "Everyone has the right to life, liberty and security of person". United Nations. (1948). Universal Declaration of Human Rights. Paris, 10 December 1948. Available at: https://www.un.org/en/about-us/universal-declaration-of-human-rights.

[28] "The aims of this Declaration are: [. . .] (c) to promote respect for human dignity and protect human rights, by ensuringrespect for the life of human beings, and fundamental freedoms, consistent with international human rights law". UNESCO. (2005). Universal Declaration on Bioethics and Human Rights. Paris: United Nations Educational, Scientific and Cultural Organization. Available at: https://unesdoc.unesco.org/ark:/48223/pf0000146180.

irrespective of the number and duration of each. It is further postulated that the consequences of a given choice are of negligible consequence, even if that choice results in the preservation of a greater number of lives.

Gutman (2020) clarifies the concept, affirming that "[t]his equal right to life means that no single life may be sacrificed, not even for a greater number of lives saved. Numbers don't count. [...] We cannot let someone die in order to save other people. So, when it comes to the right of life every life has the same value, and we must not discriminate when it comes to saving lives or to killing even, we must not discriminate on any grounds". In essence, the question is whether numbers matter. The answer to this question lies in solving the riddle (Taurek 1977).

Instead, considering the arguments given so far about the preservation of mankind, one could assume that by taking the outcomes of the cases under consideration to extremes, it is possible to recognise that numbers do in fact make a difference. Affirming, therefore, the fundamental right of each individual to live as long as possible and hypothesising an entirely plausible scenario in which the consequences of a pandemic endanger the very existence of mankind on earth, it is possible to argue for the ethical legitimacy of applying utilitarian criteria to triage in the event of an insufficiency of available healthcare resources.

This argument is predicated on several factors. Firstly, it is assumed that a principle is generally valid if the theoretical assumptions underlying it are present. In order to investigate the validity of the essence of the principle itself, it is necessary for its validity to persist in every situation in which the same assumptions are present, even if they are theoretically extreme. Consequently, the principle that numbers do not matter should remain valid, irrespective of the consequences of its application. It is important to note that, in theory, this is only possible by accepting the hypothetical extinction of the species and the violation of the resulting right to life of human beings.

Conversely, if the consequences were to be considered, and the self-preservation of the species were to be regarded as a paramount concern, then the utilisation of a utilitarian approach would be implicitly validated. This utilitarian approach would encompass a meticulous evaluation of the outcomes resulting from each choice, thereby ascertaining its efficacy for the majority of individuals.

Secondly, with regard to the question of rights, it is possible to state that there are no criteria capable of not infringing fundamental human rights in any way, since even the mere idea of choosing to whom to administer necessary treatment and to whom not to do so implies the violation of the right to health and life of at least one patient. It is evident that, irrespective of the criteria on the basis of which such a choice can be made, at least one person who would have been able to make the decision would be denied the right to receive the necessary treatment, and would in all likelihood face death, the right to life itself. It can thus be concluded that, even if the right to health is regarded as the right to the highest possible standard of health, the principle of triage would result in an individual being excluded from health treatment that is theoretically possible but becomes impossible solely and exclusively by virtue of a choice. Conversely, in circumstances where triage is conducted with the objective of allocating intensive care beds, the right to health and even the right to life itself are placed in a grave jeopardy. Furthermore, the right to survival of every human being, and indeed of the species, can be regarded as a fundamental prerequisite for the safeguarding of all subsequent rights. The preservation of the human species is, in fact, the very foundation upon which the protection of all other rights is built.

Thirdly, in order to clarify whether there are any arguments on the basis of which it is preferable to adopt utilitarian criteria, it is necessary to verify whether the argument of supporters of an egalitarian approach to triage, based on the thesis that the adoption of utilitarian criteria would necessarily give rise to the violation of the principle of equality and non-discrimination between human beings, is in fact well-founded. In order to undertake this process, it is first necessary to verify whether the application of utilitarian criteria to triage gives rise to actual discrimination between individuals.

This argument can be drawn directly from an analysis of the concept of discrimination itself. In fact, having ascertained that choosing whom to treat on the basis of purely clinical criteria is unlikely to constitute direct discrimination, since the discriminating characteristics (e.g. the patient's chances of survival) do not necessarily and inextricably correspond to those discriminated against (frailty, old age, co-morbidity or disability), it is appropriate to verify whether the application of a utilitarian approach in triage may instead give rise to indirect discrimination of the aforementioned categories. Well, the definition of indirect discrimination can be drawn analogically from that identified by Directive 2006/54/EC[29] on equal opportunities in employment and occupation, according to which indirect discrimination is a situation where an apparently neutral provision, criterion or practice may put persons belonging to a certain category at a particular disadvantage. At the same time, however, the same directive identifies a cause of justification—provided for only in cases of indirect discrimination—excluding the occurrence of a discriminatory act where the provision, criterion or practice applied is objectively justified by a legitimate aim and the means employed to achieve it are appropriate and necessary. At this juncture, it is imperative to inquire whether the implementation of specific clinical criteria for triage constitutes a suitable and essential means of attaining a legitimate social policy objective. Furthermore, it is crucial to ascertain whether this approach genuinely fulfils the intended purpose and whether it is executed in a consistent and systematic manner.

[29] Art.2 (b) "indirect discrimination: where an apparently neutral provision, criterion or practice would put persons of one sex at a particular disadvantage compared with persons of the other sex, unless that provision, criterion or practice is objectively justified by a legitimate aim, and the means of achieving that aim are appropriate and necessary; European Parliament and Council. (2006). Directive 2006/54/EC of the European Parliament and of the Council of 5 July 2006 on the implementation of the principle of equal opportunities and equal treatment of men and women in matters of employment and occupation (recast). Official Journal of the European Union, L 204, 26.7.2006, pp. 23–36. Available at: https://eur-lex.europa.eu/legal-content/EN/TXT/?uri=CELEX:32006L0054.

The aims pursued through the application of a utilitarian approach to triage appear to be legitimate (even if one agrees with the aforementioned theory of self-preservation). However, it is necessary to consider the specific criteria and how they should be identified in order to envisage their consistent and systematic implementation. This is also necessary to avoid any discriminatory outcome resulting from a lack of in-depth assessment of the rationale behind the criterion itself.

In view of the aforementioned arguments, and the balancing of the rights and interests at stake, it seems possible to conclude by affirming the ethical justification for the application to triage of criteria motivated by utilitarian ends, provided that a coherent and systematic implementation is ensured with the ends pursued. In view of the analysis that has just been completed on the principle of the self-preservation of the human species, it appears feasible to consider the ethical legitimacy of utilitarian criteria being applied to emergency triage situations. The subsequent paragraph will examine the criterion that is likely to exert the most significant influence on the utilitarian meaning of triage, namely age. It is therefore the objective of this study to ascertain whether age can be considered within the framework of utilitarian criteria.

4.6 Utilitarian Justifications and the Moral Relevance of Age: Is There a Right to Live Through All Life Stages?

The justification for a general utilitarian approach, however, makes it appropriate, given the extreme diversity of the specific criteria applied within that approach, to ascertain whether there are some that enjoy a further ethical justification over others.

The preeminent goal pursued by almost all recommendations and guidelines for performing triage is to save as many lives as possible. Given that, on the basis of the arguments given above, this objective is ethically justified, it is worth examining whether the same justification can be attributed to the second most frequently pursued objective, namely that of trying to save as many years of life as possible.

The idea of treating the patient with the *greatest number of years of life saved* expands, and perhaps further complicates, the related philosophical considerations.

In fact, placing a value on the number of years a patient has left to live, once the acute phase of the disease has passed, can only imply a prognostic judgement on the future duration of life and a valorisation of the simple age factor. It must be recognised, however, that acknowledging the valuation of the patient's life expectancy entails the acceptance of a considerable margin of error in the assessment. This is due to the fact that a substantial number of unforeseen events may occur in the medium to long term, which could result in a change to the estimated duration of a human being's life.

A considerable number of the guidelines examined in fact repudiate a priori evaluation of the patient's age in the provision of treatment. Rather, they utilise the criterion of age as either a competing criterion in the assessment of chances of survival (SIAARTI and SIMLA)[30] or as a criterion for resolving draws (DCCM, University of Pittsburgh).[31] Conversely, life expectancy is only accorded significance in certain instances where it falls below a predetermined threshold. The underlying cause of this discrepancy can be attributed to the enhanced reliability of the medical-scientific evaluation of patients' life expectancy in the immediate future. This approach is evidently designed to circumvent the utilisation of a resource by individuals who, possessing an equal probability of salvation, would be capable of benefiting from it for a highly constrained duration.

The ethical question connected with the application of this criterion is whether, given the ethical legitimacy of trying to save as many lives as possible, it is equally legitimate, given an equal chance of salvation, to save the person with the longest or shortest life expectancy.

Useful food for thought in analysing the criterion of patient age and life expectancy comes from the results of a aforementioned study conducted in the United Kingdom (Wilkinson 2020) and in the United States (Buckwalter and Peterson 2020). Participants, in deciding who should receive treatment in the event of treatment failure, not only prioritised patients with the best chance of survival, but also gave particular weight to the patient's age regardless of purely clinical aspects. It is relevant also that that all participants approved of utilitarian allocation criteria, even if these resulted in a disadvantage for the older segments of the population.

In the overall assessment of the problem, it is therefore good to take such ethical attitudes into consideration and to ask why there is this tendency, also expressed by subjects belonging to the same category, to admit age as the predominant factor in triage, almost agreeing with what Harris (1985) stated: "It is always unpleasant to die [. . .] but it is certainly more so to die prematurely".

Well, the first consideration that can be derived from the analysis of the aforementioned results, seems to confirm what the theory of the self-preservation of the species holds. In fact, the tendency—all other conditions being equal—towards the pre-eminence of the age criterion, which emerged in the aforementioned studies, is consistent with the inclination towards the self-preservation of the

[30] Italian Society of Anaesthesia, Analgesia, Resuscitation and Intensive Care (SIAARTI) & Italian Society of Legal and Insurance Medicine (SIMLA). (2021). Decisioni per le cure intensive in caso di sproporzione tra necessità assistenziali e risorse disponibili in corso di pandemia di COVID-19 [Decisions on intensive care in cases of disproportion between healthcare needs and available resources during the COVID-19 pandemic]. 13 January 2021. (2021) Available at: https://www.siaarti.it/news/382977. See also Riccioni et al. (2021).

[31] (DCCM) Department of Critical Care Medicine (2020) Allocation of Scarce Critical Care Resources During a Public Health Emergency, University of Pittsburgh, published on 15 Apr 2020, https://www.ccm.pitt.edu/sites/default/files/2023-05/Allocation_of_Critical_Care_in_Public_Health_Emergency_June2021-FINAL.pdf.

species in that choosing to treat younger patients, with a greater life expectancy and still in the biological conditions to reproduce, consequently increases the chances of survival of the species.

Secondly, one seems to be able to agree with the ethical argument based on the principle that every human being has an equal right to go through all the cycles of life and to live all the experiences that a life can actually offer. This theory originates from the idea, based on the fair innings argument, that equality between individuals on the basis of age should not be assessed at a particular point in time but over the course of a lifetime (McKerlie 1989; William 1997). The fair innings argument posits that each person is morally entitled to a "reasonable" span of life—an opportunity to live through the basic stages of the human condition. Thus, those who have not yet had this opportunity (typically younger individuals) are morally prioritized over those who have already lived through a complete or nearly complete life course. This view favours an approach to the positive discrimination necessary to ensure that the younger generation has the same opportunities as the older generation. Valuing the so-called life-cycle principle consists of ensuring equal opportunities for every human being to obtain an education, get married, have children, etc. (McKerlie 1989; William 1997). According to this principle, the age factor should play a direct role in determining to whom medical care should be administered in the event of insufficient care (Emanuel and Wertheimer 2006; Daniels 1983).

These principles are frequently invoked in triage contexts to resist the accusation of ageism, which is commonly defined as discrimination or prejudice against individuals on the basis of chronological age (Levy and Banaji 2002). Unlike ageist approaches, which dismiss the value of older lives as inherently lower, the fair innings argument justifies differential treatment based on temporal equity—the idea that those who have lived less should be granted priority, not because others are less worthy, but because they have already had their "fair share." Nevertheless, critics argue that this logic can unintentionally reinforce structural ageist assumptions, particularly if applied rigidly or without consideration of individual health prospects, quality of life, or social vulnerability (Harris 1985; Jennings 2020).

In the context of the global pandemic caused by the severe acute respiratory syndrome (SARS-CoV-2) virus, also known as the Coronavirus disease (COVID-19), Altman (2021) provided a compelling rationale for the incorporation of patient age into the triage process following a confirmed case of the virus. The primary rationale pertains to the fact that the short-term prognosis of a patient infected with the virus is significantly influenced by their age. A secondary rationale underscores the direct impact of age on the number of years of life saved. A third rationale draws upon a transposition of the 'veil of ignorance' theory propounded by Rawls (1971). The theory of the veil of ignorance, developed by John Rawls in *A Theory of Justice* (1971), was conceived as a philosophical thought experiment designed to determine the foundational principles of a just society. The core idea is that rational individuals, placed in what Rawls calls the "original position," and situated behind a "veil of ignorance"—that is, deprived of any knowledge regarding their own personal characteristics such as age, gender, health status, socio-economic background, natural talents, or conception of the good—would nonetheless possess general knowledge about the functioning of human societies and the laws of psychology, economics, and biology. In such a position of radical impartiality, Rawls argues, individuals would agree on a set of principles that ensure fairness and equality, as they would be motivated by a prudential concern to avoid being disadvantaged in whatever position they may ultimately find themselves once the veil is lifted.

Applying this same philosophical metaphor to the allocation of scarce health resources in contexts of emergency or structural limitation, it is possible to argue—as Palazzani (2020) does—that an individual behind the veil of ignorance, unaware of their actual age, health status, or social role, "could only accept the criterion of justice in the distribution" of such resources. In other words, without knowledge of whether one will be old or young, sick or healthy, privileged or vulnerable, the most rational and prudential decision would be to endorse principles that minimize the risk of extreme disadvantage for any possible position one might occupy. Within this framework, and ceteris paribus, it becomes plausible that such a hypothetical chooser would tend to prefer an allocation principle that takes age into account—specifically, one that favors those who have not yet had the opportunity to live through the basic stages of life. According to Altman (2021), this prudential logic is rooted in a common-sense intuition: each of us would find it unreasonable to assign greater moral weight to the mere extension of life (in terms of raw years) rather than to the opportunity to live years that are more likely to be free from significant physical or cognitive impairment. From behind the veil of ignorance, the decision-maker would not know whether they will be a frail elderly person or a young adult on the verge of full life development. In this condition of uncertainty, a preference for allocating scarce health resources to those who have not yet had a "fair innings" can be justified by a deeply rational concern: namely, that it is better to guarantee access to those stages of life that everyone would prudently wish to experience, rather than to maximize life-years without regard to their quality, potential, or existential significance. In this sense, the appreciation of age as a morally relevant factor is not an expression of ageism, but the outcome of an ethical reflection grounded in symmetry, fairness, and prudential neutrality.

Whilst the initial two arguments proposed by Altman may lack complete persuasiveness, the final one appears to be rather compelling. The primary argument asserts that triage systems should differentiate between patients infected with the novel coronavirus and those afflicted by other ailments. The secondary argument contends that the quantification of the number of years of life saved in the long term exhibits an excessive degree of randomness, thereby undermining the justification for the application of the criterion in question.

The age criterion applied to triage appears to be ethically justifiable. However, as Altman contends, it does not necessarily signify an indicator of greater long-term life expectancy. Instead, it is founded on the premise that every human being possesses an inherent right to progress through the various stages of life. The acknowledgement of age as a equitable selection criterion for the allocation of care is a fundamental aspect of this right.

In view of the analysis undertaken thus far with respect to the type of criteria that would be ethically tenable to adopt in a fair approach to emergencies triage, it can be stated that the following criteria are justifiable: (a) the utilitarian approach should be applied; (b) the number of lives to be saved should be maximised; (c) the fair innings argument should be taken into account, i.e. the expectation of every human being to go through all the cycles of life. It is acknowledged that, despite the preceding assertions, there are several issues that require thorough analysis. Firstly, the assessment of the criterion of the number of years of life saved must be conducted with caution, as this is not directly proportional to age, but may also take other factors into account. Secondly, the criterion of the quality of the years of life saved, i.e. the attribution of a sort of social value to the years of life of the patient, necessitates careful consideration.

4.7 Different Lives, Different Values: Focus on Quality-Adjusted Life Years (QALYs) and Disability-Adjusted Life Years (DALYs)

Among the various criteria proposed for the allocation of scarce healthcare resources, the use of Quality-Adjusted Life Years (QALYs) remains one of the most controversial. The QALY model combines both the quantity and quality of life expected from a medical intervention, assigning greater value to treatments that result in more years lived in better health. This approach, initially developed within health economics, has been endorsed by authors who argue that it provides a rational and cost-effective way to maximize health benefits across populations (Weinstein and Stason 1977; Gold et al. 1996). Proponents contend that the QALY allows for objective comparison between interventions and respects the utilitarian imperative of maximizing overall well-being (Nord 1999). Moreover, it is seen as a valuable decision-support tool in public health and resource management, offering transparency and consistency in clinical and policy contexts where difficult trade-offs are inevitable.

From an ethical perspective, some argue that the QALY model can be justified insofar as it prioritizes those treatments that produce the greatest benefit for the greatest number, while still incorporating considerations of quality rather than merely extending biological life at any cost. Daniels (2008) has argued that, when embedded within fair and accountable processes (such as his "accountability for reasonableness" framework), tools like QALYs can play a legitimate role in ensuring allocative efficiency without sacrificing legitimacy. In addition, some defenders of the QALY model suggest that ignoring the quality of life altogether would itself be ethically questionable, as it may result in prioritizing interventions that extend life in states of extreme suffering, dependency, or diminished autonomy—thus disregarding what matters most to patients themselves (Ubel et al. 2000).

However, the QALY model has also been the target of strong ethical criticism. One of the main objections is that it tends to discriminate against individuals with chronic illness, disability, or advanced age, as their projected quality of life is often lower—thus leading to lower QALY scores and reduced priority in care allocation (Harris 1987; Williams 1997). Critics argue that this form of evaluation risks introducing implicit forms of ableism—that is, a form of structural or cultural discrimination based on assumptions that certain types of physical or mental ability are inherently superior to others (Campbell 2009). Ableism can manifest both overtly and implicitly, for example by prioritizing "healthier" or "more productive" individuals while devaluing the lives of those who live with impairments, even if such impairments are consistent with a life the person deems fulfilling or worthwhile.

A similar line of criticism applies to another widely used metric in health policy: the Disability-Adjusted Life Year (DALY). Unlike QALYs, which quantify the health gains produced by a medical intervention, DALYs measure the health losses due to disease, disability, or premature death. Formally introduced by Murray and Lopez (1996) in the context of the Global Burden of Disease project, the DALY aggregates two components: Years of Life Lost (YLL) due to early mortality and Years Lived with Disability (YLD), calculated by multiplying the duration of a condition by a weight that reflects its severity. In this sense, DALYs capture the total burden that a particular health condition imposes on individuals and populations, offering a comprehensive view of morbidity and mortality.

From a utilitarian perspective, DALYs are considered a useful tool in prioritizing health interventions that aim to reduce the most significant burdens of disease. For example, public health programs targeting malaria, tuberculosis, or childhood malnutrition in low-resource settings often rely on DALY-based models to allocate limited funds to the interventions that promise the greatest health return per unit cost (Jamison et al. 2006). However, the applicability of DALYs in triage contexts, where decisions must be made quickly and often under extreme uncertainty, is much more controversial. While DALYs may appear to offer an objective criterion—favoring those whose treatment would avert the highest number of "lost healthy years"—they raise significant ethical concerns. Like QALYs, DALYs may unjustly disadvantage those living with disabilities or chronic conditions, as these individuals are assigned higher YLD scores and, thus, may be deprioritized in resource allocation. Once again, the risk is that ableist assumptions become encoded in the decision-making process: lives are ranked in terms of their deviation from a normative ideal of physical and cognitive health, rather than evaluated on their own terms.

This concern becomes particularly acute when compared to prioritarianism, which, as previously discussed, prioritizes the worst-off not based on their social productivity or future life-years, but on the moral urgency of alleviating the most severe disadvantage. A prioritarian framework might assign priority to a severely ill or disabled individual not despite their low projected quality of life, but precisely because they are worst-off in morally relevant terms (Parfit 1997). From this standpoint, the use of DALYs—or any metric that implicitly ranks lives based on future health potential—conflicts with the prioritarian commitment to fairness and moral equality. Moreover, critics have noted that DALYs tend to emphasize population-level efficiency at the expense of individual-level justice, a trade-off that may be acceptable in macro-level health planning but becomes ethically troubling when applied to micro-level triage decisions (Bognar and Hirose 2014).

Some authors have tried to reconcile these tensions by proposing hybrid models. For instance, utilitarian approaches that incorporate sufficientarian thresholds (i.e. guaranteeing a minimum acceptable outcome for all) attempt to moderate the harsh implications of pure DALY- or QALY-based allocation by ensuring that no one is left below a critical level of well-being (Crisp 2003). Nonetheless, such proposals still face the challenge of operationalizing vague thresholds and balancing competing claims under conditions of extreme scarcity. In conclusion, while QALYs and DALYs can offer technical support for cost-effective decision-making in public health, their application in triage raises profound ethical dilemmas. When life-and-death decisions must be made, considerations of equity, moral status, and vulnerability may justifiably override pure efficiency.

4.8 The Real Ethical Dilemma of Triage

As evidenced by the initial phase of the pandemic, healthcare systems were found to be inadequately prepared to address the disproportionate demand for intensive care beds and ventilators. The challenges experienced in the intensive care unit (ICU) and across hospital wards, coupled with the difficulties in managing hospitalisation, compelled physicians and professional associations to proactively identify the criteria for allocating scarce resources.[32] Simultaneously, the majority of

[32] See SIAARTI (2020) 'Clinical Ethics Recommendations for the Allocation of Intensive Care Treatments in exceptional resource-limited circumstances', https://www.flipsnack.com/SIAARTI/siaarti_-_covid-19_-_clinical_ethics_reccomendations/full-view.html; Belgian Society of Intensive Care Medicine (2020) Ethical Principles Concerning Proportionality of Critical Care During the 2020 COVID-19 Pandemic in Belgium', https://www.zorgneticuro.be/sites/default/files/general/COVID-19-ethical_final_c.cleaned.pdf; The Hastings Center, Ethical Framework for Health Care Institutions Responding to Novel Coronavirus Sars-CoV-2 (COVID-19), https://www.capc.org/documents/759/; *Sociedad Española de Medicina Intensiva Crítica y Unidades Coronarias* (SEMICYUC) *y Sociedad Española de Enfermería Intensiva y Unidades Coronarias* (SEEIUC), '*Plan de Contingencia para los Servicios de Medicina Intensiva frente a la pandemia COVID-19*' [Spanish Society of Intensive and Critical Care Medicine and Coronary Units (SEMICYUC) and Spanish Society of Intensive Care and Coronary Unit Nursing (SEEIUC), 'Contingency Plan for Intensive Care Services in Response to the COVID-19 Pandemic], Available at: https://www.medintensiva.org/es-plan-contingencia-servicios-medicina-intensiva-articulo-S0210569120300954. See also, National Ethical Committee and National Health Department on the matter of allocation of scarce resources: *Informe del Comité de Bioètica de Espana Sobre los Aspectos Bioéticos de la Priorizacion de Recursos Sanitarios en el Contexto de la Crisis del Coronavirus* [Report of the Spanish Bioethics Committee on the Bioethical Aspects of the Prioritization of Healthcare Resources in the Context of the Coronavirus Crisis], 25.3.2020; Nuffield Council on Bioethics, Ethical Considerations in Responding to the COVID-19

national and supranational ethics committees articulated divergent perspectives on the matter, delineating the fundamental rights that ought to be safeguarded during a pandemic, particularly in circumstances where there is a discrepancy between the requisite and available health resources.[33]

As evidenced by the discourse surrounding the criteria for the allocation of scarce medical resources, which witnessed a surge in the United States during the 1960s (Boyd and Potter 1986) and revived in the context of the ongoing pandemic, this issue has persisted and resurfaced in various forms throughout history, thus highlighting its enduring ethical complexities.

In such a scenario, the primary question that arises is that of determining which individual should be prioritised for medical intervention. However, of even greater significance is the establishment of the criteria by which this decision is to be made. A number of choices, along with the situations that arise when one is faced with the life-or-death decision of a patient, give rise to significant ethical and scientific questions concerning fundamental human rights.

Despite the fact that the majority of ethical reflections, in principle, identify the protection of human dignity, equality, justice, the duty of care, non-discrimination and transparency as inviolable principles, reality demonstrates that different criteria have been applied in various countries, and also within them, and that these criteria may have violated these principles. Indeed, it is evident that certain choices have had the unfortunate consequence of engendering injustices, inequalities and discrimination.

Pandemic, 17.03.2020; Department for Health, Ireland, Ethical Framework for Decision-Making in a Pandemic, 2020. Other National European Etichs Comitee pronunced in general Covid-19 (Francia, Germania, Austria) and International Comitee (IBC).

[33] *Comité de Bioética de España, 'Informe del Comité de Bioètica de Espana Sobre los Aspectos Bioéticos de la Priorizacion de Recursos Sanitarios en el Contexto de la Crisis del Coronavirus'* [Report of the Spanish Bioethics Committee on the Bioethical Aspects of the Prioritization of Healthcare Resources in the Context of the Coronavirus Crisis] Available at: https://personaybioetica.unisabana.edu.co/index.php/personaybioetica/article/view/13579; Nuffield Council on Bioethics, Ethical Considerations in Responding to the COVID-19 Pandemic, https://www.nuffieldbioethics.org/publications/ethical-considerations-in-responding-to-the-covid-19-pandemic; Ireland Department for Health, 'Ethical Framework for Decision-Making in a Pandemic' 2020. Available at: https://www.gov.ie/en/publication/dbf3fb-ethical-framework-for-decision-making-in-a-pandemic/#. The Italian National Bioethics Committee, *Covid-19: La decisione clinica in condizioni di carenza di risorse e il criterio del "Triage in emergenza pandemica"* [OVID-19: Clinical Decision-Making under Resource Scarcity and the Criterion of "Emergency Pandemic Triage"], http://bioetica.governo.it/media/4111/p136_2020_covid-19-la-decisione-clinica-in-condizioni-di-carenza-di-risorse-e-il-criterio-del-triage-in-emergenza-pandemica.pdf. UNESCO International Bioethics Committee (IBC) and the UNESCO World Commission on the Ethics of Scientific Knowledge and Technology (COMEST), 'Statement on COVID-19: ethical considerations from a global perspective', https://unesdoc.unesco.org/ark:/48223/pf0000373115?fbclid=IwAR3CZBldVi_r–TUoNLs0qWHuwyNlhZiBdK4z5LfdeZIZ9FBiw1EG0hf3JQ; European Group on Ethics in Science and New Technologies (EGE), 'Statement on European solidarity and the protection of fundamental rights in the COVID-19 pandemic'. Available at: https://research-and-innovation.ec.europa.eu/document/download/b77dbf1f-727d-4924-8a67-e99c445e9787_en?filename=ec_rtd_ege-statement-covid-19.pdf.

In contemplating the allocation of limited health resources, it is imperative to recognise that, irrespective of the decision criteria employed—even in circumstances where no decision is reached—significant violations of fundamental human rights are occurring. Firstly, the right to life[34] of at least one human being must be acknowledged. Indeed, electing to treat a single patient necessitates the acknowledgement that this decision may result in the fatality of another. Simultaneously, violations of the right to healthcare[35] and the human dignity of a patient[36] are occurring in instances where individuals deny or withdraw from necessary medical care.

Furthermore, by choosing on the basis of which criteria to allocate the available health resources, there is also the risk of violating the right to non-discrimination[37]

[34] Art.2 "Everyone has the right to life". European Union. (2000). Charter of Fundamental Rights of the European Union, 7 December 2000, OJ C 364, pp. 1–22. Article 2. Available at: https://eur-lex.europa.eu/legal-content/EN/TXT/?uri=CELEX:12012P/TXT.

[35] Art. 35 "Everyone has the right of access to preventive health care and the right to benefit from medical treatment under the conditions established by national laws and practices. A high level of human health protection shall be ensured in the definition and implementation of all the Union's policies and activities". European Union. (2000). Charter of Fundamental Rights of the European Union, 7 December 2000, OJ C 364, pp. 1–22. Available at: https://eur-lex.europa.eu/legal-content/EN/TXT/?uri=CELEX:12012P/TXT; Art. 25 "Everyone has the right to a standard of living adequate for the health and well-being of himself and of his family". United Nations. (1948). Universal Declaration of Human Rights, 10 December 1948. Article 25. Available at: https://www.un.org/en/about-us/universal-declaration-of-human-rights; Art. 14, c.2 "Taking into account that the enjoyment of the highest attainable standard of health is one of the fundamental rights of every human being without distinction of race, religion, political belief, economic or social condition, progress in science and technology should advance:(a)access to quality health care and essential medicines, especially for the health of women and children, because health is essential to life itself and must be considered to be a social and human good". UNESCO. (2005). Universal Declaration on Bioethics and Human Rights, Paris, 19 October 2005. Available at: https://unesdoc.unesco.org/ark:/48223/pf0000146180.

[36] Art. 1 "Human dignity is inviolable. It must be respected and protected". European Union. (2000). Charter of Fundamental Rights of the European Union, 7 December 2000, OJ C 364, pp. 1–22. Available at: https://eur-lex.europa.eu/legal-content/EN/TXT/?uri=CELEX:12012P/TXT; Art.1 "All human beings are born free and equal in dignity and rights". United Nations. (1948). Universal Declaration of Human Rights, 10 December 1948. Article 25. Available at: https://www.un.org/en/about-us/universal-declaration-of-human-rights; Art. 3 "Human dignity, human rights and fundamental freedoms are to be fully respected" UNESCO. (2005). Universal Declaration on Bioethics and Human Rights, Paris, 19 October 2005. Available at: https://unesdoc.unesco.org/ark:/48223/pf0000146180.

[37] Art. 21 "Any discrimination based on any ground such as sex, race, colour, ethnic or social origin, genetic features, language, religion or belief, political or any other opinion, membership of a national minority, property, birth, disability, age or sexual orientation shall be prohibited". European Union. (2000). Charter of Fundamental Rights of the European Union, 7 December 2000, OJ C 364, pp. 1–22. Available at: https://eur-lex.europa.eu/legal-content/EN/TXT/?uri=CELEX:12012P/TXT; Art.7 "All are equal before the law and are entitled without any discrimination to equal protection of the law". United Nations. (1948). Universal Declaration of Human Rights, 10 December 1948. Available at: https://www.un.org/en/about-us/universal-declaration-of-human-rights; Art. 11 "No individual or group should be discriminated against or stigmatized on any grounds, in violation of human dignity, human rights and fundamental

and equality[38] of every human being, especially if the criteria for allocating resources are not justified by a legitimate purpose and the means employed to achieve it are not necessary or adequate.

In order to circumvent the potential risks associated with this approach, scientists and researchers worldwide have expended considerable effort to establish the criteria to be employed in the allocation of scarce resources. In doing so, they have consistently sought to adhere to medical evidence and ethical principles. However, this endeavour was likely futile. A meticulous study on triage, such as the one carried out by Kuylen (which offers medical ethics a promising way to consult public preferences), confirmed that "a 'triad' of ethical principles may be a useful structure to guide ethical deliberation as societies negotiate the conflicting ethical demands of triage" (Kuylen et al. 2021). On this point, it is asserted that, irrespective of the criteria employed for the allocation of resources, it is inherently impossible to prevent the infringement of certain fundamental human rights.

The act of prioritising one individual over another constitutes a violation of their fundamental rights, including the rights to health, life, and human dignity. It is not possible to choose whether or not to violate fundamental rights in this way, because the violation would be involuntary (given the lack of resources) and driven by the need for a choice. However, when the moment arrives to determine who should be prioritised for medical intervention, the act of infringement becomes a particular decision.

From this standpoint, the allocation of limited resources according to a general utilitarian approach has the potential to result in discrimination against elderly individuals, those experiencing frailty, individuals with disabilities, and patients with comorbidities. Moreover, fundamental human rights are violated simply by denying another patient access to healthcare resources or removing them from such resources, regardless of their specific condition. The act of choosing, in addition to the act of refraining from choosing, has the potential to infringe upon fundamental human rights.

Conversely, the implementation of an equitable distribution of health resources, grounded in the principle of first-come, first-served, has the potential to exacerbate the repercussions of such violations, augment the number of violations of fundamental rights, or contradict the overarching objective of science and ethics, which

freedoms" UNESCO. (2005). Universal Declaration on Bioethics and Human Rights, Paris, 19 October 2005. Available at: https://unesdoc.unesco.org/ark:/48223/pf0000146180.

[38] Art. 11 "The fundamental equality of all human beings in dignity and rights is to be respected so that they are treated justly and equitably" UNESCO. (2005). Universal Declaration on Bioethics and Human Rights, Paris, 19 October 2005. Available at: https://unesdoc.unesco.org/ark:/48223/pf0000146180.

is to safeguard and promote the interests of both the present and future generations[39] (UDHR, art. 2, principle g). Indeed, in the absence of an efficient allocation of resources, there will be an increase in the number of patients withheld or withdrawn from necessary medical care, as well as an increase in the number of deaths. It has been posited that prioritising the interests of society would contravene the principle espoused in the UDHR (art. 3), which asserts that "the interests and welfare of the individual should have priority over the sole interest of science or society".[40] This assertion is further substantiated by the Hippocratic Oath (Dawson). However, the implementation of egalitarian criteria has the potential to result in discriminatory outcomes, particularly in cases where individuals possess greater access to healthcare due to factors such as proximity to medical facilities or economic status (Kuylen et al. 2021). It has been argued that certain policies are predicated on medical-scientific parameters, with the objective of selecting appropriate treatment for patients, thus circumventing the potential for indirect discrimination (for example, the SOFA Score, the Charlson Comorbidity Index, the Clinical Frailty Scale, etc.). The application of medical-scientific parameters to the process of triage appears to serve as a mitigating factor in the potential for discrimination. The determination of who should be prioritised for treatment is said to be substantiated by a legitimate aim pursued with adequate and necessary means.

However, as highlighted in the preceding discussion, there is a lack of adequate criteria for the allocation of scarce resources that can prevent violations of fundamental human rights. In circumstances where it is necessary to determine the individual to be prioritised for medical intervention, the requisite criteria are not met.

It can be assumed that the preceding studies are useful in identifying the most evident problem that arises from the triage dilemma (which could perhaps be avoided with adequate regulation): the discrimination between those who live in the same country, region or even in the same city. The crux of the issue lies not in the establishment of criteria for the allocation of scarce resources, but rather in the presence of divergent criteria within the confines of a single territory. This poses a risk of discrimination, with consequences for individuals' lives and deaths.

It is the contention of the present study that this inequality must be addressed through the prism of ethical reasoning, and that the regulation of the matter by law is an imperative. It is only through such a comprehensive approach that the guarantee of equal treatment, transcending considerations of territorial origin, individual policies and hospital guidelines, can be assured. This conclusion relates to the question of how to decide who should receive medical care in an emergency.

---

[39] Art 2, principle g "The aims of this Declaration are: [. . .] safeguard and promote the interests of the present and future generations". UNESCO. (2005). Universal Declaration on Bioethics and Human Rights. Paris: United Nations Educational, Scientific and Cultural Organization. Available at: https://unesdoc.unesco.org/ark:/48223/pf0000146180.

[40] United Nations. (1948). Universal Declaration of Human Rights, 10 December 1948. Available at: https://www.un.org/en/about-us/universal-declaration-of-human-rights.

It is therefore necessary to establish the criteria to be employed in the allocation of scarce resources. Moreover, it is essential to identify the body responsible for the regulation of this matter.

In the context of discussing the minimisation of violations of fundamental rights (a subject which, it must be acknowledged, is inherently impossible to avoid), it is imperative for a legitimate body to establish a procedure by which such rights may be knowingly violated. Consequently, there will be established normative criteria according to which such violations must be accepted.

Therefore, if democracy is not merely a means of providing people with a voice, but rather a process of allocating caring responsibilities (Tronto 2015), it follows that the decision regarding the criteria for violating fundamental rights should be made by the people.

Deliberative democracy (Fishkin 2009; Kim 2016; Biddison et al. 2018) has been posited as a potentially efficacious approach for eliciting public preferences in medical ethics consultations, provided that sufficient information is available. However, the ethical triage dilemma remains to be resolved by legal frameworks. The issue of the ethics of triage is not only of a legal nature, but is also of a political nature, and as such merits a response from a representative political body. In consideration of the extant medical and scientific evidence (which also incorporates deliberative study), it is incumbent upon governments and parliaments to assume responsibility for these choices, establishing the triage criteria by law.

It is proposed that the implementation of this process will ensure the establishment of a set of criteria to be applied in hospitals, thereby obliging medical professionals to adhere to these stipulated principles. Indeed, in the absence of legal provisions for triage criteria, and instead of their reliance on recommendations or guidelines, patients may be treated in divergent ways without the requisite safeguards. Moreover, in order to circumvent any potential discrimination between individuals within the same territory, it is imperative to implement a uniform regulatory framework at the national level, encompassing both the European Union and the United States.

It is therefore argued that the provision of effective regulation can only be achieved through the establishment of a representative, supranational and legislative body. This assertion is supported by the work of Gutman (2020): "[t]his question must be a question of constitutional law, the one way or the other, and as long it's not, it must be a question of a formal decision by the people in a democratic way". Indeed, given the absence of a consensus on the question of who should receive medical care, it becomes imperative to address this issue through the lens of political deliberation. In order to guarantee the legitimacy of triage guidelines, which have consequences for the general public, it is essential to take into account the public's moral intuitions, as these are not always aligned with the recommendations of experts (Kuylen et al. 2021).

Decisions that are firmly embedded in ethical dilemmas necessitate robust popular legitimacy, thereby ensuring a substantial degree of fulfilment, transparency, and certainty in the medical treatment process.

It is imperative that this is comprehended by the populace, interpreted, and made available to the legislative power. Consequently, supranational legislative bodies such as the European Parliament (Ehni et al. 2021, p. 134) and the United States Congress will be capable of establishing precise guidelines and the insurmountable principle on which each State can regulate the matter.

Despite the evident paucity of health resources during states of emergency, it is imperative to recognise that this issue has its foundations in the inherent structural injustices that are ingrained within the health system itself. Moreover, it is crucial to acknowledge that these injustices are intricately interwoven with the prevailing inequalities that characterise society at all levels. It is hypothesised that the issue may be resolved through the implementation of a more profound level of reflection and a comprehensive analysis. Nevertheless, the proposed solution has the capacity to curtail the infringement of certain fundamental human rights (deriving from the uncontrolled application of principles and criteria due to a paucity of health resources and impoverishment of national health systems) without necessitating structural changes that would require a considerable investment of time.

As indicated by the aforementioned results, it can be posited that there is an absence of appropriate criteria for the ethical approach to triage. In consideration of the fact that the ethical approach of each continent, state and hospital is directly influenced by local values, it may be posited that the question that theorists and philosophers should seek to resolve is another.

The crux of the issue pertains to the selection of the criteria for triage, as well as the relevant authorities responsible for this determination and the methodology to be employed. The fundamental issue that was highlighted at the outset of this chapter pertains to the necessity of transitioning the burden of decision-making from the micro level to the macro level.

It is evident that, irrespective of the existence of certain preferable criteria, the responsibility for certain choices must be shouldered by a legislator or a representative body, rather than being delegated to medical associations or ethics committees. In 2020, there was a significant increase in the number of academics and scientists discussing the ethical justification of the decision-making process of triage (Karahda et al. 2020; Emanuel et al. 2020; Satomi et al. 2020; Truog et al. 2020). However, these discussions have only partially addressed the legitimacy of the production process of the triage criteria.

In the wake of the publication by Jöbges et al. (2020), medical associations and ethics committees worldwide have offered their insights on the criteria to be employed in instances of equipment-to-bed ratio imbalances in intensive care units. However, concerns regarding the authority to regulate this issue have only emerged in select instances.

A comprehensive review of extant studies and opinions on this issue suggests that it has probably engendered the most significant ethical dilemma of the last few decades. The principal challenge during a pandemic is the necessity to assign priority to certain patients over those who are not receiving assistance and who, in the worst case scenario, perish (Ehni et al. 2021, p. 126). The necessity to have certain resources available gave rise to a conflict with certain principles and values, such as the maximisation of benefits and the respect of equal rights (Ehni et al. 2021, p. 126). From a consequentialist perspective, it can be argued that the principle of treating patients equally may, in certain circumstances, hinder the achievement of the best possible outcome. From a deontological perspective, the maximisation of benefits may result in discrimination or violations of individual rights (Ehni et al. 2021, p. 126). The preponderance of this phenomenon is evidenced by the fact that a significant number of countries worldwide are confronted with a similar predicament, characterised by the presence of patients in need of essential medical interventions for their survival. These patients, despite their shared need for medical care and their inherent right to life, find themselves in a state where the fulfilment of their fundamental desire to live and the provision of the requisite medical treatment are both unattainable.

The ethical challenges posed by the decision-making process in situations involving the allocation of limited resources are the subject of considerable debate. To elaborate further, the question pertains to the amalgamation of both perspectives, and the subsequent justification of the optimal outcome, in conjunction with the procedural framework by which these objectives are to be accomplished, whilst maintaining adherence to individual rights (Ehni et al. 2021, p. 126).

Indeed, as Holm (2007) asserts, the "ethical basis and practice of triage provokes conflicts in values between public health and clinical bioethics, precisely because of the tension between the rights of individuals and the need to protect the common good". Faced with a global emergency, health workers have been forced to abandon the concept of "giving everyone a fair and equal opportunity to receive medical treatment" (Kuschner et al. 2007). Applying the triage criteria, the conflict arises because, in a pandemic emergency, physicians used an ethical framework that seeks to minimise morbidity and mortality among the whole population, instead of giving primacy to the individual autonomy and the doctor-patient relationship (Petrini 2010).

Nevertheless, the divergent approach to triage is ethically justified, and is also influenced by the personal value system. It is imperative that the ethical triage dilemma provides a response to an alternative question, namely, who is responsible for making certain decisions and the manner in which these decisions are to be made.

4.9 The Need for a Common EU Framework for Triage in Times of Crisis

On the basis of a legal-philosophical analysis brought up in the previous paragraph to understand whether there were common criteria underlying triage. It was thus possible to ascertain that the approach of all the guidelines analysed was utilitarian and that therefore triage should aim to maximise the cost-benefit ratio for society as a whole, as the sum of the individual interests of its components. Attempts were subsequently made to verify the ethical justification of the utilitarian approach and consequently focus the analysis on the specific objectives most frequently adopted, saving the greatest number of lives and saving the greatest number of years of life.

Whilst the objective of saving as many lives as possible appears to be a more straightforwardly justifiable criterion, even in consideration of the principle of self-preservation of the species, the criterion of preserving the greatest number of years of life and, above all, the greatest number of adjusted years of life is more controversial. Indeed, the former necessitates the recognition of the value of having had the opportunity to traverse the various stages of life, while the latter values—arguably illegitimately—not only the resources required to overcome the acute phase of the disease but also those that the patient will consume in the future, to the detriment of society as a whole. The latter theory has the potential to engender excessive discrimination.

To resolve the ethical dilemma of triage, it is therefore necessary to consider a common protocol, at least at European level.

In order to address the ethical challenges posed by triage, it is imperative to establish a uniform protocol, at the very least at the European level. Indeed, any EU citizen who finds themselves in another Member State is guaranteed the right to receive necessary and life-saving healthcare under EU law. This is primarily guaranteed by Regulation (EC) No 883/2004 on the coordination of social security systems, which ensures access to medically necessary treatment during a temporary stay abroad, using the European Health Insurance Card (EHIC). Furthermore, Directive 2011/24/EU on patients' rights in cross-border healthcare reinforces the right to receive healthcare in another Member State, particularly in urgent or life-threatening situations, and to be reimbursed under the rules of their home health-care system. This principle is reinforced by the Charter of Fundamental Rights of the European Union, Article 35, which asserts the right to access preventive health care and medical treatment in accordance with national laws and practices.

The European Union faces increasingly complex crises and challenges that cannot be ignored. From growing geopolitical tensions and conflicts, hybrid and cybersecurity threats, to climate change and increasing natural disasters, the EU must be ready to protect its citizens and the key societal functions crucial for democracy and daily life. So, on the 26th of March, the Commission and High Representative launched the *EU Preparedness Union Strategy to prevent and react to emerging threats and crises*. The key objectives and actions of the strategy include the need for protecting Europe's essential societal functions, between which there is the development of a minimum preparedness criterion for crucial services such as hospitals, schools, transport, and telecommunications; Enhancing Crisis Response Coordination and Cooperation: establishing or improving integration among existing crisis structures and developing emergency protocols to react to crisis.

The COVID-19 pandemic served as a stark warning, revealing the structural weaknesses of many national healthcare systems within the EU. One of the most pressing shortcomings was the absence of clear, coordinated, and ethically defensible mechanisms for allocating scarce medical resources—especially in intensive care units (ICUs). In the face of limited ICU beds and ventilators, healthcare providers were forced to make life-and-death decisions under extreme pressure, often without institutional support or legal and ethical guidance. This vacuum led to the application of diverse, and sometimes controversial, triage criteria across countries and regions, potentially compromising principles such as human dignity, equality, non-discrimination, and transparency.

To overcome these problems, it might be useful to consider developing a European Ethical Triage Protocol: a shared, scientifically grounded, and publicly acceptable framework for the allocation of scarce healthcare resources during emergencies. Not to impose a one-size-fits-all model but rather to create a robust and adaptable protocol that respects both universal human rights and the diversity of European moral landscapes.

On the basis of particularly theories of bounded rationality (Simon 1955), procedural rationality (March and Olsen 1989), and multi-actor collaborative governance (Ansell and Gash 2008)—it possible to recognizes that decision-making under conditions of scarcity and uncertainty must be explicitly structured to avoid arbitrariness, cognitive overload, and ethical drift. The literature on ethical decision-making in clinical settings (e.g., Daniels and Sabin's "Accountability for Reasonableness") has emphasized the necessity of fair, inclusive, and intelligible processes that enable legitimacy in morally fraught choices.

Accordingly, to possible solution for the ethical triage dilemma go beyond identifying triage criteria and instead formalize a step-by-step decision architecture. This could include: institutional role allocation (e.g., triage officers, multidisciplinary review boards, ethical consultants), processual elements (e.g., timing, documentation, deliberation protocols), review and oversight mechanisms (e.g., appeal pathways, real-time auditing, retrospective assessment), and the integration of ethical heuristics tailored to emergency settings. These heuristics could be developed using insights from behavioral decision-making, with the aim of reducing bias and enhancing the reliability of morally defensible outcomes.

Is important to note that decision-making on triage should not be considered as a purely clinical or legal task. It conceives it as a multi-level process requiring coordination between healthcare practitioners, institutional authorities, legal frameworks, and public expectations. The protocol's decision-making process should therefore be aligned with principles of distributed governance, capable of being embedded into both national emergency frameworks and transnational cooperation mechanisms within the EU. It will also draw from socio-technical systems theory to anticipate the interaction between human actors and digital tools, thus facilitating future integration with decision-support technologies.

The COVID-19 pandemic has strongly highlighted the structural limitations of the national healthcare systems of the EU member states, particularly in coping with shortages of healthcare resources in times of crisis, such as places in intensive care units or the availability of ventilators. The absence of a coordinated and ethically justified approach to triage at the European level has generated uncertainty, moral distress, and fragmentation. In the absence of a shared protocol, the burden of the most difficult decisions has fallen on individual healthcare professionals, often forced to act under immense emotional pressure and cognitive overload, without institutional guidelines or ethical support. This unstructured environment significantly increased the risk of inconsistent practices and violations—intentional or not—of fundamental rights such as human dignity, equality, and non-discrimination.

In those cases, what matters is how decisions are made, by whom, through what procedures, and with what safeguards. These features are essential to guarantee that triage decisions, while difficult and context-sensitive, are not arbitrary, discriminatory, or opaque.

The aim is to contribute to a more resilient, just, and coordinated European healthcare system. It seeks to empower healthcare professionals with tools and processes that protect not only patients' lives but also the core values of democratic societies. Through the development of an ethical triage protocol and a corresponding decision-making framework, is possible to make Europe better prepared for the moral, medical, and political challenges of future emergencies.

From a pragmatic standpoint, it is important to adopt a stance that encompasses both procedural elements and the substantive content of a potential protocol designed to mitigate the infringement of fundamental human rights.

In light of the preceding analysis, it is possible to propose a valuation of the patient's age, not in relation to medical-clinical factors, but in recognition of the intrinsic right of human beings to progress through the various stages of life.

Conversely, this criterion appears to be both rational and widely accepted, as evidenced by the extant research cited above. This is a crucial consideration when formulating health policy, given the potentially significant ramifications such decisions can entail.

In the pursuit of ethically sustainable triage, the objective is to maximise the number of lives saved while ensuring the integrity of patients' rights. The establishment of criteria necessitates a focus on the effective and efficient administration of care, with the overarching aim being the preservation of lives. Concurrently, the short-term life expectancy could be valued, with the implementation of a parameter ensuring a degree of certainty to minimise the margin of error to a percentage close to zero (e.g. by assigning a value only to life expectancy of less than 1 or 2 years). In conclusion, it would be appropriate to value the criterion of age purely and simply, admitting the existence of a human being's right to pass through the various stages of life.

The practical application of the latter criterion is encumbered by certain weaknesses. Primarily, the identification of age brackets (as exemplified by the Pittsburgh DCCM in the United States) renders the establishment of an individual's right to traverse the various stages of life unfeasible. The limitations inherent in the practical implementation of this criterion are twofold. Firstly, the identification of age bands (as exemplified by the Pittsburgh DCCM, 12–40, 41–60, 61–75, 76+) corresponds to the same number of life stages. It is important to note that there is a risk of uncertainty regarding the correspondence between the attainment of a given age and the experiential consequences that are believed to be associated with it. Secondly, the application of these bands could result in divergent valuations for individuals aged 40 and 41 compared to those aged 41 and 60, who would be valued similarly.

In order to surmount the aforementioned issues, it would be imperative to incorporate a corrective measure into the established protocols. This would involve assigning a distinct value to each year of life lived, thereby acknowledging the significance of age in the assessment of patients.

It is evident that the realisation of the objective of ethically sustainable triage is contingent upon the implementation of guidelines that are founded upon the principles under discussion.

It is recognised that situations of emergency, such as the pandemic or war, give rise to a number of issues with regard to the protection of fundamental human rights. The resolution of these issues should, in principle, be delegated to the legislative authority rather than to guidelines and recommendations. A comprehensive analysis should also encompass additional domains, including the doctor-patient relationship, the transparency and clarity of clinical evaluations, the obligation to ensure access to palliative care and pain therapy for patients deprived of medical care, and the potential for providing access to euthanasia treatment.

Notwithstanding the aforementioned, and in consideration of contemporary geopolitical developments and the European Union's endeavours to prepare for potential crisis scenarios, it is imperative to persist in contemplating and furthering the ethical and philosophical inquiries that have been accentuated by the CoV-19 pandemic. It is essential to guarantee that future responses to potential emergency situations are more congruent with the safeguarding of fundamental human rights.

References

Altman MC (2021) A consequentialist argument for considering age in triage decisions during the coronavirus pandemic. Bioethics 4(35):356–365

Ansell C, Gash A (2008) Collaborative governance in theory and practice. J Public Adm Res Theory 18(4):543–571

Antommaria AHM, Gibb TS, McGuire AL, Wolpe PR, Wynia MK, Applewhite MK, Caplan A, Diekema DS, Hester DM, Lehmann LS, McLeod-Sordjan R, Schiff T, Tabor HK, Wieten SE, Eberl JT (2020) Ventilator triage policies during the COVID-19 pandemic at U.S. hospitals associated with members of the association of bioethics program directors. Ann Int Med 173 (3):188–194

Barilan YM, Brusa M (2016) Triage. In: Have H (ed) Encyclopedia of global bioethics. Springer, Cham

Beauchamp TL, Childress JF (2001) Principles of biomedical ethics, 5th edn. Oxford University Press, New York

Berlinger N, Wynia M, Powell T, Hester DM, Milliken A, Fabi R, Cohn F, Guidry-Grimes L, Watson JC, Bruce L, Chuang E, Oei G, Abbott J, Jenks N (2020) Ethical framework for health care institutions responding to novel coronavirus SARS-CoV-2 (COVID-19): guidelines for institutional ethics services responding to covid-19. The Hastings Center, Garrison, NY

Biddison ELD, Gwon H, Schoch-Spana M, Cavalier R, White DB, Dawson T, Terry PB, London AJ, Regenberg A, Faden R, Toner ES (2014) The community speaks: understanding ethical values in allocation of scarce lifesaving resources during disasters. Ann Am Thoracic Soc 11:777–783

Biddison ELD, Gwon HS, Schoch-Spana M, Regenberg AC, Juliano C, Faden RR, Toner ES (2018) Scarce resource allocation during disasters: a mixed-method community engagement study. Chest 153(1):187–195

Bognar G, Hirose I (2014) The ethics of health care rationing: an introduction. Routledge, London

Boyd KM, Potter BT (1986) Priorities in the allocation of scarce resources. J Med Ethics 12 (4):197–200

Broome J (1991) Weighing goods: equality, uncertainty and time. Blackwell, Oxford

Buckwalter W, Peterson A (2020) Public attitudes toward allocating scarce resources in the COVID-19 pandemic. PLoS One 15:11

Campbell FK (2009) Contours of ableism: the production of disability and abledness. Palgrave Macmillan, London

Capraro V (2019) The dual-process approach to human sociality: a review of the models and evidence. arXiv preprint

Charlson ME, Pompei P, Ales KL, MacKenzie CR (1987) A new method of classifying prognostic comorbidity in longitudinal studies: development and validation. J Chronic Dis 40(5):373–383

Christian MD, Sprung CL, King MA, Dichter JR, Kissoon N, Devereaux AV et al (2014) Triage: care of the critically ill and injured during pandemics and disasters: CHEST consensus statement. Chest 146(4 Suppl):e61S–e74S

Crisp R (2003) Equality, priority and compassion. Ethics 113(4):745–763

Daniels N (1983) Justice between age groups: am i my parents' keeper? Milbank Memor Fund Quart Health Soc 61:489–522

Daniels N (2008) Just health: meeting health needs fairly. Cambridge University Press, Cambridge

Ehni H, Wiesing U, Ranisch R (2021) Saving the most lives—a comparison of European triage guidelines in the context of the COVID-19 pandemic. Bioethics 35(2):125–134

Egan TM, Murray S, Bustami RT, Shearon TH, McCullough KP, Edwards LB, Coke MA, Garrity ER, Sweet SC, Heiney DA, Grover FL (2006) Development of the new lung allocation system in the United States. Am J Transplant 6:1212–1227

Emanuel EJ, Persad G, Upshur R, Thome B, Parker M, Glickman A, Zhang C, Boyle C, Smith M, Phillips JP (2020) Fair allocation of scarce medical resources in the time of covid-19. New Engl J Med 382(21):2049–2055

Emanuel EJ, Wertheimer A (2006) Public health. Who should get influenza vaccine when not all can? Science 312:854–855

Fishkin JS (2009) When the people speak. Deliberative democracy and public consultation. Oxford University Press, Oxford

Gold MR, Siegel JE, Russell LB, Weinstein MC (1996) Cost-effectiveness in health and medicine. Oxford University Press, Oxford

Green BP (2019) Self-preservation should be humankind's first ethical priority—and therefore rapid space settlement is necessary. Futures 115:102475

Gutman T (2020) Tragic choices: criteria for "triage" of Covid-19 patients in need for intensive care. Ordines 2:28

Harris J (1985) The value of life: an introduction to medical ethics. Routledge, London

Harris J (1987) QALYfying the value of life. J Med Ethics 13(3):117–123

Hobbes T (1651) Leviathan, or the matter, forme and power of a commonwealth ecclesiasticall and civil. Andrew Crooke, London

Hooker B (2000) Ideal code, real world: a rule-consequentialist theory of morality. Clarendon Press, Oxford

Holm S (2007) Medical aid and disaster relief. In: Ashcroft RE, Dawson A, Draper H, McMillan JR (eds) Principles of health care ethics, 2nd edn. Wiley-Blackwell, Chichester, pp 671–677
Jamison DT, Breman JG, Measham AR et al (2006) Disease control priorities in developing countries, 2nd edn. World Bank and Oxford University Press, Washington, DC
Jennings B (2020) Aging, meaning and social structure: connecting critical and humanistic. Bristol University Press, Bristol
Jöbges S, Vinay R, Luyckx VA, Biller-Andorno N (2020) Recommendations on COVID-19 triage: international comparison and ethical analysis. Bioethics 34(9):948–959
Jonas H (1984) The imperative of responsibility: in search of an ethics for the technological age. University of Chicago Press, Chicago
Karahda A, Sethi S, Prasad SK (2020) Effect of healthcare burden and resource reallocation on elderly during COVID-19 pandemic. J Geriatr Care Res 7(2):89–92
Kim S (2016) Theory and practice of democratic deliberation in bioethics research. In: Ives J, Dunn M, Cribb A (eds) Empirical bioethics: theoretical and practical perspectives. Cambridge University Press, Cambridge, pp 177–194
Kuschner WG, Pollard JB, Ezeji-Okoye SC (2007) Ethical triage and scarce resource allocation during public health emergencies: tenets and procedures. Hosp Top 85(3):16–26
Kuylen MNI, Kim SY, Ruck Keene A, Owen GS (2021) Should age matter in COVID-19 triage? A deliberative study. J Med Ethics 47(5):291–295
Leteurtre S, Duhamel A, Grandbastien B, Lacroix J, Leclerc F (2006) Paediatric logistic organ dysfunction (PELOD) score. Lancet 367–897
Leven K (1998) The invention of Hippocrates: oath, letters and Hippocratic oath. In Trohler U, Reiter-Theil S, Herych E (eds) Ethics codes in medicine. Foundations and achievements of codification since 1947, Ashgate. Aldershot, pp 3–23
Levy B, Banaji M (2002) Implicit ageism. In: Nelson TD (ed) Ageism: stereotyping and prejudice against older persons. MIT Press, Cambridge, MA, pp 49–75
Liddell K, Skopek JM, Palmer S, Martin S, Anderson J, Sagar A (2020) Who gets the ventilator? Important legal rights in a pandemic. J Med Ethics 46(7):421–426
Light DW (1997) The real ethics of rationing. BMJ 315:112–115
March JG, Olsen JP (1989) Rediscovering institutions: the organizational basis of politics. Free Press, New York
McGough LJ, Reynolds SJ, Quinn TC, Zenilman JM (2005) Which patients first? Setting priorities for antiretroviral therapy where resources are limited. Am J Public Health 95:1173–1180
McKerlie D (1989) Equality and time. Ethics 99:475
Murray CJL, Lopez AD (1996) The global burden of disease: a comprehensive assessment of mortality and disability. Harvard School of Public Health for the World Health Organization and the World Bank, Boston
Nacoti M, Ciocca A, Giupponi A, Brambillasca P, Lussana F, Pisano M, Goisis G, Bonacina D, Fazzi F, Naspro R, Longhi L, Cereda M, Montaguti C (2020) At the epicenter of the Covid-19 pandemic and humanitarian crises in Italy: changing perspectives on preparation and mitigation. New England J Med Catalyst Innov Care Deliv 1(2)
Neuberger J, Adams D, MacMaster P, Maidment A, Speed M (1998) Assessing priorities for allocation of donor liver grafts: survey of public and clinicians. Br Med J 317:172–175
Nord E (1999) Cost-value analysis in health care: making sense out of QALYs. Cambridge University Press, Cambridge
Oken MM, Creech RH, Tormey DC, Horton J, Davis TE, McFadden ET, Carbone PP (1982) Toxicity and response criteria of the Eastern cooperative oncology group. Am J Clin Oncol 5:649–655
Palazzani L (2020) La pandemia e il dilemma per l'etica quando le risorse sono limitate: chi curare? BioLaw J 6
Parfit D (1984) Reasons and persons. Oxford University Press, Oxford
Parfit D (1997) Equality and priority. Ratio 10(3):202–221

Persad G, Wertheimer A, Emanuel EJ (2009) Principles for allocation of scarce medical interventions. Lancet, pp 373

Petrini C (2010) Triage in public health emergencies: ethical issues. Intern Emerg Med 5 (2):137–144

Rawls J (1971) A theory of justice. Harvard University Press, Cambridge

Raynaud P (2003) Egalité. In: Reynaud P, Rials S (eds) Dictionnaire de philosophie politique. Presses Universitaires de France. Paris, pp 217–221

Riccioni L, Ingravallo F, Grasselli G, Mazzon D, Cingolani E, Forti G, Zagrebelsky V, Zoja R, Petrini F (2021) The Italian document: decisions for intensive care when there is an imbalance between care needs and resources during the COVID-19 pandemic. Ann Intens Care 11(1):100

Rockwood K, Song X, MacKnight C, Bergman H, Hogan DB, McDowell I, Mitnitski A (2005) A global clinical measure of fitness and frailty in elderly people. Can Med Assoc J 173 (5):489–495

Satomi E et al (2020) Fair allocation of scarce medical resources during COVID-19 pandemic: ethical considerations. Einstein (Sao Paulo), 18:eAE5775

Savulescu J, Persson I, Wilkinson D (2020) Utilitarianism and the pandemic. Bioethics 34(6):620–632

Schaller M, Park JH, Faulkner J (2003) Prehistoric dangers and contemporary prejudices: evolutionary bases for intergroup bias. Curr Direct Psychol Sci 12(1):9–13

Simon HA (1955) A behavioral model of rational choice. Q J Econ 69(1):99–118

Singer P (2011) Practical ethics, 3rd edn. Cambridge University Press, Cambridge

Taurek J (1977) Should the numbers count? Philos Publ Aff 6(4):293–316

Taylor PW (1986) Respect for nature: a theory of environmental ethics. Princeton University Press, Princeton

Temkin L (2003) Equality, priority, and the levelling down objection. In: Clayton M, Williams A (eds) The ideal of equality. Palgrave Macmillan, London

Thompson AK, Faith K, Gibson JL, Upshur REG (2006) Pandemic influenza preparedness: an ethical framework to guide decision-making. BMC Med Ethics 7:12

Tronto J (2015) Democratic caring and global care responsibilities. In: Barnes M, Brannelly T, Ward L, Ward N (eds) Ethics of care: critical advances in international perspective. Policy Press, Bristol

Truog RD, Mitchell C, Daley GQ (2020) The toughest triage — allocating ventilators in a pandemic. New Engl J Med 382(21):1973–1975

Ubel PA, Loewenstein G, Jepson C (2000) Disabling the disabled: the moral implications of valuing health states. Milbank Q 78(4):619–642

Vincent JL, Moreno R, Takala J, Willatts S, De Mendonça AD, Bruining H, Reinhart CK, Suter PM, Thijs LG (1996) The SOFA (sepsis-related organ failure assessment) score to describe organ dysfunction/failure. Intensive Care Med 22:707–710

Weinstein MC, Stason WB (1977) Foundations of cost-effectiveness analysis for health and medical practices. N Engl J Med 296(13):716–721

White DB, Lo B (2020) A framework for rationing ventilators and critical care beds during the COVID-19 pandemic. JAMA 323(18):1773–1774

Wilkinson D et al (2020) Which factors should be included in triage? An online survey of the attitudes of the UK general public to pandemic triage dilemmas. BMJ Open (10)

Williams A (1997) Intergenerational equity: an exploration of the 'fair innings' argument. Health Economics 6:117–132

Wynia MK (2005) Oversimplifications II: public health ignores individual rights. Am J Bioethics 5:6–8

Chapter 5
Conclusion

The analysis conducted thus far reveals the challenges inherent in engaging in assessments that require confronting the innermost aspects of human existence.

The investigation conducted throughout this book, which extends beyond the endeavour to furnish a comprehensive framework of the ethical, philosophical, and legal ramifications of contentious issues, ultimately seeks to propose normative solutions that encompass the diverse positions and schools of thought that have evolved within this domain.

One of the main difficulties encountered when writing about such issues without personally experiencing the conditions they entail and while attempting to suggest possible solutions lies in understanding and interpreting the strength of the desires and the wills of the individuals involved.

Indeed, it is challenging enough to comprehend one's own desires and wills, and even more so to understand those of others. Moreover, if the realisation of others' desires and wills and desires leads to irreversible consequences—such as birth or death—the difficulties in evaluation, analysis, and the identification of appropriate normative frameworks become all the more acute.

This consideration assumes even greater significance when we reflect upon the fact that desires and wills frequently emerge from the contingent voids and lacks of existence, and that, upon satisfaction, these desires and wills often lose their value.

It is imperative that legislators adopt a cautious approach, given the multifaceted factors that influence human decision-making. This approach should not be informed by a paternalistic perspective that seeks to subject human autonomy to institutional oversight. Instead, it should be grounded in the recognition of the potentially fatal consequences of such choices.

This is particularly pertinent in relation to the conditions of vulnerability that characterise the parties most affected, who raise the greatest number of questions concerning the limits within which institutions may legitimately participate in the fulfilment of desires and wills.

A. Ferrara, *Bioethical Reflections on the Border between Life and Death*, European Union and its Neighbours in a Globalized World 32,
https://doi.org/10.1007/978-3-032-09985-3_5

5.1 Surrogacy: Between Freedom and Vulnerability

Surrogacy can be regarded as one of the most contested and ethically intricate practices in the realm of contemporary biolaw. The fundamental question that this subject raises is that of the decision to generate life through the involvement of another person's body. This decision is directly associated with questions of autonomy, dignity and the rights of the child. The subject under discussion is not merely a technical arrangement of reproductive medicine, but rather a profound ethical and philosophical issue in which the boundaries between freedom and commodification, solidarity and exploitation, private will and public order are continuously tested.

The initial dimension that was examined pertained to autonomy and reproductive freedom. Advocates of surrogacy frequently portray the practice as an extension of individual self-determination: commissioning parents, unable to conceive naturally, pursue their aspiration to form a family, while the surrogate mother, fully informed and consenting, decides to make use of her body in a way that she perceives as meaningful. In this perspective, surrogacy is regarded as a manifestation of solidarity and a legitimate expression of personal liberty, akin to other reproductive choices that are legally protected.

Surrogacy has been demonstrated to engender the potential for the commodification of human life and the body. Critics have emphasised that treating pregnancy and childbirth as services to be contracted risks reducing women's bodies to mere instruments and transforming children into products of contractual exchange. This standpoint posits that even consensual agreements may serve to obscure inherent disparities, particularly in circumstances where economic divergences exist between the commissioning parents and the surrogate mothers.

A secondary tension emerges in relation to the issues of dignity and the protection of the child. The concept of autonomy in the context of surrogacy entails the prerogative of the adults involved in the decision-making process. However, the child born through surrogacy is considered a third party whose interests must be given due consideration and deliberation. The law cannot ignore questions such as: Who is the 'real' mother—the genetic contributor, the gestational carrier, or the intended parent? Is there only one true mother, or might there be several parents? What rights does the child have to know their origins? How do different legal systems protect children from potential abandonment or disputes over parental status? Consequently, the legal systems are compelled to re-evaluate fundamental concepts such as kinship, filiation, and parental responsibility, acknowledging the paramount interest to be safeguarded as that of the child, the innocent third party to the choices made by others.

A review of national legislation reveals a spectrum of regulatory approaches. In certain jurisdictions, including Italy, France and Germany, a strict prohibitionist stance is adopted, with the argument that surrogacy is inherently incompatible with human dignity and cannot be reconciled with public order. In the United States and Ukraine, for instance, commercial surrogacy has been historically tolerated, and in some cases even facilitated. However, this practice has frequently resulted in significant inequalities and cases of exploitation. A third approach, found in countries such as the United Kingdom and Canada, permits only altruistic surrogacy under strict regulation, seeking to balance individual freedom with protection against commercialisation. The oscillation between prohibition, tolerance and partial recognition is indicative of the manner in which each legal order prioritises different values, such as dignity, equality and liberty, while grappling with the same ethical dilemma.

From a philosophical standpoint, surrogacy functions as a paradigmatic case in which individual choice collides with collective values. It tests the limits of liberal theories of autonomy: if one accepts that individuals are free to make choices about their own bodies, can this freedom extend to the creation of life and the contractual transfer of parental rights? Conversely, communitarian and feminist critiques remind us that choices are shaped by social and economic contexts, and what appears voluntary may in fact conceal coercion, vulnerability, or structural injustice. Consequently, surrogacy cannot be considered as a matter of private agreement alone; rather, it must be understood within broader frameworks of justice and social responsibility.

The second chapter puts forward the proposition that surrogacy serves to underscore the pressing need for the establishment of normative frameworks that are capable of both the limitation of harm and the protection of the dignity of all parties involved. It is imperative that such frameworks not only regulate contractual aspects, but also safeguard against exploitation, ensure the rights of children, and preserve the integrity of motherhood as a biological-relational experience. Consequently, the concept of surrogacy is presented not as an isolated bioethical issue, but as a reflection of the profound conflicts within contemporary societies concerning the concept of autonomy, the limits of the market, and the function of law in guiding ethically contested choices. In this regard, the objective has been to delineate a normative solution that can simultaneously sustain the various objectives in question. This has been achieved by reinterpreting the Kantian notion of the human being as an end rather than a means. The solution has been developed through an institutionalised process and is grounded in the valorisation of the concept of altruism.

5.2 End-of-Life: Autonomy and Protection at the Threshold of Death

While surrogacy raises dilemmas at the threshold of birth, end-of-life decisions confront the equally delicate boundary of death, where autonomy, dignity, and protection come into sharp conflict. The question of whether human beings should have the capacity to decide whether, and under what circumstances, it is acceptable to bring life to an end is one that is of significant moral and ethical concern. A common thread between these two scenarios is the pivotal role of human choice: the decision to bring life into being through the involvement of another's body, and the decision to bring life to an end when suffering becomes unbearable. In both cases, the determination of the law is to ascertain the recognition, regulation or restriction of such choices, and the manner in which they can be reconciled with the broader demands of justice and social responsibility.

The ethical underpinnings of end-of-life decision-making are predicated on the principle of self-determination. Proponents of assisted dying and euthanasia posit the argument that personal autonomy extends to the final moments of existence. In essence, this position asserts that if individuals are at liberty to shape the course of their lives, they should also be entitled to determine when and how to bring their lives to a close. From this standpoint, the right to die can be regarded as a corollary of the right to live with dignity. The legal recognition of assisted dying is thus defended as an affirmation of respect for individual will. It is argued that this act protects against unnecessary suffering and secures ultimate control over one's body and destiny.

However, it should be noted that this position is not without contention. Critics emphasise the intrinsic value of life, often grounded in religious, philosophical, or human rights traditions, and argue that life is an inalienable good not subject to individual disposal. It is contended by the aforementioned parties that the legalisation of physician-assisted suicide would risk the erosion of the collective societal responsibility to preserve life, particularly in circumstances where individuals are susceptible to vulnerability due to factors such as illness, disability, or psychological distress. In this context, the focus transitions from autonomy to protection, giving rise to concerns regarding abuse, coercion, and the normalisation of death as a response to suffering.

Following a thorough examination of the extant legal-philosophical debate on end-of-life issues, it becomes imperative to turn to the variety of legal approaches adopted across different jurisdictions. In countries such as Belgium, the Netherlands and Canada, the practice of assisted dying has been legalised under strict conditions, typically requiring the presence of unbearable suffering, repeated voluntary requests for the procedure, and medical supervision. However, the Belgian and Dutch experiences suggest that the range of admissible cases has gradually expanded over time, a development that appears to confirm the empirical relevance of the so-called 'slippery slope' theory. The application of comparative perspectives illuminates the manner in which normative evolutions have not only reflected but also reshaped moral perceptions. Furthermore, it demonstrates how the law itself has functioned as a testing ground for the boundaries of autonomy and protection. In contrast, the majority of other European countries, including Italy, France and Germany, have formally adopted legislation that prohibits euthanasia. Nevertheless, judicial decisions in these jurisdictions have increasingly established exceptions, thereby addressing the gap left by parliaments that remain politically unable or unwilling to legislate on such contentious issues. These judicial appointments signify a gradual shift in the practical management of end-of-life choices, even in the absence of comprehensive legislative reform. The outcome is an evolutionary process that is driven by the courts rather than the legislatures. The absence of clear statutory frameworks gives rise to legal uncertainty and gradual shifts in practice.

The fundamental question under consideration is whether there exist circumstances in which human beings should be permitted to exercise a legitimate right to terminate their own life, or to seek assistance in doing so. Simultaneously, the issue of suffering and its intolerability remains pivotal, particularly when the extension of end-of-life decisions is contemplated in contexts involving mental illness, where the assessment of capacity and voluntariness becomes particularly problematic. The issue of informed consent and awareness is of equal significance, particularly with respect to advance directives, as illustrated by the Koffie case. These questions demonstrate that end-of-life cannot be reduced to a mere confrontation between autonomy and protection. Rather, a broader reflection is required that holds together vulnerability, responsibility, and justice.

Utilitarian arguments emphasise the reduction of pain and the maximisation of well-being, suggesting that assisted dying may, in certain cases, serve the greater good. Conversely, deontological perspectives, which emphasise the inherent value of human life, challenge this consequentialist logic. They contend that intentionally ending a life constitutes a violation of a categorical duty to respect human existence, irrespective of the consequences. Meanwhile, communitarian and relational approaches underscore the impact of end-of-life choices not only on individuals but also on families, communities, and the medical profession. These approaches emphasise that such decisions have ramifications that extend far beyond the person making them. The discussion also addresses the role of medicine and medical professionals, who frequently find themselves at the intersection of ethics and law. The medical profession is traditionally bound by the Hippocratic Oath, which includes the imperative to 'do no harm'. However, physicians are also called to alleviate suffering. The legalisation of assisted dying transforms this role: it redefines the physician's responsibilities, sometimes positioning them as agents of death as well as life. This dual role raises profound questions about medical ethics, professional integrity, and the trust between doctor and patient.

Equally significant are the sociopolitical implications of end-of-life regulation. Legalising assisted dying risks creating pressures on vulnerable populations—such as the elderly, disabled, or economically disadvantaged—to view death as a 'duty' rather than a choice. At the same time, denying access to assisted dying may perpetuate suffering and deny individuals the agency they value most. End-of-life decisions are therefore situated within broader debates about equality, justice, and the role of the state in mediating life's most intimate boundaries. This conflict can be considered a paradigmatic example of the tension between autonomy and protection. On one side of this conflict is the claim of the individual to self-determination over their body and destiny. On the other side of the conflict is the collective responsibility to safeguard life, prevent abuse, and uphold the intrinsic value of existence. The aforementioned competing principles elucidate the rationale behind the enduring contention surrounding assisted dying as one of the most contentious issues in contemporary bioethics and biolaw.

The conclusion draws attention to the necessity of meticulously formulated normative frameworks that demonstrate deference to individual autonomy, whilst concurrently incorporating substantial safeguards. It is imperative that such frameworks are able to differentiate between authentic autonomy and choices that are distorted by vulnerability or coercion. Furthermore, it is essential that these frameworks provide guidance that achieves a balance between compassion and justice. This phenomenon is exemplified by end-of-life decisions, which serve as a testament to the continuous effort of the law to navigate the delicate balance between personal autonomy and collective responsibility, dignity and protection, freedom and life itself.

In any event, in view of these divergences and the variety of approaches, normative frameworks should be guided by a principle of precaution. As end-of-life choices are associated with consequences that are both absolute and irreversible, it is argued that access to assisted dying should be based on the highest level of certainty that human judgment can provide. The termination of a life cannot be approached with a lesser degree of rigour than that applied to the restriction of liberty. This is because it represents not only a legal decision, but also a profound moral boundary.

5.3 Triage Under Crisis: Justice and Democratic Legitimacy

In circumstances of scarcity, the process of medical triage represents a critical juncture where the line between life and death is delineated. In contrast to the decision-making processes involved in surrogacy, which pertains to the initiation of life, and assisted dying, wherein an individual asserts autonomy over the termination of life, triage does not empower the individual who is subject to its consequences. Instead, the responsibility for such decisions lies with the institutions and professionals tasked with the allocation of resources in cases where all cannot be saved. In this sense, triage can be regarded as a normative act rather than merely a medical practice. It is imperative that this act is guided by clear legal and ethical structures, which are capable of defining both the criteria and the procedures by which life-saving interventions are prioritised.

The COVID-19 pandemic has cruelly highlighted the fragility and fragmentation of these structures. In circumstances where intensive care units were overwhelmed, no democratically legitimate authority had issued binding rules to guide physicians in the distribution of ventilators or beds. Conversely, the responsibility was transferred to professional associations, ad hoc hospital committees, or regional health authorities, each of which produced its own guidelines. The result was a patchwork of criteria, which were sometimes focused on maximising survival, sometimes privileging the young, and sometimes protecting healthcare workers, without uniformity or democratic endorsement. The absence of legitimacy in this context is a matter of significant concern, as triage decisions fundamentally impact the fundamental rights of individuals. The process of determining who receives treatment and who does not constitutes a fundamental ethical dilemma, as it essentially involves the decision of who lives and who dies.

The absence of consistent, democratically sanctioned rules gives rise to several critical risks. The present situation places an intolerable burden on medical professionals, who are compelled to make tragic decisions without adequate legal protection and under conditions of extreme urgency and emotional exhaustion. In the absence of binding criteria, medical professionals must rely on personal judgment or local guidelines, which vary from one hospital or region to another. This phenomenon has the potential to engender profound moral distress and to expose professionals to the prospect of legal liability. The role of healthcare professionals is subject to change, whereby they transition from the exclusive advocacy of individual patients to the administration of scarcity. This transition obliges them to achieve a balance between collective outcomes and individual needs.

Concurrently, the absence of democratic legitimacy erodes public trust in the fairness of health systems. Rules drafted by technical bodies without open deliberation risk appearing opaque or arbitrary, especially when factors such as age, disability, or social role implicitly determine access to care. Such dynamics give rise to the risk of structural discrimination, whereby already vulnerable groups—such as the elderly, the disabled, or those suffering from chronic illness—suffer disproportionate exclusion. Within a sociopolitical environment wherein decisions regarding life and death are made, such perceptions of injustice have the potential to erode social cohesion and exacerbate pre-existing inequalities.

The ethical debate has long highlighted the tension between competing theories of justice. Utilitarian perspectives are concerned with the maximisation of survival or life-years saved. In contrast, egalitarian views emphasise the equal worth of every patient. By contrast, prioritarian approaches give precedence to the worst-off, while sufficientarian models seek to guarantee everyone a minimal threshold of care. Each of these moral intuitions is capable of capturing an important aspect of the subject, yet none are able to fully resolve the tragedy of choosing who will be saved and who will not.

The pandemic has thus exposed the fundamental problem of triage, which lies not only in the scarcity of resources but also in the absence of legitimate infrastructures to guide choices that implicate the most fundamental human rights. In a domain where decisions mark the boundary between life and death, the acceptability of arbitrariness and fragmentation is not a matter that can be taken lightly. It is imperative that the principles underpinning such decisions are characterised by transparency, territorial uniformity and a democratic foundation. Only under such conditions can triage, despite its tragic nature, be conducted in a manner that safeguards human dignity and sustains the trust on which healthcare systems ultimately depend.

5.4 Future Challenges for Bioethics and Biolaw

The reflections developed in the preceding chapters converge on a unifying concern: how the legislator ought to address human desires, wills, and choices when regulating matters that touch upon the thresholds of life and death. Such an inquiry requires balancing the normative force of individual aspirations with the protection of fundamental human rights, while also acknowledging the condition of vulnerability from which these desires often emerge.

Each scenario under consideration highlights the tension between two distinct concepts: the tension between individual autonomy and collective responsibility, between the assertion of personal freedom and the protection of vulnerable lives, and between the legitimacy of private decisions and the need for public norms. The questions raised are not merely transient or peripheral. These ethical considerations are of paramount importance in the contemporary context of biolaw, and their significance is set to increase in the face of ongoing scientific and technological advancements that are redefining the boundaries of human capabilities in relation to life and death.

It is anticipated that the landscape of biolaw will be increasingly influenced by emerging biotechnologies. Advancements in the fields of genetic engineering, artificial reproduction and synthetic biology are already precipitating profound transformations in the conceptualisations of parenthood, kinship and human identity. Surrogacy is anticipated to evolve beyond the present dichotomy between prohibition and regulation. The advent of new technologies, such as artificial wombs (ectogenesis), has the potential to profoundly transform the discourse, thereby diverting ethical concerns from the exploitation of women's bodies to the broader commodification of gestation itself. The fundamental question, however, remains constant: to what extent should human beings be granted the autonomy to determine the manner in which life is generated, and what limitations must law and ethics impose to safeguard dignity and prevent inequality?

Conversely, technological progress is set to have a profound impact on end-of-life decisions. The augmentation of life-sustaining treatments, in conjunction with the emergence of novel forms of artificial intelligence in medicine, will engender a marked increase in the feasibility of protracting life under conditions of extreme dependency. This has the potential to intensify the ongoing tension between autonomy and protection, as individuals may begin to demand the right to terminate lives that technology is capable of extending, while legal systems may encounter challenges in determining the scope and implementation of such demands. Furthermore, the potential for predictive algorithms to contribute to the assessment of suffering, prognosis and capacity is a matter of considerable concern. Indeed, it raises unprecedented questions regarding the capacity of technological systems to mediate or influence decisions regarding life-ending actions. The challenge for biolaw will be to ensure that human dignity remains central, preventing both the normalisation of premature death and the uncritical extension of life without quality.

If end-of-life decisions highlight the ethical tension at the level of individual existence, the dilemmas of triage reveal how similar questions of life and death emerge on a collective scale when resources are scarce.

The issue of triage serves to illustrate the dilemmas that future societies will face with even greater acuity. The ongoing global pandemic has brought to light the vulnerability of existing systems when confronted with sudden scarcity, and the inadequacy of legal frameworks in such circumstances. In the context of imminent global crises, including climate change, pandemics, and geopolitical instability, there is an increased probability of scenarios in which resources become inadequate for all parties. In such scenarios, triage will not be an isolated practice, but rather a recurrent procedure. It is imperative to emphasise the significance of the development of decision-making processes that demonstrate resilience to the pressures of crisis. The utilisation of technological tools, encompassing algorithmic systems, has the potential to serve a supportive function. However, it is imperative that these tools are integrated within structures that are characterised by transparency and accountability. Such structures are essential for ensuring the safe-guarding of human dignity and fundamental rights. The pressing task is to design mechanisms that combine openness, responsibility and fairness. It is vital to ensure that technological instruments serve human values rather than replacing them.

In the context of biolaw, the domains of surrogacy, end-of-life and triage represent specific areas of concern. However, the broader outlook for the field is characterised by an escalating degree of complexity and interdependence, which renders an increasingly interdisciplinary approach imperative. The confluence of biotechnological innovation and digital transformation is set to generate novel scenarios in which the boundaries between the biological and the technological become increasingly indistinct. For instance, the field of artificial intelligence is not only relevant to triage but may also play a role in reproductive medicine, genetic counselling, and end-of-life care. The challenge for legal philosophy and bioethics will be to articulate principles that remain coherent and human-centred across diverse contexts, avoiding fragmented or contradictory responses.

From this standpoint, justice, autonomy, and dignity emerge as the indispensable values that should guide the future of biolaw. The fundamental principle of justice is predicated on the equitable distribution of resources and opportunities, with the objective of eradicating discrimination and structural inequalities. Autonomy is defined as the ability to make one's own decisions, free from external influence, and this concept is particularly relevant in the context of powerful technologies and institutions. The concept of dignity asserts that human beings must never be regarded as mere means, whether as gestational carriers, patients in irreversible conditions, or numerical values in an algorithmic triage system. However, it is imperative to recognise that these values cannot be sustained as mere abstract ideals. It is imperative that these principles be concretely embodied in normative structures, encompassing legislative frameworks, policy directives, ethical guidelines, and institutional practices. These structures should facilitate the limitation of potential harms, the direction of choices, and the provision of safeguards.

Finally, the outlook of this book is not merely descriptive but normative and forward-looking. The issues discussed are not destined to disappear; on the contrary, they will intensify as societies confront new scientific and technological possibilities. What is at stake is the capacity of law and ethics to evolve without losing their humanistic foundations. If today's critical frontiers are surrogacy, end-of-life, and triage, tomorrow's challenges will extend to genetic editing, artificial gestation, neuroenhancement, the governance of artificial intelligence in medicine, and assistance in end-of-life decision-making, both for patients and for their families and physicians. The guiding thread will remain the same: when fundamental rights with profound and irreversible implications at the boundaries of life and death are concerned, the task is to ensure that choices are exercised within systems that safeguard the dignity, equality, and justice of all individuals.

In conclusion, the volume's overarching message is one of prudence and responsibility. The power to decide over life and death is at once the highest expression of human freedom and the greatest source of ethical challenge. The future of biolaw will be contingent on our ability to ensure that these powers are retained within structures that are both effective and efficient in facilitating choice while also ensuring that it is not subject to arbitrary influences. Achieving the optimal balance between freedom and protection, autonomy and justice, innovation and dignity will require constant effort. It is only through such a process that societies are able to navigate the complex and contested terrain of biotechnological and medical progress while remaining faithful to the fundamental values of humanity. Ultimately, it is imperative that bioethical reflections and biolegal principles serve as the custodian of human values, particularly at the most vulnerable junctures of human existence.

MIX
Papier aus verantwortungsvollen Quellen
Paper from responsible sources
FSC® C105338

If you have any concerns about our products,
you can contact us on
ProductSafety@springernature.com

In case Publisher is established outside the EU,
the EU authorized representative is:
Springer Nature Customer Service Center GmbH
Europaplatz 3, 69115 Heidelberg, Germany

Printed by Libri Plureos GmbH
in Hamburg, Germany